ACCESS YOUR ONLINE RESOURCES

Developing Educational Plans for Learners with SEND is accompanied by a number of printable online materials, designed to ensure this resource best supports your professional needs

Go to https://resourcecentre.routledge.com/speechmark and click on the cover of this book.

Answer the question prompt using your copy of the book to gain access to the online content.

DEVELOPING EDUCATIONAL PLANS FOR LEARNERS WITH SEND

This accessible and informative resource provides practical ideas and resources to develop educational plans for learners with SEND enabling access to a daily curriculum.

Divided into four main development areas: Communication and Interaction; Cognition and Learning; Sensory and Physical; and Social Emotional and Mental Health, the book highlights evidence-based approaches and outlines strategies and interventions for both speaking and non-speaking pupils. Chapters:

- Cover a range of core themes from environments and managing anxiety to inclusion and progression through provision.
- Introduce tracking and assessment tools to measure progress and to ensure all learners can access quality-first teaching 100 per cent of the time.
- Provide provision and assessment tools which can be used to inform all types of plans, including EHCPs, individual education plans, personal education plans, behaviour plans and daily classroom plans.

With further reading signposts, practical takeaways and case studies woven throughout to highlight key success components and their impact, this is an essential resource for anyone working in any primary and secondary settings.

Darleen Matoe Grimsby is a Trust SENDCo and Inclusion Officer at Unity Education based in Norfolk, UK. She now leads SEND across a diverse range of schools including Mainstream, SEMH settings, Alternative Provision, Specialist Resource Bases and Complex Special Needs. Darleen has proven expertise in creating, developing and implementing programmes and strategies to support students with diverse learning needs.

DEVELOPING EDUCATIONAL PLANS FOR LEARNERS WITH SEND

How to Support Speaking and Non-Speaking Children in All Settings

Darleen Matoe Grimsby

LONDON AND NEW YORK

Designed cover image: Getty Images

First published 2026
by Routledge
4 Park Square, Milton Park, Abingdon, Oxon OX14 4RN

and by Routledge
605 Third Avenue, New York, NY 10158

Routledge is an imprint of the Taylor & Francis Group, an informa business

© 2026 Darleen Matoe Grimsby

The right of Darleen Matoe Grimsby to be identified as author of this work has been asserted in accordance with sections 77 and 78 of the Copyright, Designs and Patents Act 1988.

All rights reserved. The purchase of this copyright material confers the right on the purchasing institution to photocopy or download pages which bear the support material icon and a copyright line at the bottom of the page. No other parts of this book may be reprinted or reproduced or utilised in any form or by any electronic, mechanical, or other means, now known or hereafter invented, including photocopying and recording, or in any information storage or retrieval system, without permission in writing from the publishers.

Trademark notice: Product or corporate names may be trademarks or registered trademarks, and are used only for identification and explanation without intent to infringe.

British Library Cataloguing-in-Publication Data
A catalogue record for this book is available from the British Library

ISBN: 978-1-032-98051-5 (hbk)
ISBN: 978-1-032-98043-0 (pbk)
ISBN: 978-1-003-59682-0 (ebk)

DOI: 10.4324/9781003596820

Typeset in Interstate
by Apex CoVantage, LLC

Access the Support Material: https://resourcecentre.routledge.com/speechmark

CONTENTS

Acknowledgements ix
Introduction x

Part I   Communication and Interaction 1

   Preface 3

1   Inclusive Practice: The Delivery of Inclusive Education for Learners with SEND 5

2   What Does the Physical Environment Look Like? 27

3   How to Implement a Communication-Supportive Environment 56

4   Opportunities that Pupils Have to Practise Their Communication Skills 69

Part II   Cognition and Learning 77

   Preface 79

5   Understanding How Children Learn: The Crucial Role of Working Memory in the Classroom 83

6   Interventions: Pre-Programme and Reading 95

7   Writing and Maths Interventions 129

8   Assessment and Tracking 144

Part III Physical and Sensory — 155

    Preface — 157

9 Sensory Processing and Regulation — 159

10 Sensory Integration Interventions — 168

11 Sensory Impairments and/or Physical Needs — 179

Part IV Social, Emotional and Mental Health (SEMH) — 193

    Preface with Jade Collinge Long — 195

12 Research into Mental Health Strategies for Non-Speaking Autistic Pupils — 199

13 Mental Health Support — 209

14 TOOLBOX: Practical Regulation and De-escalation Strategies for Both Speaking and Non-Speaking Pupils — 219

    Conclusion: Putting It into Practice — 237

    References — 238
    Index — 241

ACKNOWLEDGEMENTS

I am passionate about supporting as many SEND learners as I possibly can: this passion may have stemmed from a family connection. I grew up with my cousin who got meningitis at a young age; her language became limited to three words accompanied with an infectious laugh! I built a trusted relationship with my cousin, accepted by all of my family as who she is and still today, 59 years later, she is with us alongside my aunt who has cared for her all of her life. Another contributing factor to this book was the loss of one of our non-speaking pupils who sadly passed away, some of this due to not being able to communicate. The family continues to fight and educate others to ensure this doesn't happen again. This book is a dedication to both families for what they have taught us; to ensure that no one is left behind and everyone has a voice somehow, in some way.

I would like to thank my father, David Matoe, and my husband, James Grimsby, I learned to fly on your wings. A special thank you to my sister, Joanne Matoe Watson, one of the most resilient people I know, and to Edna Rooke, my mother-in-law, for all of your support. A message to my beautiful children, Hemi and Sana, I wanted to show you that if you put yourself out there, you never know what might come back. So chase your dreams and passions, they can come true! Thank you to you all for your ongoing support, this would not be possible without you.

I wrote this book because I wanted to showcase all of the **phenomenal talent** and hard work from my colleagues at Churchill Park Academy in King's Lynn both past and present. A special mention to those specialist contributors, including Sophie Finney, Molly Lucas, Abbey Howling, Charlotte Housden, Carl Harris, Hester Howells, Jade Collinge Long, Lisa Dodge, Hannah Nicholas, Kerry Taylor, Kerry Goldsmith, Aimee Stebbings, Michelle Carpenter, Hester Howells, Samantha Howlett, Priscilla Crane, Sam Birkinshaw, Emma Adcock and Ellie Weatherall. You are all amazing. Finally, thank you to my colleagues at Unity Education Trust; this is dedicated to the commitment and passion that you show, all day, every day.

A special thank you to the Rout Family for sharing your insights and family's journey.

INTRODUCTION

Welcome to *Developing Educational Plans for Learners with SEND: How to Support Speaking and Non-Speaking Children in All Settings*.

Dear Reader,

The first thing I want you to know is that I have taken into account the struggles schools have with time, resources and staffing. Not to mention the rigour and expectations that are placed on them. Therefore, I have aimed to equip schools with as many resources as possible to minimise those struggles and maximise the impact for the pupils.

This book is designed to be accessed in two ways:

1. Reading it in full as a holistic approach: Engaging in the core themes that run through the book as a whole. These core themes include:
   - 'What' and 'How'. The book aims to identify what can be put in place and how it can be achieved.
   - Enabling environments.
   - Managing anxiety and distress.
   - Practical takeaways to meet the broadest of needs, with a focus on non-speaking pupils.
   - Progress through provision.
   - Inclusive teaching through anticipating and planning.

2. Dipping into parts to get a snapshot. Chapters have been organised so that readers can use subheadings to find and pull-out specific information.

So, however you choose to read this, the aim of the book is to use the contents to inform any type of SEND educational plan (which informs teaching, learning and assessment), in any setting, for any young person, to enable them to access a daily curriculum and most importantly, daily life. I wanted to include well-known 'universal' approaches, but also research and acknowledge those that have had significant impact but are not yet as well-known as others. I have worked with colleagues from specialist school settings, mainstream and alternative provisions, as well as therapists and education psychologists who have kindly taken the time to share with me the resources they have found or developed.

Introduction xi

The book is organised into four parts which are the four development areas: Communication and Interaction; Cognition and Learning; Sensory and Physical and Social, Emotional and Mental Health. These areas are typically the focus of Education, Health and Care Plans (EHCPs) and most other educational plans. These four parts are then further broken into chapters. The chapters inform and clarify **what** support can be put in place for learners with SEND and **how** this can be achieved. Each chapter uses both headings and subheadings to further group the information, aiming to achieve as much flow and clarity as possible. The information is designed to support and develop your thinking and planning.

As you make your way through the book you will naturally make links between the four development areas. In Part III of the book there are specific examples which highlight how the body uses all four of these to create a response to a need or a want.

A Summary of the Chapters

I think it is important, here, to highlight that the aim is to provide an environment that enables communication, regulation, independence and accessible provision. The main focus for the adult is to think about shifting the environment from what the adult wants it to look like, to what the children need from it. Therefore, I aim to provide practical approaches to building those enabling environments so that all pupils can thrive.

Chapter 1 – Inclusion

This standalone chapter gives an evidence-based interpretation of inclusion and how to achieve this in our current climate: how to teach all areas to 100 per cent of pupils while still maintaining the rigour and high expectations that are placed on schools. This chapter includes education plan templates and examples for both SEND (K) and specialist support (EHCP).

Part I – Communication and Interaction

My understanding is that this development area is being split into two different sections:
  Speech and Language
  Communication and Social Interaction

However, for this book, Speech, Language, Communication and Social Interaction will remain as one part, but the chapters will cover both areas. This part of the book will look at how to achieve communication-supportive environments, focussing on three aspects:

- The **physical environment**
- The **strategies** that **adults** use
- The **opportunities** that children have to practise their communication skills

This section of the book will focus heavily on supporting pupils that are non-speaking, non-verbal, selective mutes and those with limited language. With the increase in pupils coming to reception classes with limited levels of speech, this is a great tool for all early year environments.

There is a chapter dedicated to supporting non-speaking pupils, most importantly equipping adults with **how** to teach pupils and **how** they can use their tools to communicate. For this chapter I worked with Molly Lucas who is a Speech and Language Therapist, and Charlotte Housedon, Carl Harris and Aimee Stebbings who are Pastoral Support and Behaviour Specialists. Abbey Howling, a Speech, Language and Behaviour Specialist, supported with ensuring information regarding Augmentative and Alternative Communication Devices was most up-to-date.

Part II - Cognition and Learning

This section is dedicated to listing evidence-based curriculums, interventions and assessment tools, accompanied by case studies which offer an in-depth example of practice and impact. Working memory is included to identify how pupils learn. There is a separate chapter dedicated to reading, and then writing and maths are joined together. The reading chapter includes a reading framework that is aimed at all pupils at any stage of their reading journey. The writing chapter includes a programme designed to bridge the gap for those struggling to go from Reception to Year 1 (with links to phonics and spelling), combined with a maths chapter that discusses concrete, pictorial and abstract methods. Abbey Howling shares personalised wordbanks that she uses with learners with profound and multiple learning difficulties. Lisa Dodge and Kerry Goldsmith, who both have over 30 years' experience working with mild, moderate and complex needs, share examples of word sets and sensory days of the week plans. Kerry Taylor, Michelle Carpenter, Frankie Follen, Louise Mienczakowski and Hannah Cragg, with both mainstream and special needs teaching backgrounds, were part of a writing team I set up to ensure the programme was effective. They supported me with tweaking the programme and measuring the impact.

Part III - Physical and Sensory

This part of the book looks at sensory support through lots of different lenses. These include sensory processing and sensory difficulties, identifying what these can look like and strategies that can be implemented into a daily curriculum or in the moment. Sophie Finney, a Behaviour Specialist who leads in this area at a Complex Special Needs School, provided some of these key approaches and strategies. There is a chapter focussed on sensory regulation and the connection between the senses, emotions and emotional regulation. This section will also include how to support those with sensory impairments and/or physical disabilities.

Part IV - Social, Emotional and Mental Health (SEMH)

This section of the book includes a dedicated chapter outlining strategies that can support non-speaking pupils with anxiety, distress and their mental health based on a recent study and its findings. Dr Hester Howells, a Senior Education Psychologist, provides key information regarding neuroception and attunement, and Charlotte Housedon supported with the initial stage of teaching emotions. The following chapters include a list of interventions, websites and professionals that provide support for pupils and their SEMH, ending with a chapter providing strategies to support regulation and de-escalation. It is a list grouped into different themes. The idea is that you can use these to make toolboxes and put practical strategies into educational plans. It also provides brief descriptions where needed to support the 'what' and 'how'.

Further Reading

Some chapters will have a further reading section at the end. This has additional websites and resources that have been referenced in the book or are good tools to look up.

Clarify Thinking

I believe that we have to think about what works best for our pupils, being aware of what I call the 'bandwagon' approach: jumping into something that later you find wasn't the most effective approach and so consequently jumping back off the 'bandwagon'. Think about taking bits from here and there to make it work for the pupils you work with. Therefore, to help clarify your thinking when looking at an approach, to ensure it is effective all round, ask yourself these questions:

Who is this for? Identify your target audience.
What is this for? What are you trying to embed? What outcomes are you looking for?
Is this approach going to meet that? Will it have the desired outcome? Is there evidence to support this?

Points of Reflection

Don't be afraid to be critical and ask questions. When I visit schools for observations and ask to see provisions in place, often they are 'just in the cupboard' or 'we normally use them, just not today, they should be here somewhere'. When you are looking at plans, honestly reflect and be confident to ask yourself: 'Are these resources effective? If not, why not?'

Take this time to dive a little deeper and think about practices and processes that you have in your setting. A lot of the Points of Reflection are encouraging you to think using two different lenses. First (if it was you in that position), as adults we need certain things, so if *we* need it, surely pupils do too. Second (look at things through the pupils' lens), they have not yet had those experiences that we as adults have, so they need to be taught and guided rather than assume they know it. It is all about putting processes in place to support success rather than setting pupils and adults up to fail.

Definitions Adopted in This Book

Non-speaking: For this book, non-speaking is defined as a term which means a person does not form and utter mouth (speak) words (Marnell, 2023).
 Non-verbal: Pupils who have no words or sounds and are not selective mutes.
 Limited language: Pupils who are beginning to use single words.

The Chain: From the Book to the Pupil

Although this is last in this section, it is possibly the most important! From this book to the pupil on the chair, you need to think about the chain that the plans go through. Ask yourself, are there any kinks in that chain that could pose barriers and how do we get around these? The most important thing is getting the strategies right **for** and **to** the pupil: that is the aim of this book.

We have the 'what' and 'how' to deliver the provision; you need to think about ensuring it happens and continues to happen.

Finally, the contents of this book are from years of trial and error (some call it intellectual trial and error), experience and extensive research. I ask you to keep in mind that these are my own experiences, ideas and conclusions from which you can select, think about, play around with and make work for you. I always say that when it is a 'square peg, round hole' situation that we use the approaches listed in this book to help shave the sides of the peg.

I wanted to give educators a one-stop shop starting point: providing a base that you could start from, in all four areas. I wanted to share as many resources as I possibly could, for you to then decide what to look further into. I think that is how the book has evolved into a training-like manual. At the end of the day, it is so you have practical strategies to implement for all pupils.

Part I
Communication and Interaction

Preface

Communication is key in the journey towards independence and the management of anxiety. People with a learning disability and/or learning difficulty may communicate in a range of different ways. Whereas some people may use spoken language, other people may communicate in different ways such as signing, objects, pictures, facial expressions or body language. Often, it is a combination of all of these. Lots of people with a learning disability and /or learning difficulty find it harder to understand and remember what people say.

There are three things we all need to communicate:

- Means or a way to communicate.
- Reasons to communicate.
- Opportunities to communicate.

This is called the Means, Reasons and Opportunities model and is a useful way to think about how we can support the communication skills of children and young people with a learning disability. It can be helpful to think about the young person's communication using this model. The 'Means, Reasons and Opportunities model of communication' resource is a model developed by Money and Thurman (1994).

This part of the book will focus on those three key areas, providing you with practical strategies on what you can put in place to support speech and language needs and how you can do that in the classroom.

> *Points of Reflection: If a student is non-speaking and does not use spoken words, what do they use to communicate and how do you teach them to use it?*

4 *Developing Educational Plans for Learners with SEND*

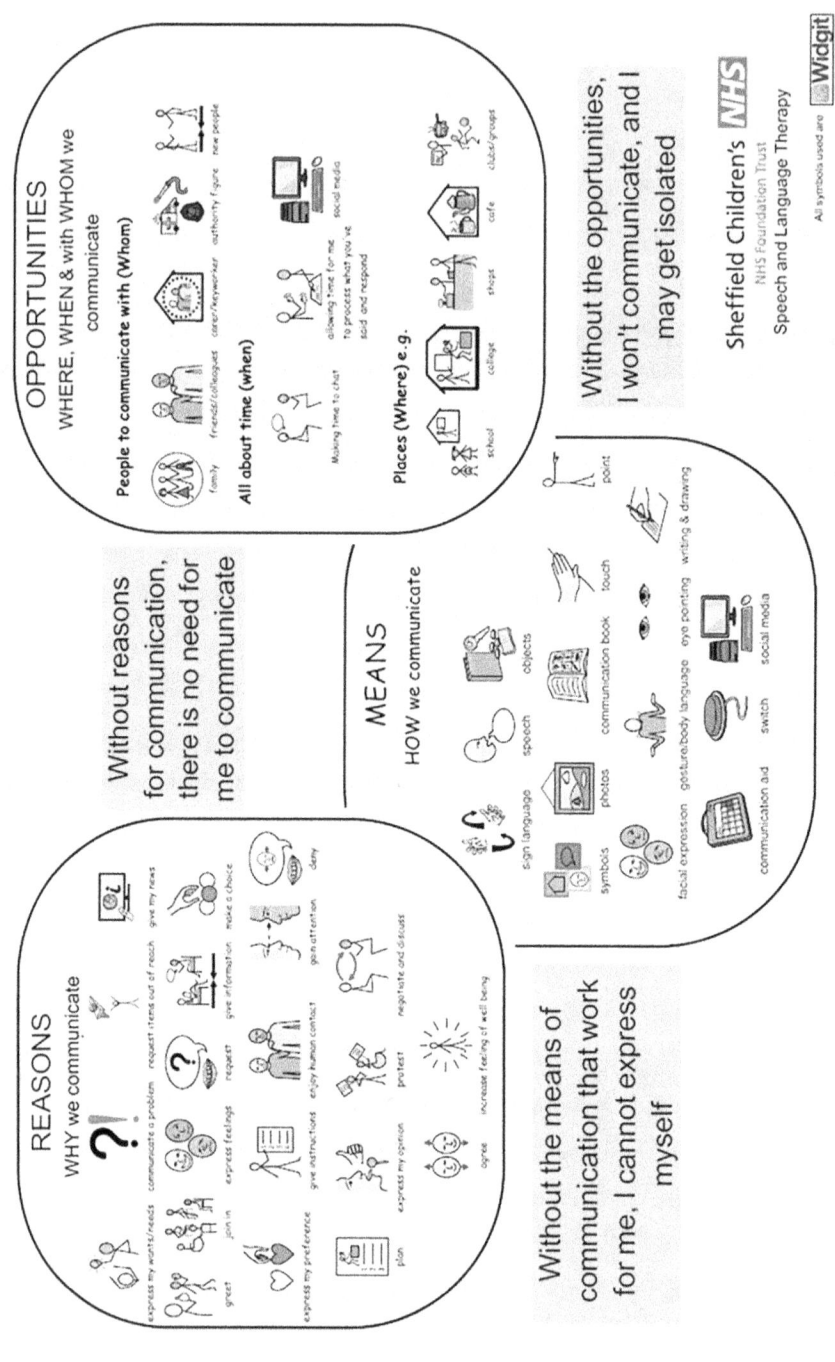

1 Inclusive Practice
The Delivery of Inclusive Education for Learners with SEND

When a young person starts at your school, their journey begins. What they bring with them is their starting point that we identify. Schools have a National Curriculum that guides us to where we want to get pupils to. For learners with SEND we need to build in support, whether it be reasonable adjustments, subtle changes or plans, to provide those pupils with the best chance of getting them as close to 'there' as we possibly can. This is what I believe to be inclusion – building in, so everyone gets something. Therefore, this book shares the 'what' and 'how' and the plans are there to 'house' the information.

Achieving inclusion can be a challenge especially as SEND is so broad in schools. Therefore, making identifying and anticipating barriers part of your school culture can ease some of those challenges. If you anticipate and plan ahead as much as you can, then you can build in interventions and support, rather than as an afterthought. You may find that you read through some of this and think to yourself, this might not be possible, but what I am encouraging you to think about is when you plan a lesson, plan for all of your pupils. If the pupil with SEND cannot access the other material, what can they access to make progress? What could they access independently and what tools can I put in place to support this before adult input?

What Is Inclusion?

> *Points of Reflection: What does inclusion mean for you? What are you aiming for when it comes to inclusion? Is everyone on the same page?*

'Inclusion is a multi-dimensional concept around which there is much scope for misunderstanding and disagreement' (Farrell et al., 2007). Therefore, do we really know what it is? Sometimes there is a misconception that this means to simply include the pupils in the classroom, no matter what they are doing, as long as they are there because getting this right for pupils with SEND can be a tricky balancing act. The aim is to have a culture where SEND isn't an afterthought, it is part of the initial plan, ensuring it is a built-in not bolt-on approach.

After researching the evolution of inclusion and what has been deemed as best inclusive practice, this is an interpretation of what inclusion can be:

Inclusion = the same time and value given to pupils = the same treatment.

My philosophy which underpins this is for every pupil to be able to access a daily curriculum with an equal amount of time and value given. Therefore, if a neurotypical pupil can access a curriculum (that is, National Curriculum) for argument's sake let's say 95 per cent of the time, a learner with SEND should also access some form of a curriculum 95 per cent of the time. They should be planned into the school curriculum and daily timetable just as a pupil accessing the National Curriculum would. For example, where most pupils would access Year 5 Maths National Curriculum – White Rose and a pupil with SEND is not able to, then can they access the same objective but differentiated appropriately from a lower year level, that is Year 1. This would prevent pupils with SEND completing 'holding task' style worksheets for example writing over numbers to 10 when it is only 9 they need help with.

A further example would be a learner with cerebral palsy who needs careful physical management which requires the family and a range of professionals working together with an integrated therapy programme, in order to promote learning, communication and inclusion.

However, are mainstream schools able to provide these programmes and individualised plans while maintaining an ideology of inclusion? To answer this question, there is a small body of research by Farrell and colleagues (2007), funded by the Department for Education and Skills (DfES) (Farrell et al., 2007) which addressed inclusion of SEND pupils in England mainstream schools. They found that schools which were highly inclusive managed their special educational needs (SEN) provision in different ways. 'Customisation of their provision depended on careful assessment, planning and monitoring at an individual level. Students were neither rigidly segregated from their peers nor "dumped" in mainstream classes, but were offered careful mixtures of provision in a range of settings' (Farrell et al., 2007).

According to this, the balance comes from giving the pupil what they need, however that may look, which could be both in and out of the classroom. What I believe this looks like is inclusion through curriculum and inclusion through environment, offering those careful mixtures of provision in order to meet the needs of the pupil.

Points of Reflection: Inclusion through a curriculum may mean accessing this in another space other than the classroom and inclusion through the physical environment may mean joining back into the classroom with a focus purely on social interaction (which, one could argue, is also inclusion through curriculum because it is still part of their daily curriculum). Of course, there are numerous challenges; hopefully this book will provide some ideas in breaking down those barriers or jumping over them.

Reflective question: Do leaders create a culture whereby staff anticipate barriers through their planning? Do leaders have a process that asks 'How do 100 per cent of pupils access this?' For example, how does next week's English lessons look for 100 per cent of the pupils? By incorporating this process, your school's curriculum becomes inclusive by design, creating those right conditions for inclusion and developing thinking colleagues. This will upskill staff so that they have the knowledge of what they can put in place and the confidence to do it. What we want to encourage is thinking and networking rather than problem dumping, otherwise we end up with problem dumping and a fixer.

Where Did Inclusion Come From?

Knowing the background and history can help to provide more of an insight into the journey of inclusion and the difficulty in achieving it. 'The inclusion "ideal" is one which has been both celebrated and maligned. It paved the way for equality but also, out of its diversity, sprang many misconceptions and concerns for children with Special Educational Needs and Disabilities (SEND)' (Smith and Broomhead, 2019).

In 1994, the Salamanca Statement focussed on and urged governments to 'concentrate their efforts on the development of inclusive schools' (Smith and Broomhead, 2019). It was also in this year that the Code of Practice from the Department for Education (1994) established the role of special educational needs coordinator (SENCO) to help facilitate the inclusion of pupils with SEN in mainstream schools (Maher and Macbeth, 2014).

Then in 2014 the SEND Code of Practice was introduced. This document is considered to be the single most important guidance on the provision expected in settings. This states the expected vision for children with SEND: 'Education is the same as for all children and young people – that they achieve well in their early years, at school and in college, and lead happy and fulfilled lives' (Department for Education, 2015). One of the key principals is inclusive practice and removing barriers to learning (NASEN, 2015). However, in the drive towards inclusive education for learners with SEND, why is there still so much debate and misinterpretation? Is it because inclusion became an illusion, to become what Žižek (2009, cited in Hodkinson, 2012) would call a symbolic fiction?

How Do You Achieve Inclusion for Learners with SEND through Planning?

Ask yourself:

A – Can they access the National Curriculum with some additional forms of support, reasonable adjustments and scaffolding?

Or:

B – What needs to be in place of the National Curriculum (all or some) to create a pre-National Curriculum, like a stepping stone?

Identifying A or B allows pupils with SEND to access a curriculum that is designed to meet their needs the same as a typically functioning pupil would access the National Curriculum designed to meet their needs. Equal time and equal value.

Tier 3 – Specialised	Education plan	Bespoke curriculum
Tier 2 – Individualised support	Education plan	NC + additional provisions
Tier 1 – Universal support	National Curriculum NC	NC + reasonable adjustments

Choosing A – Structuring support to access the National Curriculum.

Tier 1 – The first step is how we identify pupils with SEND, whose additional needs cannot simply be met through 'quality first teaching'. This is typically achieved through observations and assessments, analysing those pieces of information and then considering what that might be indicating or telling us. Next is how you go about getting support (whether it be big or small); most schools already have these systems in place and they are typically through the SENDCo. For example:

SEN Referral Form		
Pupil name:		**Class/Year:**
Teacher name:		**Date of referral:**
Areas of concern (tick the relevant boxes)	Other (please specify)	
☐ General learning difficulties	☐ Communication and interaction	☐ Emotional, social and mental health
☐ Specific learning difficulties (e.g. dyslexia)	☐ Speech and language	☐ Physical (gross/fine motor skills, visual or hearing impairment)
What difficulties does the pupil have accessing the curriculum?		
What support has already been put in place?		**Impact of support**
What next steps would you like to see?		
Any further comments?		
Attached documents e.g. observations, pupil information, work samples, parent discussion notes		
Created By Priscilla Crane and Samantha Joyce.		

Most counties have published their own inclusion support documents, which do include identification of need and Tier 1 quality first teaching. The following example has been taken from Norfolk County Council's Provision Expected at SEN Support (PEaSS), Identification of Needs section.

This helps to identify and create a profile of need, then the idea is that these needs can be supported by provision, which is listed later in the document. Another similar document is from Suffolk County Council, which can be found at: https://suffolklearning.com/inclusion/suffolk-mainstream-inclusion-framework.

I would suggest looking into your local offer and what documents have been provided by your county. I know the amount of expertise and specialist knowledge that went into the PEaSS and Suffolk Mainstream Inclusion Framework (SMIF) documents, which is why they are really useful tools.

3.1.1 Need: Communication and Interaction (Speech, Language and Communication)

Children and young people may have one or more of these learning profiles and may experience one of more of these difficulties:

Attention and Listening	Tick box
Difficulty paying attention during a shared activity, to an activity for an age-appropriate length of time and listening to instructions whilst busy doing something else	
Finds tasks with spoken instructions harder to complete than tasks where listening is not required	
Easily distracted and tends to prefer activities of their own choosing	

There are also numerous documents online that support putting in place 'quality first teaching'. One particular document dedicated to inclusion is the *Teachers Handbook: SEND Embedding Inclusive Practice*. It is very comprehensive. There is one section called 'Barriers to learning and reasonable adjustments', which can easily be adopted into the classroom aiming to provide practical and basic approaches that will help everyone. Another common tool that is used by educators is the Education Endowment Fund: they have evidence-based resources to improve teaching and learning. Their blogs are also a quick and easy way to catch up on snippets of updated information.

Tier 2 – Providing more individualised support, but still accessing the National Curriculum. This would be achieved typically through a more bespoke and targeted type of educational plan. The starting point of the plan is to identify what the pupil can do and what are the barriers that make it difficult for the pupil to access the National Curriculum. The 'can do' identifies starting points and where to move from, to avoid pupils doing things already embedded (not to be confused with over learning), that is, 'doing to do' and not learning anything. The SENDCo can be a good person to support with observations to identify these barriers. It is also good for them to sit with the teacher and try to unpick what the barriers may be, looking at both the obvious and what is at the heart, which can be the not so obvious. There are so many documents that are provided by local councils and specialists like Speech and Language to help identify what these barriers may look like. Once the barriers have been identified, it is then that you are able to look into provisions to try to overcome these and make progress, hence the term, progress through provision. This helps to ensure that you pick an effective provision that allows that progress. If not, why not?

SEND Support Plans

These plans are typically used when pupils are added to a register of those that receive additional support for SEND. The plans 'house' personalised targets and provision aimed to support the pupil to overcome barriers to learning. Following is a SEND support plan that incorporates the Norfolk County Council expected provision for SEND separated into three graduated levels.

These plans were created by Sam Birkinshaw who is an Academy Trust SENDCo. One of the aims of the template is to reduce the time it takes to write these. Therefore, by trying to make these more effective, hopefully it makes planning easier, less like an additional chore and more a place to refer to. Teachers can use specialists, for example, Speech and Language, Occupational Therapist and Educational Psychologist reports to highlight provision, taking away guess work. This can help to make planning more efficient and 'streamlined'.

There is also a version of the plan for those with an EHCP or in the process of applying for one. The EHCP/ECHNA plan is designed so that you can take the provisions straight from the EHCP and just highlight them in blue (use the rhyme: *blue you do*) in the *how will you help me* section. There is then a second page for additional EHCP information.

School SEN Support Plan – (year)

Name:		Year:	Teacher:	M
Primary need:	Speech & Language	Social Comm. & Interaction	Cognition & Learning	Social, Emotional & Mental Health (SEMH)	Physical and/or Sensory
Vulnerability:	School support (K)	EHCP (E)	PP	LAC	EAL	Home Lang:
Why do I need extra support?					

Area of need	My current SMART targets	Key Adults

Copyright material from Darleen Matoe Grimsby (2026),
Developing Educational Plans for Learners with SEND, Routledge

How will you help me? Highlight all adaptations/supports in place to achieve targets   **BLUE = EHCP Section F Provision**

Speech and Lang.	Social Comm.	Cog. & Learning	SEMH	Phys & Sensory
• Dual coding through visuals/objects (e.g. visual timetable, comic strips) • Cue in instructions by name • Simplify instructions • Thinking time before responding • Check understanding • Cue in changes of topic • Model how to ask for help / to clarify an instruction • Word banks • Pre-teach vocab • Considered partners for group work • Targeted questioning (based on Blanks levels) • Speech sound modeling when repeating back (My Turn,Your Turn)	• Dual coding through visuals/objects (e.g. visual timetable, timers) • Clear, consistent routines (e.g seats) • Prep. for changes (e.g timers, now/next phrasing) • Adapt to special interests • Agreed calming area or strategy • Modelled emotional language (I think you are feeling ....) • Explicitly teach social/ emotional skills (e.g. Zones of Reg.) • Adult-guided play/ group work to model social communication • Adapted play/lunch routines	• Dual coding through visuals/objects (e.g. visual timetable, manipulatives) • Assessment for Learning & adaptive teaching methods to pitch tasks appropriately • Simple, clear language • Revisit prior learning more frequently • Use real-life experiences for child • Thinking time before responding • Check understanding • Break down tasks into smaller chunks • Use alternatives to writing where poss. • Multi-sensory teaching • Small group in-class/ catchup/ pre-teach • Considered seating near adult/ role model • Fast-track Phonics	• Dual coding through visuals/objects (e.g. visual timetable, emotions visuals) • Responsibilities/roles to boost self-esteem • Clear modeling of positive behaviours and praise when seen ("Catch me good") • Fix it folder / restorative approaches to any challenging or harmful events • Positive Behaviour Strategies (Norfolk Steps) • PATHS / Zones of Regulation strategies around regulation • Adults 'annotate' or model their own feelings to the child	**Physical** • Fine/Gross Motor skills group interventions • Adapted equipment (pencils, grips etc) • For specific physical issues (such as hearing, sight or mobility) see SENDCo for guidance **Sensory** • Sensory audit to identify triggers / calming strategies • Considered seating • Movement breaks • Adapted resources (fidget bands / cushions) • Multi-sensory teaching • Sensory Circuits • Ear defenders • Adapted play/lunch routines

Universal Supports (INDES 1+)

Copyright material from Darleen Matoe Grimsby (2026),
Developing Educational Plans for Learners with SEND, Routledge

			Other
• SLCN screening tool used to identify personalised targets • 1-1 Speech sound intervention, guided by speech screener • 1-1 or small group Blanks intervention (vocabulary) • Personalised visual aids / prompts (e.g. core board) • SENDCo to consider referral to SaLT/ATT Attention Autism sessions • Colourful Semantics support / intervention	• 1:1 or small group work on specific issue • Lego/Brick-based Lego therapy intervention • Social stories • Personalised visual timetable and prompts (e.g. Now and Next board) • Adult support in managing transitions • SENDCo to consider referral to Ed Psych. / ASD outreach / SCT • SENDCo to meet with parents/carers to consider NDS referral	• Screening tools used to identify barriers & set personalised targets • Consistent adult support in small group work in core lessons • Booster / pre-teach sessions on key skills • Additional 1:1 booster learning sessions • 1:1 or small group memory skills sessions • SENDCo to consider referral to Ed Psych. / ATT/Dyslexia Outreach	• Regular 1:1 check in time with an adult to discuss daily events & strategies to manage feelings or anxieties • Increased Home-school communication to share positives and track triggers • Small group/1:1 work on nurture/emotional reg. • Personalised ZoR toolkit • Personalised 5-point scale • SENDCo to consider referral to Ed Psych/ Inclusion & SEND / SCT	• 1:1 Gross/Fine motor skills intervention • Personalised equipment (scissors, writing area) • Individual sensory kit • Additional sensory breaks or strategies • Personalised workspace/ alternate working area • SENDCo to consider referral to OT/Physio • SENDCo to meet with parents/carers to consider NDS referral	
• SaLT input and plan • Alternative communication strategy (e.g. Obj. Of Ref; PECS; sign language) • SRB referral / outreach placement • Intensive Interaction	• 1:1 support at breaks and lunchtimes • 1:1 support in class to help manage social interactions • Pos. Behaviour Support Plan (PBSP) for scripting • SRB referral / placement	• 1:1 support in class to help access a personalized curriculum • Personalised alternative recording method (e.g. ATT resources) • SRB referral / outreach / placement • TEACCH Workstation	• 1:1 classroom support • CAMHS referral / support • 1:1 counselling • Pos. Behaviour Support Plan (PBSP) for scripting • SRB Referral / outreach/ placement • Short-term reduced timetable	• Physio or OT input • 1:1 support for PE or other physical tasks • Personalised adaptive technology (ATT / medical team) • Personalised sensory diet (informed by OT) • Virtual Schools	
•	•	•	•	•	
Targeted (4+)			Specialist (6+)		Other

Copyright material from Darleen Matoe Grimsby (2026),
Developing Educational Plans for Learners with SEND, Routledge

School SEN Support Plan – EHCP or EHCNA pathway

Name:		Year:	Teacher:	
Primary need: *(Highlight)*	Speech & Language	Social Comm. & Interaction	Cognition & Learning	Social, Emotional & Mental Health (SEMH)	Physical and/or Sensory
Vulnerability:	School support (K)	EHCP (E)	PP	LAC	EAL	Home Lang:
Professionals Involved/ Reports:					

What are my strengths?	What do I like?	What do I find difficult / not like?

My needs	INDES Score Date:	Brief summary of barriers to learning / diagnoses (taken from EHCP Section B / Professional Reports)
Speech and Language		
Social Communication & Interaction		•
Cognition and Learning		•
Social, Emotional & Mental Health (SEMH)		•
Physical and/or Sensory (State area if VI,Deaf, sens)		
INDES Score Guide	1+ – Universal supports	4+ Consider targeted support	6+ Consider Specialist supports

Copyright material from Darleen Matoe Grimsby (2026),
Developing Educational Plans for Learners with SEND, Routledge

Area of need	Long Term outcomes/targets (EHCP Section E / Professional Reports)
Speech & Language	•
Social Communication & Interaction	•
Cognition and Learning	•
Social, Emotional and Mental Health (SEMH)	•
Physical and/or Sensory Area:	•

Copyright material from Darleen Matoe Grimsby (2026),
Developing Educational Plans for Learners with SEND, Routledge

The second part of the plan is the Meeting Record (Assess-Plan-Do-Review cycle) to be used in the termly meetings with families. Teachers can add in the plan, do, review sections prior to the meeting, then discuss these in the meeting with families and decide on the next steps. This way everyone has been involved. If interventions are or are not successful then you can have those discussions, while sharing what other actions you are going to implement.

SEN Support Plan review Meeting Record (Print out)	Meeting attended by:	Date of meeting:

Pupil and Family views

What is going well?	What are the things I need most help with now?

Current Academic Attainment (Regression, Maintained, Accelerated Progress)

	Phonics	Reading	Writing	Maths

	Plan	Do	Review	Assess
Current Targets (include area of need)		Who will help me? When? How often? (adaptations, intervention, resources) Use the highlighted grid on the support plan to guide this	Have I achieved my target? Green – Achieved Yellow – Part achieved Red – Not achieved Provide brief comments on why	What happens next? Do I need a new target? Or adapted targets / provisions? Draft targets
				.

Signatures	Parent/carer		Teacher / Staff member	

Copyright material from Darleen Matoe Grimsby (2026),
Developing Educational Plans for Learners with SEND, Routledge

The idea is that you meet with the parents and record that meeting on that document. Therefore, the Meeting Record document will keep record of all of the targets and provision changes, creating a recorded 'target' journey for that pupil. The SEND support plan will be a 'live' working document holding 'live targets'.

Once the plan has been agreed, parents will then sign it in the meeting. The next stage is implementing any amendments. Question the intervention or scaffolding that is being implemented. Ask yourself why you have chosen this and what is the desired outcome? Has everyone been properly trained? If teaching assistants are delivering it, have they received appropriate training? Do they have a clear understanding of what the learning outcomes should be?

> *Points of Reflection: When implementing plans, have we managed the implementation of that plan or have we just asked people to do the plan, for example: has the information been passed down through a 'just do this' conversation in the corridor? Or is there a process in which provision is highlighted if people have not been trained? Is the implementation of plans monitored or just the plans themselves?*
>
> *A friendly reminder: Where you find new interventions, be mindful of that 'bandwagon' approach, use the assess, plan, do, review cycles to ensure that you don't become led by the intervention and not the pupil. Dive as much as you can into the actual purpose of the intervention and what it is teaching. What is the student learning? Evidence-based Practice Unit Logic Model (covered in Chapter 9 under the heading Assessing Interventions) is a model that can be used to identify and review an intervention.*

Choosing B – Create a pre-National Curriculum bespoke to meet the pupil's needs?

Tier 3 – This is putting in place a balanced curriculum that gives that pupil the skills they need to function every day independently and lead them closer towards the National Curriculum. For non-speaking pupils it would be giving them a voice, means of communication and teaching them how to use it to communicate, providing an environment that can address their wants and needs.

Learners with SEND do not typically develop in the same way; their development is delayed or disordered. Educational practices for children with SEND increasingly focus on functionality instead of developmental milestones. This is due to the slow rate of development and learning. Therefore, it is necessary to create a bespoke curriculum with the balance of interventions to meet their needs, so that you can offer a careful mixture of provision in a range of settings. The content in this book aims to provide those interventions and strategies to build that curriculum- those stepping stones.

Personalised Learning Goals

This type of plan incorporates personalised targets that the pupils work on, which can dictate their daily curriculum. The main difference between these plans and the SEND support plans is that one is used in mainstream and the following has been used in a special school setting. The first example is a plan created for a pupil who has limited language and would access a semi-formal curriculum (mostly intervention-based, pre-learning skills, early reading, early writing). The second plan is for a non-speaking pupil with profound and multiple learning difficulties.

Key Barrier to Learning: Communication difficulties, regulation of behaviour					
Area	Learning Goal - 'What?'	Teaching Strategies - 'How?'	Outcome - How will we 'know?'	Review
Communication and Interaction	PLG: To be able to use a snack board to request least three items.	1. Adult to model using symbol to request a snack. 2. Encourage pupil to point to symbol to request a snack. 3. Encourage pupil to touch symbols and then receive snack item.	By the end of the term pupil will select and use at least three symbol cards to request their snack.	Achieved Partially Not achieved
EHCP Outcome: Pupil will communicate using symbols, gesture and begin to build up his vocabulary to get his wants and needs understood. Curriculum: Equals My Communication: Imperative Communications Assessment: Word sets tracker, Engagement Model				
Cognition and Learning	PLG: To be able to match letters in his name and then trace E using a pen.	Morning task is matching letters of their name, placing them on their name card in the right order and then holding a pen to overwrite (first letter of name) independently.	By the end of the term evidence will show pupil can match all the letters in their name and overwrite (first letter of name).	Achieved Partially Not achieved
EHCP Outcome: Pupil attention and engagement increases by participating in a range of different learning activities. Curriculum: Writing model: match then trace. Assessment: Pre-Key stage standard 1				

Social, Emotional and Mental Health	PLG: To request a walk using a symbol when feeling anxious and heightened.	Self-Regulation: Use the AIC curriculum to teach what dysregulation feels like for pupil. Communication: When pupil is beginning to cry and pace the classroom. Adults to go to the door and ask pupil to use symbol to request a walk.	By the end of the term pupil's amount of dysregulation will be reduced (by at least 20%).	Achieved Partially Not achieved

EHCP Outcome: Pupil will be supported to manage his own regulation by participating in self-regulation activities.
Curriculum: Adapted Introception Curriculum (AIC) Assessment: Engagement Model

Sensory and Physical	PLG: To engage in daily TACPAC and sensology sessions.	Pupil will sit in circle and engage in sensology days of the week daily sessions. Pupil will access daily TACPAC interventions.	Pupil will ask for a reduced number of walks during daily sessions. Decrease in amount of dysregulation (by at least 20%).	Achieved Partially Not achieved

EHCP Outcome: Pupil will actively participate in a range of different sensory experiences daily to regulate sensory needs.
Curriculum: Interventions: TACPAC and Sensology. Assessment: Communication Tracker, Engagement Model

Independence: To be able to complete Cognition and Learning and Social, Emotional and Mental Health targets on their own.

Key Barrier to Learning: Communication difficulties, regulation of behaviour				
Area	Learning Goal - 'What?'	Teaching Strategies - 'How?'	Outcome - How will we 'know?'	Review
Communication and Interaction	PLG: Pupil will show symbol/photo discrimination when choosing between a preferred and non-preferred symbol/photo, e.g., light up windmill and a pencil.	1. Give the pupil a choice from two symbols, one a preferred item and one a non-preferred item, ensuring the preferred item is more motivating than the non-preferred. 2. Encourage pupil to point/touch the symbol to make a choice. 3. If the pupil chooses the non-preferred item, give it to them to explore and try again. 4. Try different objects, with different staff and in different environments.	By the end of the term pupil will be able to discriminate between two symbols.	Achieved Partially Not achieved
EHCP Outcome: Pupil will have the language and communication skills necessary to support their understanding and ability to make choices between options offered (indoor/outdoor play, snack time, mealtime, activities to access within free play etc.).				
Cognition and Learning	PLG: Pupil will look for their favourite objects when she sees them hidden.	1. To hide motivating objects nearby and then move the objects and hide them further away. 2. To be enthusiastic to show where you are hiding the object, so they understand where to find it. 3. To try this is different environments, with different staff and objects.	By the end of the term evidence will show pupil can find their favourite items when hidden.	Achieved Partially Not achieved

22 Developing Educational Plans for Learners with SEND

EHCP Outcome: Pupil will show interest in activities and resources within the classroom environment and will engage in aspects of exploratory, functional and sensory play, demonstrating developing understanding of the world around them.				
Social, Emotional and Mental Health	PLG: Pupil will play in soft play with a peer, they will show a response of happiness or frustration during the interaction.	1. Staff will model playing with pupil and another pupil. 2. Staff will support the interaction between pupil and another pupil. 3. Staff will label pupil responses, e.g. I can see you are happy when playing with	By the end of the term pupil will show clear responses when interacting with their peers in soft play.	Achieved Partially Not achieved
EHCP Outcome: Pupil will share experiences and participate in small group activities alongside her peers.				
Sensory and Physical	PLG: Pupil will take a fork which is loaded by an adult and guide it to their mouth to eat their dinner at least six times.	1. An adult will cut their dinner and load their fork with food. 2. An adult will place the fork in their hand. 3. An adult can support pupil initially by guiding their hand to their mouth. 4. Using a forward chaining approach, with the end goal of placing the loading fork on the plate and pupil will pick it up independently and feed themselves at least six times.	( ) will pick up a loaded fork, guide it to their mouth to feed themselves, six times independently.	Achieved Partially Not achieved
EHCP Outcome: Pupil will be able to participate in a variety of learning activities within her daily programme to develop her independence including fine and gross motor skills and self-care.				

Essentially, the aim of the plan is to form a cycle:

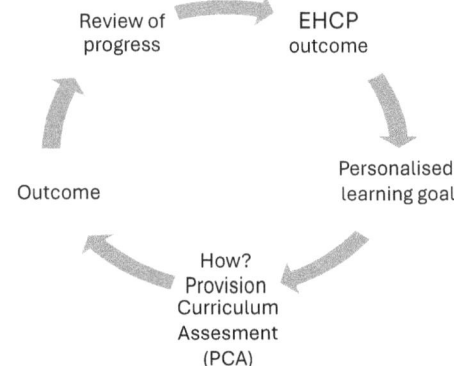

How Do You Achieve Inclusion for Learners with SEND in the Classroom?

As we all know, trying to achieve the ideal of inclusion is not always straightforward especially as complex cases are on the increase and funding is on the decrease. Following, are two common features from schools embedding inclusion, forming a model of provision:

1. Inclusive schools tend to share an ethos which is positive and welcoming but which also have a strong achievement orientation. Strong achievement orientation meaning: strong achievement towards ambitious targets, set for all pupils. Typically functioning children would work towards SATS and GCSEs. Learners with SEND would work towards independence, communication of their needs and wants and the possibility of acquiring some form of accreditation for example: functional skills entry-level qualification. For these pupils their journey is typically made up of small steps; these are their achievements, not necessarily a large target all at once (to support with small step teaching try looking into task analysis and backward chaining). When a small step has been achieved, what is the next one? For example, if a pupil is using symbols and language to request a snack, and that is achieved, then move to the next step. Do they need that symbol sentence or can they now just request the snack using the language?

2. Classroom practice in inclusive schools is recognisably like 'good' practice everywhere. This can be hard to achieve, as to be 'on it' all of the time is tiring; however, incorporating a lot of the strategies throughout this book into your everyday teaching will help you to achieve this. Reflect and think: is there anything else I can put in place to redirect, for example a visual?

How Do We Transfer these Strategies into the Classroom to Achieve Inclusion?

- During target setting meetings, you are identifying universal, targeted or specialist provisions. Leaders could look for commonalities between plans in the universal offer and use these to inform the schools 'offer' to all pupils. They could inform whole-school expectations, development plans, briefings, trainings, key consistencies (non-negotiables), learning walks and adaptive plans.
- In the same meetings, identify what is specific to the child by asking the question: Does everyone know what the intervention is? Is everybody suitably trained? Are there any potential barriers to implementing the provision? Then use the answer to these to inform your training needs.

24 Developing Educational Plans for Learners with SEND

So, how can we put the expectations and plans into the classroom? An effective approach is to break it down into steps. The first step is in line with the anticipate and plan approach and that is to look at your timetable.

For example:

Register	English	Snack	Maths	Reading	Lunch	Playtime	Topic	Home

Some questions to ask:

Access – Can 100 per cent of pupils access the subject (English)?

Who – who will need staff support and what will this look like? Can I put a smaller group within another group that could be supported by the same adult? Can I use visual aids, for example checklists rather than prompts from an adult?

When – When during the activity are staff available? When and what can pupils access independently? Incorporate Now and Next boards into your planning to help organise what will happen, with whom and when.

Where – Can all pupils successfully access activities in the same room? What does this look like?

These questions will interlink, and help to shape what lessons will look like, thus creating an inclusive daily timetable for all pupils to access. Once this is in place it ticks over, and then it just needs reviewing. For those that have bespoke timetables, it may be beneficial to have them displayed alongside the whole class timetable so that everyone involved is on the same page.

- Also, once you have built your timetable, you are further building your school's curriculum. You are building what the class and, therefore, the school now offers. This can be built-in to your curriculum documents. For example, part of the offer for Literacy is: Pre-Programme stage – Branch maps and Engagement Model – Pre-Key Stage standards – National Curriculum. Something like this will also highlight the broad need that you have at your school.

For example:

Sensory Circuits	EHCP-targeted teaching: Attention Autism	Snack	Maths	Reading Phonics Intervention	Lunch	Playtime	Topic	Home

Or a provision timetable with who is doing what.

Monday
Registration Sensory Circuits (pupil initial)
English EHCP targets ()
Snack
Maths
Reading Phonics Intervention ()
Lunch
Playtime
Topic

When I talk about using Now and Next boards in the planning process this helps with organising staff. For example, if Attention Autism (EHCP targeted teaching) is first, followed by 'choosing' then the adult may be able to support elsewhere during this time. By involving that in the planning process, you know who is where and when.

Now	Next
Attention Autism	Choosing

Inclusion in Special School Settings

With the breadth of need and provision growing in special schools, it can be a challenge to provide that inclusive curriculum for all pupils in one classroom, without having periphery learners. The following case studies explore this further.

> ### Case Study: Complex Special Needs School Curriculum.
>
> This special school has 232 pupils aged from 4–19 years old. The pupils that attend have mild, moderate, severe, profound and multiple learning needs and disabilities making the breadth and depth of need very wide. Almost 50 per cent of the school are identified as non-speaking.
>
> Therefore, taking the idea of time and value, the setting restructured classes to build curriculum pathways in each key stage forming *Pre-formal (Experience), Semi-formal (Engage) and Formal (Enhance) curriculums with a focus on inclusive practice, independence and communication. This re-structure achieved two things:
>
> - All learners could access a curriculum in a classroom with peers, avoiding pupils operating on the periphery of the class.
> - Lessen the range of abilities and therefore the breadth of differentiation so that teachers would then have more time to focus on a narrower amount of need supporting all students in equal value.
>
> *It is important to note that these titles are under review as Formal learners are still not formal learners as the title would suggest. Titles such as Pre-formal, Informal and Semi-formal are emerging alternatives.

Chapter Summary

In conclusion, the idea of inclusion can be a challenge. My interpretation is to provide all learners with a daily curriculum that they can access most of the time. This can be achieved by anticipating and planning access for all. It is important to stress that when writing this book, I have kept in mind the 'typical classroom', that is, 30+ pupils, one teaching assistant (TA) (sometimes) and the pressures on schools that come in the form of two words: rigour and expectations.

Therefore, the strategies that follow keep the typical classroom (as outlined above) in mind, in order to make this book practical, realistic and a supportive tool in providing inclusive educational plans for SEND.

 Further Reading

- How to identify learners with special educational needs: https://sendpathways.co.uk/identifying-learners-with-sen/

2 What Does the Physical Environment Look Like?

Chapter Introduction

This chapter focusses on how we can create that enabling environment when it comes to communication. This chapter shares the '**what**' we can put in place to give a voice for those specific pupils so that they can express their needs and wants.

What Is a Communication-supportive Environment?

Communication-supportive environments may have evolved from language rich environments, creating the shift in focus from language to using the language to communicate wants and needs. Speech and Language UK (2025) provide the following definition:

> A communication-supportive environment is one that ensures that children's speech, language and communication skills are planned for and supported throughout the day. It will look slightly different in early years settings and in school environments, but in general, it covers three aspects:
>
> - The **physical environment**
> - The **strategies** that **adults** use
> - The **opportunities** that children have to practise their communication skills.

> *Points of Reflection: This is something for those in early years to think about, especially with the increase of non-speaking pupils coming into Nursery and Reception classes.*

The idea is by enabling pupils to communicate, this should then decrease anxiety and frustration throughout the day. Following, I have listed ideas that you can refer to, that will help to build that environment.

> *Points of Reflection: Are our environments led by what the pupils need/want?*

Speech and Language Screeners

I feel it is important to begin with how speech and language have significant links with emotions, behaviour, trauma, recalling and retelling to name a few. Pupils with speech and language needs can miscategorise emotions and misinterpret intentions of others. They may not have developed emotional granularity and therefore aren't able to articulate how they are feeling. For those that have had traumatic experiences, this can have a significant impact on language development, making things like recalling and retelling difficult. Narratives can be very fragmented, missing out thoughts and feelings. This can also have a significant impact on the pupil's reading and writing. Therefore, working on their oral skills would support this. If a pupil struggles to tell a story and the significance of that story, then it may be speech and language difficulties; or those pupils that can show challenging behaviours you want to rule out speech and language needs, so, it may be helpful to use a screener. When writing this book, what was becoming common practice in secondary schools and youth justice services was the use of screeners. Some secondary schools were blanket screening all of Year 7s and others were using screeners as and when. SEMH alternative provisions were also beginning to screen all of their pupils on admission to then be able to build in support where needed. Special Schools use specific assessments to assess pupil's blank levels. Most local county councils have speech screener information on their websites. Following are two links to screeners that are commonly used, one for primary and the other for Secondary:

- WellComm (ages 6-11): https://www.glassessment.co.uk/assessments/products/wellcomm/
- Ages 11-18: https://shop.speechandlanguage.org.uk/products/progression-tools-from-the-communication-trust-for-secondary-years-set

Speech and Language UK are also a great place to go to for any speech- and language-related resources.

AAC: Augmentative and Alternative Communication

AAC refers to different ways that people communicate, either as well as or instead of using speech. People might use AAC if they have difficulties with their speech. This can include everything from body language and simple signs or gestures, to symbol boards and electronic communication aids. Almost everyone uses some form of AAC in addition to speech, for example using facial expressions or a gesture to add to what is being said.

- Smartbox (2025) https://thinksmartbox.com/what-is-aac/

Following are different types of AAC and some brief definitions:

- Unaided AAC: This doesn't need any equipment or resources. It includes strategies such as facial expressions, sign language and gestures such as wave or pointing to something.
- Paper based AAC: This is also called 'low-tech'. This includes printed resources like alphabet boards or symbol flashcards.
- Electronic AAC: Also called 'high-tech'. This includes devices which speak your message out loud, sometimes called speech-generating devices or voice output communication aids.

The rest of the chapter will list examples of AAC beginning with high tech and then moving on to low-tech starting with visuals. However, 'visuals' will have several examples under its own heading. Each example will introduce what it is and how it can be utilised.

High-Tech AAC

Pro-Talker: Enables independent verbal picture communication for pre-verbal users of all ages. This device allows you to place any photo, symbol or object of reference on to a sound tag card and record the corresponding word. To activate voice output, place the sound tag card on any one of the buttons and push. It can be recorded using a voice similar to that of the user, for example child/male/female and the voice recorder should use language appropriate and relevant to the user. Ideal for users that:

- engage well with auditory feedback;
- have low muscle strength or a light touch as the tiles can be adapted to 'light touch mode';
- are visually impaired as there is a large tag option;
- are a wheelchair user, it can be mounted and is portable (it comes with a backpack).

GoTalk+: Offers a variety of high-tech devices, which are lightweight and robust. There is a choice of communication aid; they include devices from one button messengers to devices with 20+ locations including lanyards, watches, talk books and grids. These devices allow you to place any photo or symbol to a tile and record the corresponding word. To trigger voice output, push the tile. Then it can be recorded using a voice similar to that of the user, for example child/male/female and should use language appropriate and relevant to the user. The GoTalk Grids in particular can also be set up like a core board. Ideal for users that:

- engage well with auditory feedback;
- have achieved targets with OoR and are looking for the next progression.

For tablet and mobile phones there are a variety of communication apps that enable the user to communicate through a collection of core boards. These are easy to edit and amend, and can open up a vast amount of topics/vocabulary for the user. The devices are lightweight and easily transitioned. Ideal for users that:

- engage well with auditory feedback;
- have low muscle strength or a light touch as the sensitivity can be altered;
- are visually impaired as there is a large view option;
- are accomplished users of core boards;
- have a divergence between their receptive and expressive language skills;
- eye gaze users.

Visuals

Using visuals with pupils with SEND has a large number of benefits in terms of developing communication and independence, while reducing challenging behaviours. Visuals can take away the uncertainty of an environment, making it predictable, trustworthy and safe and can therefore reduce anxiety. For an adult it can also help to redirect, set expectations, embed independence and free up time. Visuals do work! Sometimes it just takes time.

Most schools rely on symbol-based tools like Widgit software, valued for its intuitive and user-friendly design. This powerful program enables the seamless creation of visual aids that combine symbols with text to enhance communication. Users can also personalise their materials further by incorporating photos or images. With hundreds of templates and a vast library of pre-made resources, the system makes it easy to design custom flashcards, task cards, timetables, visual stories and a wide variety of other tools to support learning and communication.

Following is where you are able to sign up for a free trial: https://widgitonline.com/en/sign_up/trial?trial_type=standard

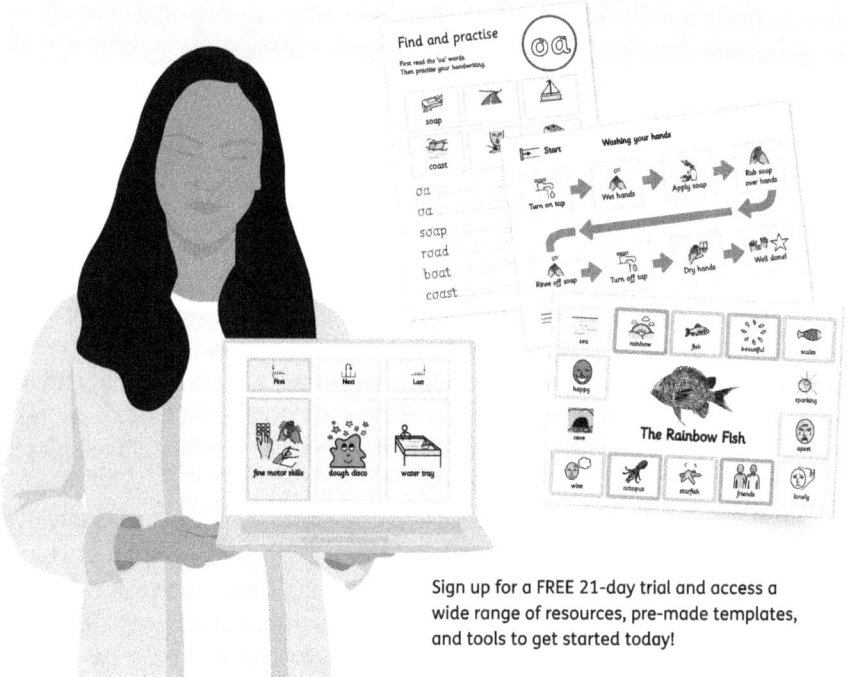

Visuals can have a significant impact. Following are ways in which visuals can support pupils:

- Comprehension: First of all, processing spoken language relies heavily on auditory memory skills. For many young people with additional needs, auditory skills are an area of difficulty, but visual skills can be an area of strength. Therefore, using visual supports, helps pupils to comprehend information. Visuals can provide a concrete reference for individuals to understand and remember information, which can help reduce confusion and frustration. Using visuals is a way of introducing/developing the concept of time (e.g. Now, Next, Then). Using consistent vocabulary alongside a visual increases the pupil's understanding of the word, the image and the activity/event or information at the same time, making all of those links.
- Communication: Visual supports are commonly used to support communication, especially for individuals who are non-speaking, have limited language or in moments of difficulty/crisis, struggle to find words. This is explored more in the following chapter.
- Independence: By providing clear and consistent visual cues, individuals can learn to navigate their environment more independently. This can include using a personalised timetable where pupils can put activities into a finished container and/or checklists where the student can tick or cross things off as they work through them.
- Reducing anxiety: Visuals are a way of providing the pupil with trust in that the environment will meet their need, therefore reducing anxiety and building trust. Visual timetables provide knowledge of the day and what is happening. Think about ourselves as adults – we keep diaries not only to remember the dance lessons, football and drama shows, but also so we know what is going on. We need that information or we worry as we need to know the plan for the day.
- Reducing the mental load: Use of visuals can reduce processing load and help to cope with demands and reduces reliance on working memory.
- Equipment is clearly marked with a label saying what it is.
- Planned seating arrangements so that children are encouraged to work together and communicate with each other. Children with challenges are sat closer to the front and facing the teacher.
- Managed background noise levels so that children are able to listen and think.
- Clear and consistent routines – how does the environment help children to know what to expect and when? Minimising grey areas.

Overall, the use of visuals can be a powerful tool in supporting communication, promoting independence, reducing anxiety and preventing challenging behaviours. Visuals can be used in the moment or throughout the day to reduce those times of escalation and support regulation. By providing clear and consistent visual cues, individuals can better understand their environment and develop the skills needed to navigate it successfully.

Objects of Reference (OoR)

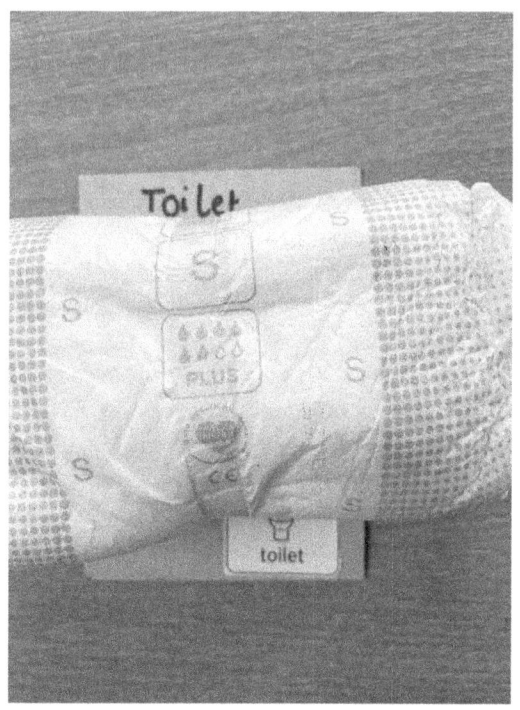

What Does the Physical Environment Look Like?   35

36 *Developing Educational Plans for Learners with SEND*

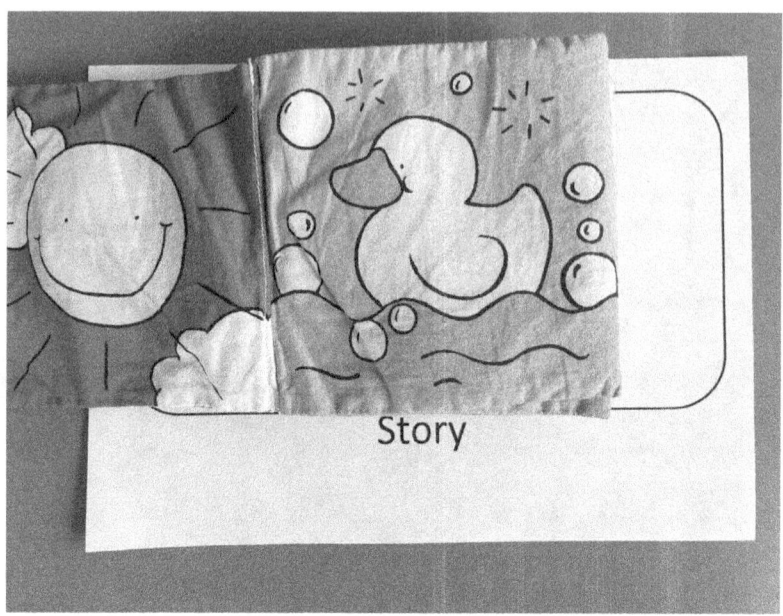

What Does the Physical Environment Look Like? 37

An Object of Reference (OoR) is an object, or part of an object, that has a particular meaning. They stand for something, each acting as a symbol in much the same way as words do, whether spoken, signed or written (McLachlan and Elks, 2017). It is used to refer to a:

Person e.g. physio, Speech and Language Therapist (SaLT)
Object e.g. car, computer
Location e.g. playground, library, sensory room
Event e.g. personal care, snack time, circle time

otherwise known as POLE. For example, a certain ball might be associated with going outside or an armband might represent swimming.

Objects of Reference are used to:

- Increase pupils' awareness and understanding of their environment and of the world.
- Develop anticipatory skills – make their world more certain, so they know what is about to happen or is happening.
- Help a pupil to make choices, e.g. the pupil can be shown a bucket or a watering can to enable them to make a choice between sand or water play. (McLaughlan and Elks, 2017)

When choosing items as OoR, keep in mind the following four points:

1. Real life objects used in the activity
   - e.g. a cup that is used every time the learner has a drink would become an OoR for a drink
2. Objects not used in the activity
   - e.g. set of keys for car, piece of towel for bathroom
3. Objects with a shared feature
   - e.g. sandpaper for sand pit
4. Miniature objects
   - e.g. a toy cup from the role play area for drink

Consider the following:

- Relevance and motivation – the object should be meaningful to the pupil.
- Ease of use – is it easy for the OoR to go with the pupil, so think about size and weight.
- Hygiene and durability – think about how long it will last and is it easy to clean.
- Expense and availability – it should be easy to replace if it goes missing. (McLaughlan and Elks, 2017)

There are at least three schemes:

- A shared scheme – all pupils in a setting use the same object of reference to represent a POLE.
- A differentiated scheme – all pupils use the same object but that object may vary slightly dependent on the pupil. It may be different in size, colour or texture.
- An individualised scheme – each pupil has a specific object to represent each POLE. (McLaughlan and Elks, 2017)

When thinking about objects of reference for your class or pupil, think about:

- Who are frequent visitors to your setting?
- What objects are needed for different activities?
- Do you have a sensory room? What might be the consistent object that you could use in every class?
- What transitions do your children make through the day that they might need consistent support for?

Objects of Reference are an effective tool for those pupil's that need that tangible support to help to understand what is being communicated.

First and Then Boards

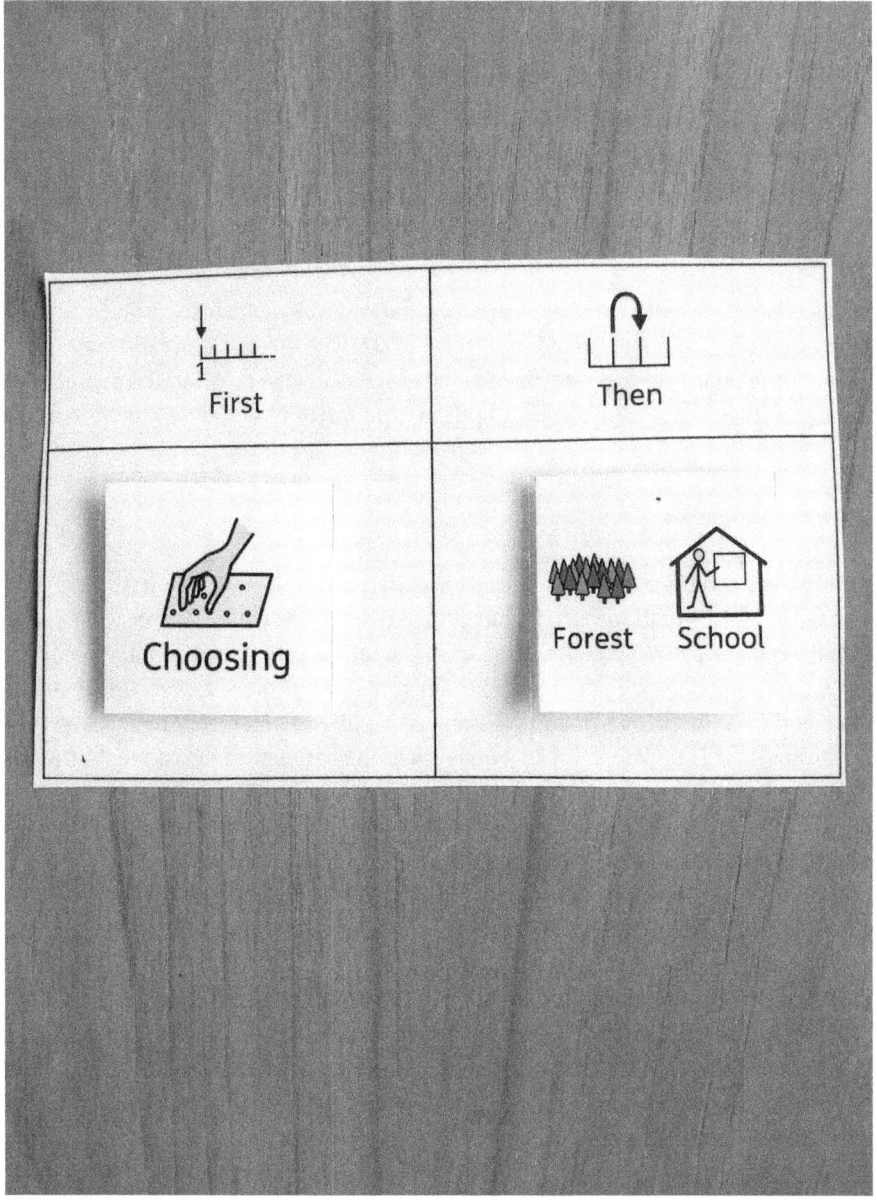

First of all, there is some debate over which words to use: First, Now, and so on. For the purpose of this book although First is being used, it is up to you which language you prefer. The aim is that it is consistently used with the purpose that the pupil understands that in that moment, this is what is happening followed by that.

- These can be used to support transitions between activities, encourage children to do 'less preferred' activities and support understanding the language around sequencing and time concepts, e.g. First, Next, Then. When pupils engage in 'less preferred activities', these boards show that there is an end to the activity and that it will not go on forever.
- These boards help with consistency of expectations. All adults (especially in a change of face situation) and pupils know what the expectations are and can remain on the same page. These boards give direction and clarity for all involved. When the adult builds the timetable, they can decide how flexible and descriptive they need to be for example:

First	Then
Write two sentences	iPad

- Alternatives can be drawing on a piece of paper or a whiteboard so that the visual can be used in every situation, even if you don't have a photo/symbol. Tip for when pupils are becoming distressed: if you are using a whiteboard and the child is not in a calm state, show the whiteboard; do not give it to them in case they throw it. Also, if they are in this state and they know the symbol, you can just point and add in language when they are ready. Sometimes adding in the language when they are not ready can make the learner more frustrated.
- First and Then boards are typically made up of two sections, one labelled 'First' and the other labelled 'Then.' The 'First' section displays the current activity, while the 'Then' section shows what activity will come next. This can help students with complex needs to understand what they are currently doing and what will happen next, which can reduce anxiety and increase their sense of control.
- First and Then boards can be tailored to meet the specific needs of each pupil. For example, pictures or symbols can be used to represent each activity, which can be particularly helpful for pupils with limited verbal communication skills. Additionally, the boards can be used to support social and emotional learning, with pictures or symbols representing emotions or sensory needs.
- These do not have to be restricted to Now and Next. They could be done in three sections, Now, Next and After. For example, Write sentence/Draw picture/Snack.

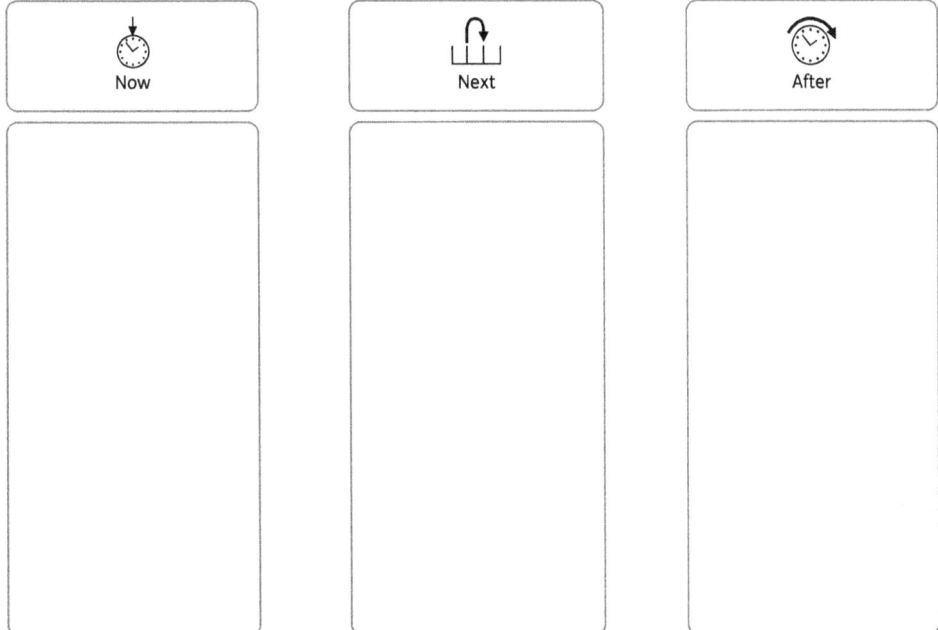

Overall, First and Then can be a useful tool for pupils with complex needs as they provide a clear visual structure to help with communication and routine. By using this tool, pupils can better understand what is happening in their day and feel more in control of their environment.

Visual Timetables

> *Points of Reflection: Think about it as an adult, if we went to a room for a day but were never told what we were going to be doing. Take some time to think about and imagine how that would feel for you. What if someone took your diary away and said don't worry, I will tell you what you are doing just before you do it?*

Visual timetables are a type of visual support that uses pictures or symbols to represent tasks or activities in a sequence or schedule. Most classrooms use these. Visual timetables typically consist of a series of pictures or symbols that are arranged in the order in which tasks or activities will occur. For example, a visual timetable for a school day might include pictures or symbols for arriving at school, register, phonics, snack, playtime, maths, lunch, and so on.

Visual timetables can be used to help individuals in several ways:

- Provide predictability: Visual timetables provide a predictable sequence of events or tasks, which can help reduce anxiety and increase feelings of control. Again, providing

an environment that meets the pupil's needs. The environment meets the need which manages the anxiety.
- Support understanding: Visual timetables can help individuals understand the sequence and duration of tasks or activities, which can reduce confusion and frustration.
- Promote independence: Visual timetables can help individuals to complete tasks or activities independently, by providing a clear sequence of steps to follow.
- Can be personalised: Visual timetables can be customised to the individual's needs and preferences, by including specific tasks or activities that are relevant to them.

Overall, visual timetables can be a powerful tool in supporting communication, understanding and independence by providing predictability, and being customisable to individual needs. Visual timetables can help individuals to navigate their daily routines, reducing anxiety and frustration.

Timers and Countdown Visual Aids

Visual timers and countdowns provide a clear visual representation of the passage of time. This can be particularly helpful for pupils who struggle with abstract concepts like time, or who have difficulty understanding spoken instructions. Visual timers can be used to help pupils:

- Manage their time more effectively. For example, a teacher might use a visual timer to show pupils how long they have to complete a task or how long they have for a break.
- Understand and follow routines. For example, a teacher might use a visual timer to show pupils how long they have for each activity during a lesson.
- Who struggle with transitions. For example, a visual timer can be used to show pupils how long they have until the end of an activity, which can help to reduce anxiety and increase their understanding of what is expected of them.

Remember, if a pupil is heightened don't give them the timer as they may be inclined to throw it. I would also recommend reflecting on when is the right time to use a timer, is it going to make the situation worse.

Visual Routines/Schedules/Personalised Routine Charts

These visuals provide clear steps needed to complete particular activities. This could include the sequence of washing your hands. You can decide how simple or detailed you would like it. Remember to make the cards as easy to follow as possible; this includes the layout of the cards. Sometimes these are sequenced using a grid, which is hard to follow. Things need to be simple and clear to follow, eliminate grey areas. These could also include personalised routines for example, bedtime routines.

What Does the Physical Environment Look Like? 43

Task Management Boards

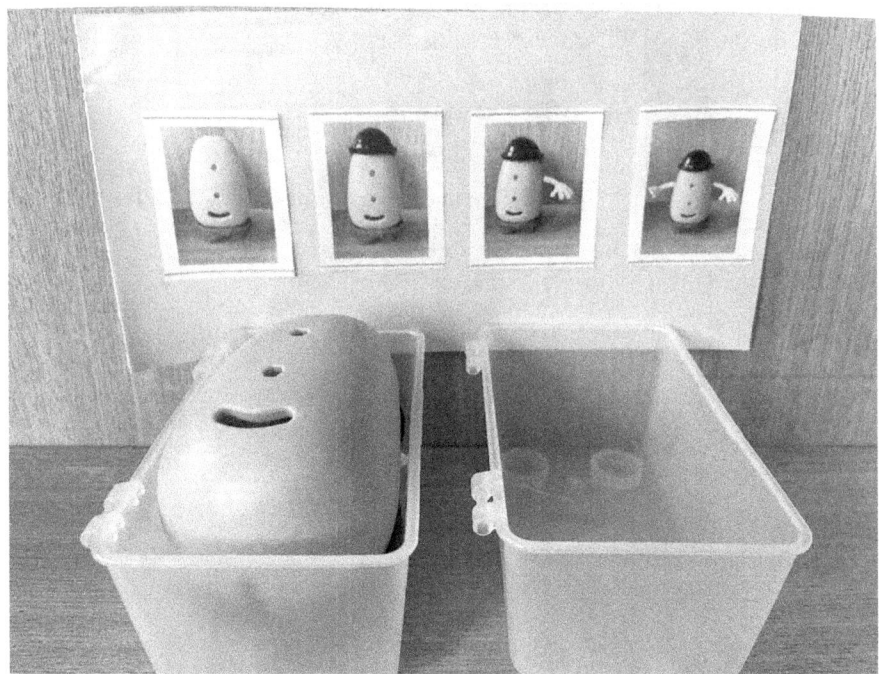

These are an effective way to support a pupil's ability to understand instructions, track, decode (skills reinforced by sensory circuits) and stay on task throughout, without need for adult support at each stage. Adult support could be tagged on to the end for those pupils that depend upon adult interaction. This way they will know that they will get adult attention once they have completed the task. Alternatively, a Now, Next and Then board could have: task board, show teacher, next activity. Task boards can be differentiated to include text, accompanied with a First and Then board so the pupil knows what to go on to next.

Below is just an example of a task board. Take the idea and make it fit for purpose for that pupil. For example: symbols and more text could be added (it is always dependent on the level of the pupil).

| To do: | Draw | Cut | Glue | Write | Show teacher |

3, 2, 1, Finished

The 3, 2, 1 symbol helps pupils who struggle with transitions, waiting, giving items back (find a neutral place rather than in your hand) and knowing what comes next. It provides a visual countdown, reducing anxiety or frustration and offering structure. For some pupils, this approach can be more effective than traditional sand timers or verbal prompts alone. You can use the example provided. The aim is for it to be just a simple visual that supports a countdown: 3 → 2 → 1 → Finished (or another suitable ending symbol). The most important and crucial takeaway is that it is used consistently by all staff across all settings.

Choose/Request Board

This is an effective way of pairing and connecting if I touch this, then I get what I am wanting/needing. Therefore, using this board around things that pupils really want is a fast way of teaching pupils how to communicate using symbol cards or visuals. The key to introducing this type of visual is to make the board using pictures/symbols of things that the pupil really likes. If you are using Widget, you can drop the pictures into the flashcard boxes. It is up to you what size you would like them to be. Essentially, they are specific pictures/symbols on a piece of paper with 'I want' on it. You can have them for different topics, for example places, food and so on. For instance, when a pupil is upset then you can have a board that contains relevant calming items like pictures/symbols of ice, weighted blanket, dark den and so on. Another example would be if the pupil uses the iPad or wants something on a screen, then have pictures of their favourite videos on a request board so that the pupil uses the board to choose from. The following is an example, you would just need to add in a visual:

I want . . .

| Wheels on the bus | Old Mac Donald had a Farm | 5 Little Monkeys |
| 5 little ducks | Incy wincy spider | Twinkle Twinkle Little Star |

Checklists

Checklists can be used to provide a visual representation of what needs to be done during a transition or in a lesson. For example, a checklist could include pictures or icons of tasks such as packing up materials, walking to the next location and settling in. Checklists can help to promote independence by providing clear and consistent expectations. These can also be used to support those with friendly reminders while completing tasks. For example: capital letters and full stops.

Like and Don't Like Boards

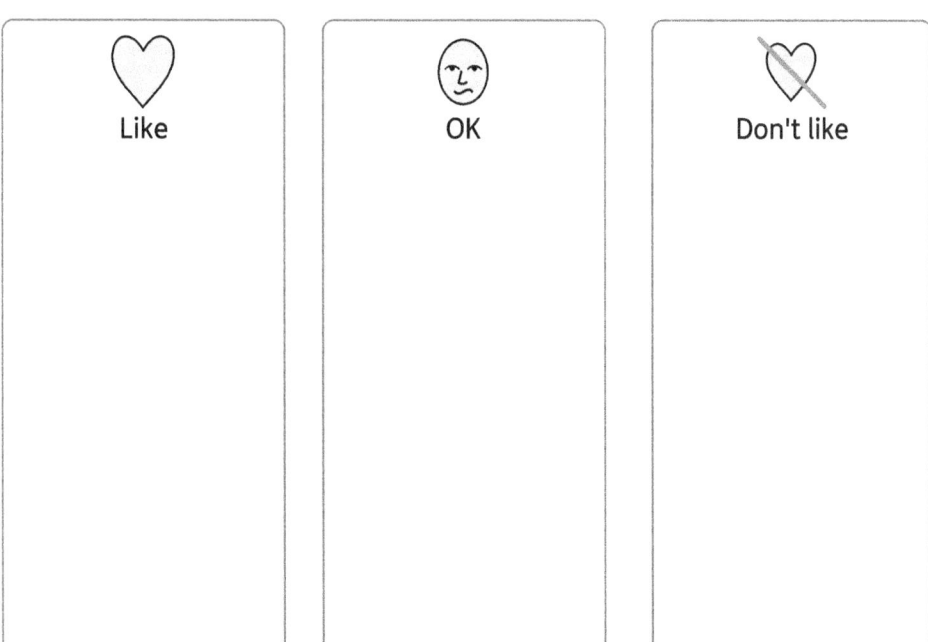

These can be used to identify what pupils like and dislike. It is also an 'in the moment' tool for when you see pupils dislike something, then you can then refer them to the 'Don't Like'

column. Or if it is something they are enjoying you can refer to the 'like' side. This board can be used as a de-escalation strategy. By using symbols, pupils can then tell you things they like and don't like.

Talking Mats

Talking Mats give pupils and young adults with a variety of communication barriers the opportunity to communicate preferences. These can be tailored to individuals, for example using photos instead of pictures, changing the topics needed and so on. Talking Mats can be introduced on a smaller scale and progress on with the learners. Each learner has their own Talking Mats which can be saved to show progression, patterns and barriers. With more formal-style learners we can use to build on independence, giving them a sense of pride in completing self-assessments at the end of lessons. In some studies, Talking Mats are highlighted as a way of supporting non-speaking pupils manage their anxiety and mental health. More information can be found at: https://www.talkingmats.com/

Core Boards

Core boards are a common tool provided by speech and language therapists. Just One Norfolk, NHS Speech and Language define Core boards as a tool that 'can support children to communicate for lots of different reasons including requesting, commenting, informing instructing, questioning and sharing opinion'. Core boards can come in various ways, they can be A4- or A3-sized paper with a grid and different language options using text and a symbol. There are a lot of different options out there via a Google search on Core boards or core word board.

Social Stories

Social stories are short, personalised narratives that are designed to help pupils to better understand, process and navigate social situations. An amazing support tool! More information can be found at: https://carolgraysocialstories.com/social-stories/what-is-it/

Draw It Out

Another way of using illustrations is when you are working through a conflict with a pupil. The visual element of drawing out what happened can support the conversation. Having pupils see what they were doing might help them to understand why it may have been a problem.

Visuals When Working with Specific People

Sometimes it is good to have a visual to show whom the pupil is working with, what they are doing and how long for. An alternative is if it is in the style of a reward then the pupil could have a choice of three activities to choose and from and two different times to choose how long for.

Blank Levels

When writing this book, these are used a lot by speech and language services. The blank model separates questions and directions into four levels. Bedfordshire Community Services has a document that clearly outlines 'What are Blank Levels and How to Use Blank Levels'; however, there is so much information out there around these levels. These play a key role in identifying pupils' understanding as well as giving adults knowledge of the next set of questions they would work towards. The test of Abstract Language Comprehension can be used to assess the level of abstract language a child can understand.

Communication Devices

For pupils who struggle with verbal communication, communication devices such as a tablet, a speech-generating device or a portable communication board and switches can be helpful in facilitating communication and reducing anxiety in the classroom.

Communication Books

> *Points of Reflection: Two-way communication. Teachers having symbols on a lanyard, does this also allow for the pupil to communicate or just the teacher to the pupil? If the pupil wanted to use it to communicate, the child would then be pulling on something around someone's neck. How does the pupil respond if they are non-speaking? Communication books can be accessed and used by both adult and the pupil.*

These are basically where you can house visuals for pupils, therefore they are typically for pupils who have limited to no language and can act as their 'voice'. The aim of these books is a resource for both adults and most importantly those pupils to use to communicate a want/need. They are typically A5 binder sized; however, this is led by the pupil. The boards act as a home for their visual supports so the pupil can access their symbols to communicate wants/needs and the adult can use them to model to the pupil how to use them. What goes in them is a combination of what the pupil needs and what adults need to teach the pupil how to use it. It can be as basic as it needs to be to start and then build it up, so eventually the pupil realises that he/she can use their book to let an adult know what they want.

Example of a Communication Book

These are ideas that could be included in communication books. However, they need to reflect the pupil as the purpose of these are to give a pupil a voice. These books house the individual visuals for that pupil to use and communicate with. Communication books must always be accessible to the user and must always travel with the user.

Example of what a communication book could look like:

- Front cover – Name and communication book.

> (Name)
> My Communication Book
> (add in symbol)

48 *Developing Educational Plans for Learners with SEND*

- Inside cover – Now and Next.

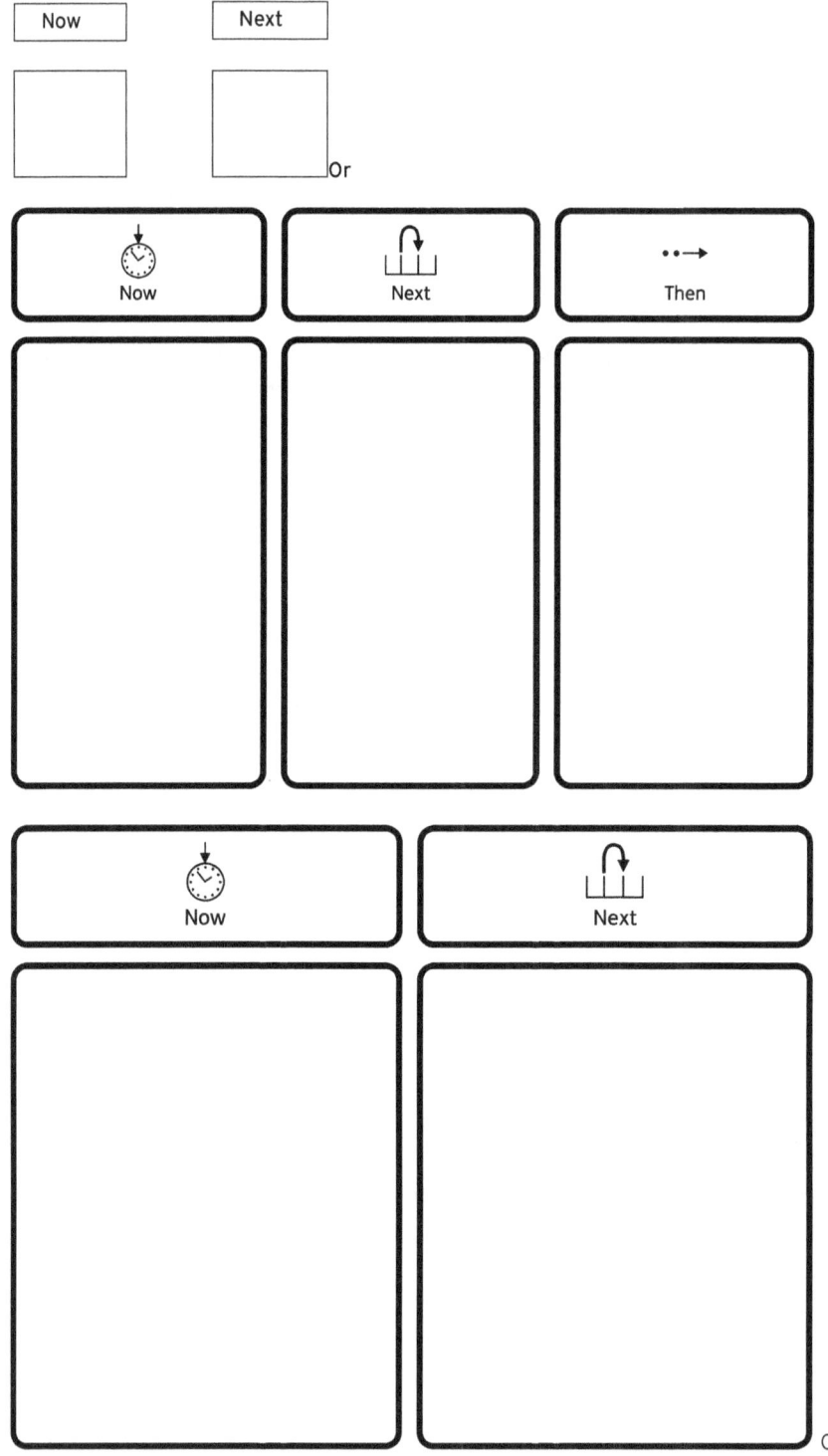

What Does the Physical Environment Look Like? 49

- Personalised Timetable strips. This example shows half of a day (just before lunchtime) in two strips.

- Accompanying symbols (cut and separated, ready to go on the board) for Now and Next boards.

50 Developing Educational Plans for Learners with SEND

- Request boards.

What Does the Physical Environment Look Like? 51

Widgit Symbols © Widgit Software Ltd 2002-2025. Link to website http://www.widgit.com.

- 3, 2, 1 finished.

- Inside the back cover – Like/Don't Like/Ok boards.
- Following are grid examples for those pupils that are more advanced:

52 *Developing Educational Plans for Learners with SEND*

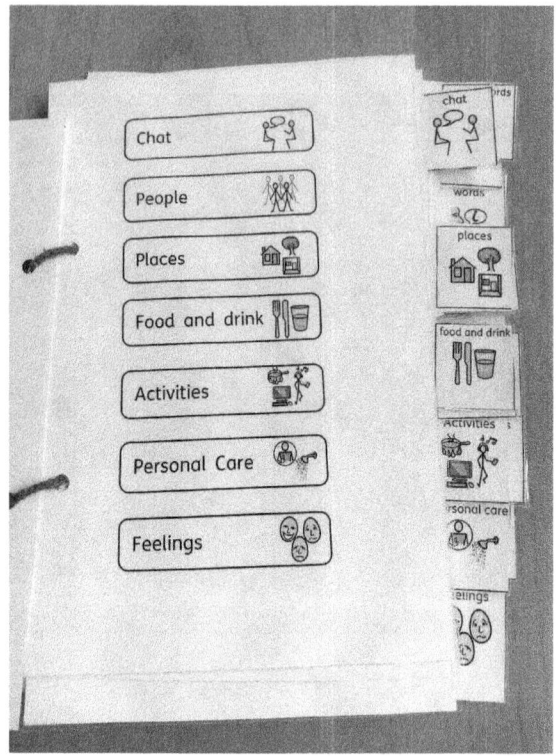

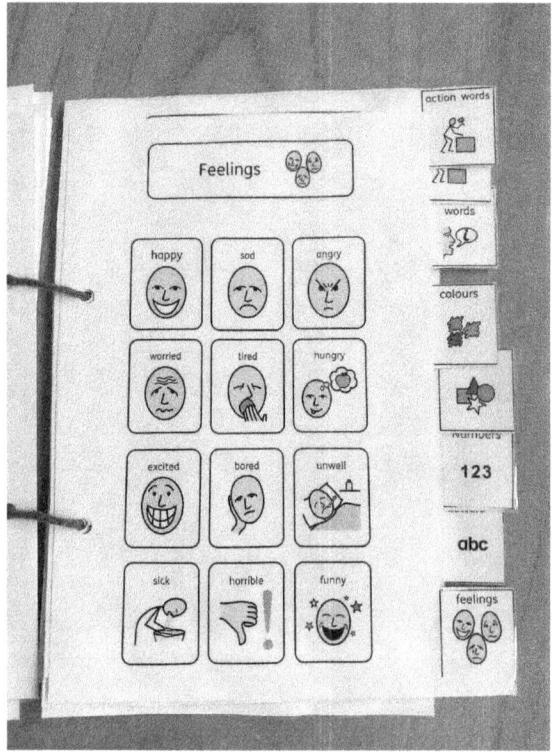

What Does the Physical Environment Look Like? 53

App Wheels

Call Scotland is a great resource especially regarding Apps for complex communication support needs and AAC. More information can be found at: https://www.callscotland.org.uk/downloads/posters-and-leaflets/

Chapter Summary

The key takeaways for this chapter are examples of 'what' resources you can use to build communication-supportive environments. The more the pupil develops, the more it informs the environment. If they are speaking, then just listen. You will be able to unpick and get that knowledge and understanding from what they are saying. If they are non-speaking then listen through their sounds and their body language as that will be their language. We just have to learn it. Then, we can use that information to support implementing visuals and teaching them how to use it. Which leads us to the next chapter, which will focus on '**how**' we can put these examples in place.

3 How to Implement a Communication-Supportive Environment

Chapter Introduction

This chapter explores how we, as adults provide a communication-supportive and enabling environment for pupils, especially those that are non-speaking or have limited language. This chapter outlines ideas that can be implemented through key contributors such as modelling, teaching and opportunities.

If we think that the child in that moment is not able to communicate, then we need to give them a voice as well as **teach** them how to use it. This typically comes from the adult using approaches to teach the child how to use something to get their needs/want met:

> *Points of Reflection: What do we do for a child that doesn't like eye contact, but we want their attention toward us? This can be tricky as we need to take care and be sensitive to what the pupil is comfortable with. It may be that the adult needs to learn other communication preferences. For those pupils who can look toward you, one approach is to ask the child to look at your nose (sometimes I get creative and ask if there is a bogey on my nose); this way it is not as intense, you have the pupil's attention and they are also looking at your mouth.*

First of all, before the chapter goes into more detail, it is important to highlight 'pairing' and how pupils will then start to transfer this. We want them to pair the following: 'If I do this, then I get this'. When it comes to communication, we want pupils to associate that way of communication to meeting that need, for example for the pupil to think if I touch that symbol (drink) then I get my drink. This is what we want to embed when teaching pupils how to use symbols to communicate. Use something they are motivated by to teach how to use symbols. This is covered in more detail throughout this chapter.

'I have tried visuals, they don't work' or 'Visuals will only work on a good day'

These can be common responses that come up when mentioning implementing visuals. Some of the reasons as to why they don't work is because the pupil doesn't like what is on the board. There is a demand on there that presents as a barrier to what they want, and what they want usually lives on the next side of the board.

How to Implement a Communication-Supportive Environment 57

When using visuals, this can help you to predict what their timetable will look like and therefore predict what strategies to put in place and when: for example, the pupil doesn't like reading, therefore the pupil may react in this way so I will: use this transition support tool + reading activity + then activity = management of distress and anxiety, around that demand. This helps us to build in that anticipate and plan process, and as you become more familiar with the pupil, that process becomes a natural response. It is not meant as a big separate plan, it can be as easy as: fidget toy + Now and Next symbols (to highlight that own choice is next) = manage anxiety and clear communication.

Visuals can help to make what is uncertain certain and it is a form of communication but also acts as part of those small things that manage anxiety throughout the day to prevent escalation. If we add in those little 'regulation enablers', they are what can help to prevent escalation.

We teach these things on a good day and build that environment, so we can resort to them on a wobbly day. For example,

We use this everyday:

When	Then
The counting beads are in the container	We can play operation

So that we can use it as an in the moment strategy:

When	Then
Screaming Shouting Finished	Calm Sat down talking to me Reading your book together

Use multiple visual aids together so they are clear and concise and adults themselves don't get confused. Take the time to get your head around what you are doing first, so when you use visuals with the pupil, you can focus on implementing it for the child and not teaching yourself at the same time and therefore you already having that buy-in. For example:

Timetable
| Reading |
| swimming |
| snack |
| play |

58 Developing Educational Plans for Learners with SEND

Reading

Now	Next
My story	Colouring characters

(Then)
(Swimming)

Task Board (transition)

| Colouring pencils in container | Container on shelf | Walk and get bag | Walk to the pool |

It doesn't need to look pretty. Here is one completed in a lesson using a whiteboard:

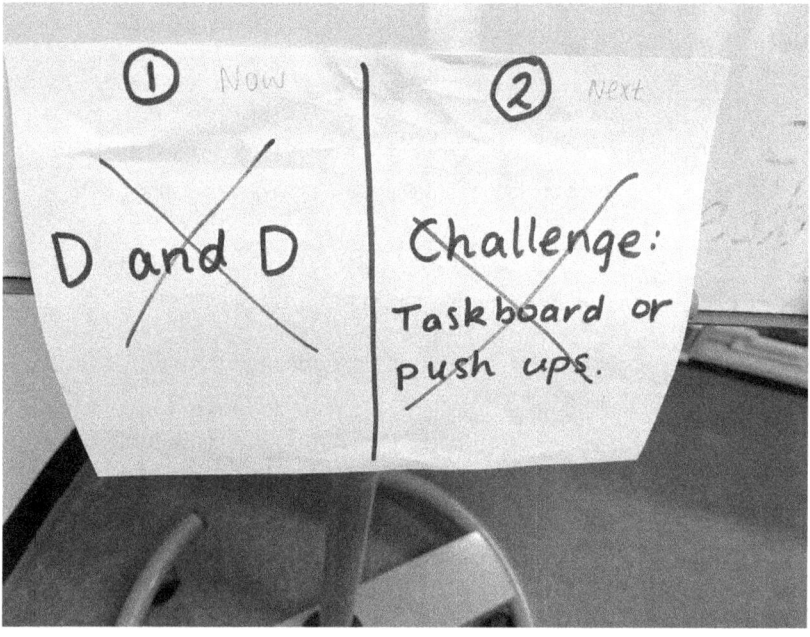

This is for pupils that like to sit next to adults and constantly ask for what is next, what should I do, is this right and seek that attention and/or attachment. Following is an example of visuals that can be put in place, this specific example is for writing:

Now and Next Board:

Now	Next
Write a sentence	Draw picture

Task board:

| Sentence in your head | Share with teacher | Write sentence Read sentence | Share with teacher | Draw picture |

Checklist:

- Sentence in your head
- Sound out word (depending on phonics scheme)
- Write word
- Finger space
- Finish writing sentence
- Read sentence

Implementing Visuals

When implementing visuals, following are points for you to consider:

- Think about trying to keep things simple and clear to eliminate grey areas. These visuals keep clear expectations and language concise for everyone.
- If repeating what is on the visual becomes a trigger, say it once and then put it away. You can refer to it again later or just pull out the visual and point without using language.
- Timetables highlight when favoured activities will be, that way pupils know that the answer is not necessarily no, it is not yet and then when it will be.
- Visuals support with scripting, so language is consistent and keeps it to a minimum, this can also prevent getting into a back-and-forth argument with the pupil.
- When you are presenting a visual, think about where you are and if you are wanting a pupil to leave the room, ensure that you aren't in the doorway and that your body is positioned to allow the pupil access as well as indicating where you would like them to go.
- Visuals show an end to a less preferred task and highlight when the start of a preferred task is.
- Think about and anticipate the pupil's behaviour and having access to the visual when needed. If they are likely to throw or tear it up, then don't let the pupil have it. If they do not like it, again present and then remove it. Use paper instead of a whiteboard or use a whiteboard but you have it or put it in a place that you can easily remove it.
- Allow the learner processing time. Sometimes they just need to process what is in their minds already and then they will process what you have said.

Points of Reflection: Think about as adults, when we are talking with someone then a few moments later or even later that day, we will say, 'Oh, I should have said that'. Therefore, think about processing time and giving pupils a moment before they respond or before you respond again. You will then learn their processing time and can use this when you are anticipating and planning throughout the day.

Teaching Pupils How to Use Symbol Cards from the Beginning

A common way to teach pupils how to use symbols for communication is through something that you know they will want. A common example is food. At snack time have photographs of their snack or even just a food symbol card in front of the pupil and you have the snack. Encourage the pupil to touch or hand the symbol card to you, then give the pupil the snack/food. If they are reluctant to touch the card, then you can guide their hand to touch it and give the snack/food straight away, therefore pairing those behaviours together. This can be transferred to requesting a piece of equipment – if you know that every day they go to the Lego then have the Lego symbol with you and put it in front of them. Encourage the pupil to tap or hand you the symbol then give them the Lego.

> *Points of Reflection: You may be asking yourself, 'but they can just go and get the Lego on their own why do they need a symbol?' You are using the Lego or snack to teach them how to use symbols to make requests. You know they want the Lego, so they will tap the card to get it. If we use something they don't want, as a way of teaching them, they won't engage and tap the symbol, so they won't learn how to use the symbol cards. Then everyone says that it is not working. But we know using visuals does work. This can be a stepping stone to then using a grid on an iPad or core boards.*

- The use of more and finished symbols. These are effective two-way communication cards instead of using yes and no. A way to introduce these cards: play a game they really enjoy (development appropriate) like peek-a-boo. Do it a few times and then stop. Encourage the pupil to touch the 'more' card and guide their hand if needed. When it is touched, play the game again. Stop and ask 'more', encouraging the pupil to touch the card. Repeat these a few more times and then say peek game has 'finished' while touching the finished card.

  This can be transferred to snack: if the student has one snack, for example. crackers. Hand the student a cracker then encourage or guide tapping the 'more' card. As soon as they have tapped or handed you the card then give the cracker. When the crackers are all gone, show the empty packet and say, 'Crackers finished' while tapping the card.
- The key is for the adult to model and guide. When the adult says 'more' or 'finished' they also tap the card and this is where pupils should have access to symbol cards, like in their communication book so both the adult and the pupil can use these. You are also building a relationship and trust with that pupil; trust that the environment will meet the needs of the pupil managing that anxiety and frustration.
- Choose/Request board is another 'in' with pupils, providing that opportunity for them to communicate their wants/needs and for us to teach them. For example, if a pupil likes particular things on the screen/iPad, have these on the request board. This would be a

piece of laminated paper with several pictures of what they may want on it. Present the board to the pupil, encourage them to point to their choice, then the adult plays that particular thing on the iPad. The idea is that they will begin to follow: if I do this (point to 'Babyshark') then I get it on the screen, again going back to that idea of pairing. Once that need is met, that will be the motivator to repeat that behaviour. Therefore, when the clip finishes, say 'Finished', and present the pupil once more with the board. Repeating the sequence they choose, the adult plays the clip. You can then transfer this over to other request boards, for example for particular items. If these are housed in the pupil's communication folder, the idea is that the pupil will then go to their folder, pull it out and use it to request items.

Once the adult has supported the pupil with how to use symbol cards then you can add more symbols to their communication book for both the adult and pupil to use. Refer to the previous chapter for what these symbols may look like.

Objects of Reference (OoR)

Initially the number of Objects of Reference used should be limited to between 3-5 and should represent POLEs (People, Objects, Location and Events) that occur regularly and frequently, for example snack, lunch, toilet, drink or specific teachers.

When the OoR has been chosen, the adult would introduce the object and then it would be used consistently. Try to ensure that it is easily accessible and if it is child-specific then it can be in a bag that goes with the child or if the item is for the whole class, then it could go where it can be accessed in that part of the classroom, for example hanging near the door if it represents going to the toilet.

Show the OoR immediately before the change in Person, Object, Location or Event. This could go alongside Now: Soft play. Show the Object of Reference. After using the OOR, it would be put away, for example back in an OOR bag/box. The idea is for the adult to have the child pair the next activity with a physical object.

For those pupils who have visual impairments, then objects would be tactile and students would explore these through touch. For example: relate the object to those adults that work with the pupil. Kerry rubs her ring on the pupil's hand, Rachael uses her watch.

Trouble shooting:

If the pupil drops or throws the OoR, the adult would pick it up and repeat the activity. This should happen approximately three times on each occasion. The adult can then carry the OoR him/herself and accompany the learner to the new POLE, occasionally displaying the OoR for the learner to see. If the learner ignores the OoR, the adult should attempt to get the learner to acknowledge the presence of the OoR and then place it in line of vision (on the learner's knee for example) before moving to the POLE.

Once the pupil becomes familiar with the Objects of Reference, more objects can be introduced and added to the bag (McLachlan and Elks, 2017).

Stages of Development for Objects of Reference

Stage	Presentation or OoR	Responses
One	The pupil is given the OoR and is taken to the activity	The pupil may have little interest or tolerance for the object and this may result in it being thrown, ignored or dropped
Two	The pupil is given the OoR and will go to the activity with prompting. Prompting may be physical, gestural or verbal. The aim being to gradually fade out the prompts	The pupil may carry or hold the OoR but at this stage will still have little understanding of what it means
Three	The pupil is given the OoR and will go to the activity or demonstrate understanding of an event without prompting e.g might look towards the activity	Pupil begins to show some understanding of the meaning of one or more OoRs, e.g if shown an OoR might look/move in direction of activity or show excitement
Four	The pupil will be able to select the appropriate OoR from a range of OoRs presented by a supporting adult to make a choice and go to the chosen activity	The pupil now has several OoRs that they link to activities and events
Five	The pupil can select the appropriate OoR independently and will go to the activity or use it to request something	The pupil selects and uses OoRs independently to make a choice or express a need

Source: Jones, 1995.

First and Then Boards

When you are using this with the pupil especially in the beginning, have the board in front of you and the pupil with two activities. Use the script: 'Now is reading a book', point to the symbol, then say 'Next is snack', again point to the symbol.

Now we are reading a book, have the book out and begin reading. When that has finished, we would say 'Reading has finished', put the book away and take the symbol off. Say 'Now is snack'. At this point transfer the snack over to the Now and put the next activity card on to the Next section saying what is next. Some people prefer Now and Next using two symbols without transferring them over, crossing them out when finished. For example, Now is reading, when reading has finished, cross it out. Next is snack, when snack is finished, cross it out.

When deciding what symbols to use on Now and Next boards, it depends on the child. Some pupils need them to be very descriptive, for example: instead of maths they would need Now is worksheet or activity then snack. For those needing specific symbol cards they could be on the back of the Now and Next boards or already in their communication books. You could model and involve the pupil when transferring them on to the Now and Next boards. If you are using symbol cards from the daily timetable, then you would take them from there and put them straight on to the Now and Next board. When finished, they could be put into a finished container, turned over or put back into the pupil's communication book under finished or just put back. Ensure that resources are ready and accessible, having correct symbol cards for that day in communication books and ready to be used.

Some pupils respond to three sections: First, Next and Then. The board is then presented in threes. For example: first read a book, next picture, then is choosing. Each one is taken off or crossed out as they are finished. While the pupil is choosing, the adult would put the next three activities on.

Timers and countdowns: When using these, they can also be a trigger so keep the timer where the pupil cannot access it, while using it to decide if it is effective or not. This is also a good time to use the 3, 2, 1, finished visual aid.

> Points of Reflection: Reflect back to the first chapter and timetabling, Now, Next and Then boards can also play a part in the timetabling of the entire class. You can use the board to help with timetabling who, what and when for that particular group or pupil. Move activities around, depending on when the adult is available or what activities the pupil can do independently or with a friend. This will help to inform planning for all groups, all pupils and adults.

Visual Timetables

These could be up in the classroom for all pupils. There are many variations on how these could be used. For example, turn over each card when the activity is finished. Use an arrow or peg to move along the timetable – this could also be a 'star of the day' job, or pupil who needs 'job' style activities to support regulation.

For individual pupils, you want it to be visible for them; this could be on the wall or on a strip of card. When implementing the timetable:

1. At the start introduce 'Maths' referring to the timetable.
2. When Maths has finished, you can have the pupil turn it over, cross it out, take it off or put it into a box labelled 'finished'.
3. Then refer back to the timetable for what is next.

Remember to keep it as clear as possible because if you are getting confused then the pupil will too. For those pupils that may need this visual, add in home at the end of the timetable so they can see the end point is home.

3, 2, 1 Countdown

This would be implemented into daily routines and educational plans, so that adults can use this to support pupils with transitions, waiting and predictability. Adults would use it to communicate to pupils that something has ended and to replace the adult continuously saying finished, finished. Putting this in place requires adults to be consistent, clear and calm in their delivery.

For example, at the end of the activity, the adult would say slowly, 3......2......1....... finished. Then move on. If the activity is a preferred activity and/or with a preferred object then variations could be:

- Finding a neutral space for the object as the pupil may not want to put the object in your hand but might put it on a table (neutral space).
- Showing the pupil on the timetable when they may have it again at a later time.

- If it is an object, can they take it with them to the next activity?
- Refocussing the pupil with what is next.

If you know that transitioning to the next activity may be difficult, while the pupil is engaged, ensure you have your 3, 2, 1 finished board and anything else you may need ready during that time.

Times that an adult would use 3, 2, 1 finished would be:

Transitions

- Finishing activities.
- Moving between areas (e.g., to the toilet, changing classrooms).
- End of lunch, playtime, or other regular activities.

Additional Situations Using 3, 2, 1 (Countdown)

- Calming Down: Signals a transition to a calming activity or space. Example: 'Let's go to the quiet area in 3 . . . 2 . . . 1 . . .'
- Starting an Unpreferred Task: Builds predictability for starting tasks that may be challenging. Example: 'We'll start our work in 3 . . . 2 . . . 1 . . .'
- Group Activities: Prepares pupils for moving between group and individual tasks. Example: 'We'll stop talking and start working in 3 . . . 2 . . . 1 . . .'
- Regulating Volume: Signals the need to quiet down in various settings. Example: 'Let's bring our voices down in 3 . . . 2 . . . 1 . . . quiet.'
- Physical Activities: Prepares pupils for starting or stopping movement activities. Example: 'We'll stop jumping in 3 . . . 2 . . . 1 . . . stop.'

Practical Examples

- Ending an Activity: 'In 3 . . . 2 . . . 1 . . . finished!' Move on to the next task or area.
- Waiting for a Toy or Person: 'You can have the toy in 3 . . . 2 . . . 1 . . . here you go!'

Key Reminders for Staff

1. Consistency is crucial: For this method to be effective, every staff member must use it regularly and across different settings.
2. It is not only for difficult moments but for every transition and waiting situation.
3. Support predictability and reduce pupil anxiety by giving them a clear visual cue.

Like and Don't Like Boards

We can use these alongside any communication boards or in any activity to model preferences. When a pupil is eating their snack, we can ask if they like or don't like what they are

How to Implement a Communication-Supportive Environment   65

eating. If the pupil is happily eating the snack and we know it is something they enjoy then we could point to like. If we see them spit it out, we can point to 'don't like'. We can also use picture symbol cards to put pictures of them on 'like' and 'don't like', to help reinforce their meaning.

This can also be used as a distraction tool. The board can be used to talk about preferences, encouraging the pupil to tell us what they don't like (talking out frustration and regulating) followed by what they do like. You can use the board to put physical items into categories like books and DVDs. Following are other examples of when and how these can be used:

- Sharing wishes and feelings for pre-verbal learners.
- As a plenary for end of session evaluations as a class or individually.
- A tool to establish an understanding of anxieties and well-being.
- Modelling –when starting out with pre-formal learners it is helpful to model your own preferences/feelings; however, try not to influence our learners' choices.
- Only using one symbol/picture with some pre formal learners if needed.
- You can use for many types of activities such as Attention Autism, Sensology, Sensory drama games etc.
- When choosing initial symbols/pictures also make sure to use options that your pupils have a definite preference to as well as ones you are unsure of.
- Good to use as a grab bag activity, especially as a lot of plans have targets around preferences and feelings.
- Find the right language for each pupil when expressing feelings/preferences.
- Talking partner activities, planned frequently throughout the day so that children have the opportunity to discuss thoughts and ideas with each other before sharing with the wider group.

Once the pupil has the understanding of 'like' and 'don't like', it can be used as a restorative tool for after a crisis. We can share what the pupil or the adults dis-like and what we would like to happen instead.

> ### Case Study: Year 7 Pupil Selective Mute.
>
> This pupil would communicate through sometimes speaking the odd English word but most of the time using 'grunting' noises or gestures. During an observation to try and capture his voice I used pages in my book to write out choices that the pupil could use in response to my questions. For example,
>
>

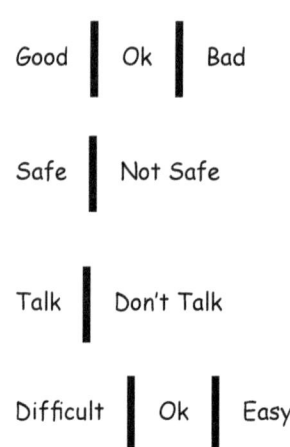

Through these, the pupil was able to tell me that they didn't feel safe and that's why they didn't want to talk, the work was difficult and pointed out what questions were difficult. They shared with me things they liked and didn't like. We were able to gather the pupil's voice through using these types of aids.

Waiting

This was written in collaboration with Charlotte Housedon, Complex Special Needs Behaviour Specialist. She wrote this programme to support pupils who find waiting difficult.

When introducing waiting, it is important to use a visual alongside the verbal request. This can aid in processing time, all the while reducing anxiety and reinforcing the request. This is an intervention focused on teaching and learning how to wait. It is not intended to be delivered while pupils are distressed. This method is best suited for students who are confident with requesting, as we do not want to deter students who have only just learnt this skill.

Timers – Using a timer can help show how long is expected for our students to wait. A one-minute sand timer works well for young students, but a digital timer can also be used.

Method: When introducing 'waiting', always start small and achievable. For example, waiting for 10 seconds to make a drink, turn on a desired device or wanting to go outside. Make sure you have all your visuals in place:

1. Once the student has requested their want or need, acknowledge their request.
2. Verbally reply with 'waiting', hand them the waiting symbol and set the timer (showing them while doing so).

3. Stay with your student while they are waiting in case they find this time period tricky. Always reinforce with visuals and verbal 'waiting'.
4. When the time has finished, praise the student and carry out the request.

Next step: Once your student becomes confident with this method, you can slowly increase the amount of time on the timer, because they have learnt to trust you and understand they have to wait but they will get what they have been told. You can then also transition this skill outside the classroom. For example, if a student is waiting for everyone else to be ready to go swimming.

End goal: This technique can help in many circumstances in the future: going out for meals with family, waiting for transport and waiting in a queue. The knowledge of knowing that waiting comes to an end is extremely important for students.

Augmentative and Alternative Communication (AAC)

Following are key considerations when implementing AAC into a pupil's daily curriculum as well as previous ones mentioned throughout the chapter.

- Model the use of AAC to the user consistently throughout their daily routine/activities/in varied locations.
- Repetition is the key to supporting the user.
- Processing time: Once you have used AAC to communicate something, pause to let the user process, and respond if they would like to.
- Everyone who is communicating with the user should use the AAC; this supports the user to learn how to use it to communicate by watching, and may motivate them to communicate in the same way.
- Use the users interests to motivate them to communicate using AAC.
- Make sure AAC is available to the child at all times to allow communication to take place. The AAC should travel with the user everywhere as it is their voice.
- All high tech AAC users should have a low/no-tech back-up.
- Do not expect the user to use grammatically correct phrases. Instead, concentrate on the meaning and context.
- Do not use AAC to 'test' the user, for example 'Can you find . . . . ?', it is for commenting and chatting.
- Continue to use and model AAC even if the user doesn't choose to use it.

The focus is to teach the pupil how they can use the AAC so that the pupil can refer to it when they need to communicate their wants and needs. Again, this is one way we can help to provide an environment that manages a pupil's frustrations, distress and anxiety.

Chapter Summary

The key takeaway for this chapter is really about how we can teach the pupil to use communication devices so that they can use these tools to communicate their wants and needs. The more they communicate, the more their needs can be met in some way, the more trust they have in their environment and the more they are regulated. This highlights the links between communication, emotional distress and regulation. Providing an environment where they are taught how to communicate their wants and needs can have an impact on managing their frustration, distress and anxiety. Now that we have covered the **'what'** and **'how'**, the following chapter will help us to identify those opportunities that we can use to encourage and reinforce those.

4 Opportunities that Pupils Have to Practise Their Communication Skills

Chapter Introduction

The two previous chapters provided what tools we can use and how they can be used. This chapter gets you thinking about providing opportunities and finding times so that pupils can practise their skills and use those communication tools, almost like the 'when' and 'where'. Part of building that communication-supportive environment means that pupils have lots of opportunities to practise using their speech, language and communication skills throughout the day. This chapter helps you to identify those opportunities and turn them into times for pupils to practise using their tools and getting their needs met through them communicating.

> *Points of Reflection: Do we provide opportunities for pupils to communicate or do we anticipate what the pupils are wanting and then go and provide them with it? How many times does someone say 'I know what they want, I will go and get it?'*

Anticipation vs Opportunities

Anticipation of what pupil's want/need – we all do it, we are so busy that we just grab things for pupils. Therefore, take the time to really reflect upon this. Reflect upon how you can change the mindset of 'I know what they want I can just get it' to a 'communication practise opportunity'. If you do know what they want, then you can use that to your advantage (plan and anticipate) to manipulate and differentiate as needed. That way you know when and how to support the pupil, so that you keep that challenge but without escalation. Following are some common phrases that encourage communication (rather than anticipation):

- 'Show me what you need?'
- '(Name) wants . . .'
- 'Let's try using your pictures or words to tell me.'
- 'You did a great job telling me!'
- 'Let's practice asking for help together.'
- 'Can you tell me more about that?'

Opportunities to Communicate

First of all, it is important to think broadly regarding opportunities, from those small moments to larger amounts of time. For example, think about the opportunities we give pupils to:

- need to communicate their wants and needs;
- access to communication tools;
- communicate to an adult and the adult gives time and attention to the pupil;
- get a response.

Reason

There are so many opportunities in the classroom to provide a pupil with a reason to communicate. We need to ensure that we leave these opportunities open for pupils to communicate rather than us predict and jump in. Allow that child to be in a position so they need to communicate and our role is to ensure they have the tools and know how to use them to manage any anxieties and frustration. At first, it may be us making our way into using situations they may not need to communicate. However, we may need to add in communication tools when they don't need it, to teach them how to use them. Then using those times as opportunities to practise, even though we know they want some food, we need to use that time as an opportunity to practise communicating.

Case Study: Reception Pupil, Non-Speaking in a Mainstream School.

This pupil was non-speaking, therefore we put a communication book together for them; however, we were trying to decide what to put in there and how we could motivate them to use it. It was quite difficult as they often appeared not really interested in anything. The pupil liked to sit on a specific apparatus in the classroom, which they liked to access throughout the day. So, what we decided to do was take a photo of the apparatus and use this to teach them how to use the communication book. The aim was every time they wanted to go on to the apparatus, we would stand in front with the symbol card and encourage them to touch it, then we would move out of the way for them to access it. This was our way in; this was how we were going to get symbol cards into their daily curriculum.

Opportunities

One common way to provide opportunities to communicate is through choice-making. We provide structured choices, which encourage the pupil to communicate preferences. Here are some other examples of when we can use situations as 'practise' times, creating opportunities to practise their communication skills that we wouldn't normally utilise.

Following are some variations on what adults already do when pupils want to request specific items:

- Put these items in a cupboard, on a shelf, in a container. Put a picture of the item on a symbol card and in their communication book or on the cupboard door. The aim is that the pupil has to refer to the card to receive the item.
- Having items in a locked cupboard, symbol cards located on the door. Pupils can request items by pointing or taking the symbol card off the door. This can be differentiated to also include I want (item) and (item) or I want (item) and I am playing with (person).

Case Study: Key Stage 1 and 2 Pupils in a Complex Special Needs School.

Sets of things that pupils liked to access were all put into containers and put in the cupboard. The cupboard was locked. On the door were symbol cards of the items. When it was choosing time, pupils would come to the cupboard and point to the symbol on the cupboard to request the item in the cupboard. Then they would wait for the adult to hand them the container that matched their request. This was a very effective way of non-speaking pupils accessing toys etc. that they wanted to play with using low-tech communication. This is an example of manipulating the environment to create opportunities where pupils can practise their communication skills. Such a simple thing then becomes a 'communication lesson'.

- Having items in containers: these could include oral processing items for example frozen carrots, pasta, Rice Krispies with labelled photos on the top of the container. Pupils can request by pointing to the symbol picture card that they want or have the symbol card in their communication books. They can then come and match or give you the card to receive the item. This way you are not only providing an opportunity to practise communication, but also to practice a key skill i.e., matching.
- During snack time, pupils have to request their snack using symbol cards.
- During any 'fun' activity, take pauses throughout and encourage the pupil to request 'more' or 'finished'. If the pupil isn't ready for both cards, then stop the activity and encourage the pupil to request more (knowing this is what they want). At the end countdown 3, 2, 1 and you show the finished card. Move on to another activity.

- Nursery rhyme/song time, using a picture from YouTube to represent the rhyme/song, create a board or laminated Widget template with several rhyme song choices on it. Hold it up for the pupil to point and choose what rhyme/song that they would like. Instead of anticipating what songs they like and putting these on, use a request board so the pupil can communicate their request.
- Role-playing everyday scenarios (for example, asking for help or greeting others) helps build social communication confidence.
- Use play-based learning. Engage in imaginative play or games that require communication (for example, building a story together, playing shop, or asking for pieces during puzzle building).
- Arrange group activities where the pupil can practice communication in social settings, under your guidance or with support.
- Use a visual schedule to guide tasks for example, morning routine: dressing, eating, and packing a bag for school and use these to talk through and reinforce vocabulary.
- Use a request board to help the pupil decide what they want to eat. This could be done choosing their lunch or mealtimes at home.
- In social situations you can use emotion cards to help the pupil express feelings in social interactions or during moments of frustration.

The aim is to use obvious and easy opportunities to teach pupils how to use their communication tools so they can transfer the skill and use it when they need to communicate. Giving them time to practise and reinforce also doubles up as giving them opportunities to communicate throughout the day and therefore linking it to building an enabling environment and managing distress and anxiety.

Not only do opportunities come in the form of 'practice times' for pupils but also opportunities for us to teach through modelling. For us to model effective communication. For example,

- **Demonstrate communication strategies:** Show the pupil how to communicate by modelling active listening and taking turns in conversation.
- **Describe your actions:** While doing everyday tasks, talk through what you're doing. This helps build vocabulary and understanding of concepts.
- **Practice turn-taking:** Playing games that require turn-taking helps learners understand conversational dynamics.

When we provide 'practice times' and anytime that we communicate to pupils we need to remember to:

- **Use short, clear sentences:** Break instructions or information down into small, manageable pieces.
- **Repeat key points:** Repetition helps reinforce understanding. Ensure you maintain a calm tone when repeating phrases.
- **Pause for processing time:** Give the pupil extra time to process what you've said before expecting a response.

- **Use open-ended questions:** Encourage the pupil to communicate more by asking questions that require more than a yes/no answer, though balance this with simpler questions when needed.

Access

Here I want to highlight a step before we think about access to tools and that is the communication preferences of the pupil. Before we provide access, we need to identify access to 'what'. Previous chapters do support with listing resources but to gain a better understanding of which of those resources pupils may benefit from or respond to, we can observe their preferences and/or consult with specialist support. Remember to be patient as communication challenges can be frustrating, but allowing the pupil to express themselves in their own time helps and builds confidence.

Ensuring that pupils have access to communication tools is key. Otherwise, this can be an addition to their frustration and anxiety. If the pupil cannot find their communication book, then they cannot get their need or want met. This also takes building trust in the environment longer and fractured. It comes back to ensuring the environment can meet the need/want, in this case, through enabling communication. Therefore, whichever tools we are implementing into the pupil's daily curriculum, they are part of the morning resource preparation. Inclusion must be built in, rather than an after-thought: pupils have pens, pencils, books; these pupils need their communication tools as well. This comes back to that theme of what do all pupils need to access the day or the lesson.

Some examples of how pupils can access their communication tools:

- Placing symbol charts on the wall or door. Use Velcro, so that pupils can take them easily from the wall and hand to you. Having a toilet card on the back of the classroom door.
- Resource cupboards. Have 'I want charts' on the cupboard so that pupils can point to 'I want' and then make a request. Or, have symbol cards with photos of items on the door and pupils use these to make requests for items/toys.
- Request boards in communication books or symbol cards to accompany choosing. Pupils make that request when they are choosing. Even if they can just go and get the items, take symbol cards to them and ask, 'What do you have?' Encourage a response using symbol cards.
- Desks and tables.
- Grab bags. Grab bags can house personalised targets and tools. These can house specific visuals to use with that pupil. Grab bags can be hung on walls as part of a display but are really there so you can easily access pupil-specific tools.
- Communication books. These can also be hung on walls, doors or on pupils' tables. The main aim is that they must be accessible for pupils to use. Do acknowledge when the pupil is dysregulated as the adult may need to be in control of the book at this time, in case the pupil throws it.
- Have a grid with key core words taped on to desks and tables, providing easy access for pupils. This can also be accessed by adults so they are able to model.

Time

Time is precious and in classrooms there is not a lot of it. Everything that we put in place requires time and therefore where we choose to dedicate our efforts can be a bit of a tricky balancing act. In relation to communication in particular, when a pupil communicates using a visual aid then this would be when you dedicate time to acknowledge and respond. At this point, if we do not give the time then the pupil is less likely to repeat the behaviour because they did not get a response before, so there is no motivation to do it again. It is also possible that no response could be a trigger and escalate the situation. The pupil's behaviour could escalate because they are trying to communicate something and if we give it the time it deserves first, then the pupil has been heard and their needs/wants have been met in some way.

Response

Respond to the communication by acknowledging and then responding accordingly. This creates a learned behaviour; pupils will pair the communication tool with getting a response. Learning: 'If I use this, then I will get this'. This creates a learned behaviour: cue- routine - reward. In relation to communication: the cue is the use of a communication tool - routine is that they use the tool to communicate to an adult who gives then a response - reward is getting what they communicated. Once the pupil has the reward, they will be motivated to repeat this. They more they repeat, the more they learn it and use it. The more embedded in their memory it becomes.

Chapter Summary: Independence

The idea behind implementing communication tools, teaching pupils how to use them and providing opportunities for them to practise is simply to build pupils' independence. These tools empower individuals to be able to express themselves, make choices and participate without someone doing that for them. This is a key message and takeaway for adults. For them to think about anticipation vs opportunity. Use your knowledge of what they want and turn it into an opportunity for them to communicate their wants and needs. Therefore, the key driver behind this section of the book is really giving pupils a voice using these tools. This is then woven into the education they receive because that is what they need to access life.

 Further Reading

- https://speechandlanguage.org.uk/educators-and-professionals/resource-library-for-educators/
- https://speechandlanguage.org.uk/educators-and-professionals/resource-library-for-educators/creating-a-communication-supportive-environment-primary/
- https://speechandlanguage.org.uk/educators-and-professionals/resource-library-for-educators/strategies-to-support-primary-aged-learnerss-communication-skills/
- https://library.sheffieldlearnerss.nhs.uk/the-means-reasons-and-opportunities-model-of-communication/
- ASD Bright Ideas. https://asdbrightideas.co.uk/

Part II
Cognition and Learning

Preface

> *Points of Reflection: What has the most focus: what we need to teach or what is learnt by the pupil? Do they inform each other? How?*

One of the focus areas of this book is enabling environments. Although there is a huge focus on those environments being around communication and behaviour regulation cognition and learning also intertwines. Once we have the pupil's attention, we need to be ready to teach them at that time before we lose their attention. Cognition and learning can routinely become a regulator also.

Therefore, this part of the book is dedicated to providing you with provisions and interventions enabling pupils to make progress through their provision, which also links to their regulation. The chapters in this section include a progression from pre-programme and emerging learning through to subject specific learning. The chapters will highlight:

- Subtle changes/support tools to access the National Curriculum.
- Interventions and Pre-Key Stage Standards.
- Provision and The Engagement Model.

While reading through the chapters in this section consider the following two points.

> *Points of Reflection: Hiding and transferring*

Sometimes when pupils struggle to access something they will hide it by taking on another role so no one knows they can't do something. For example, if a pupil struggles to read or write similar to their peers, they will hide this by becoming the class clown or the tough one to avoid being the 'not so smart one'. Especially for older students where this is the case, it may be that they cannot read or have speech and language difficulties. This is where referring to any previous assessments and taking time to unpick behaviours may identify some of those barriers for pupils. One suggestion is to talk with the young person, get their views and make a plan moving forward by offering realistic options that you know can be put in place.

I have spoken to (. . . . .) and we could put this in place (. . . .). What do you think? Those options could be technology based or intervention-based disguising it with another name. Or maybe empowering the student to be able to share with their friends that actually, 'I can't read but Ms (. . . .) has a programme that is going to help me'. Or it may be that you identify a group of similar students that do it together, building a small intervention group.

> Points of Reflection: Purpose

It is difficult to meet everyone's interests in one classroom; however, for those that find something a chore it is difficult to motivate them when the topic is not of interest. Writing is one subject that comes to mind that is a good example of this.

Although the example is specific to writing, the ideas are still transferrable to other subjects. This is where we can implement subtle interventions using Pre-Key Stage Standards to build confidence back up and bridge any gaps back to the National Curriculum. Still using writing as an example: this would be stripping back on the number of skills and focussing on embedding one thing at a time in small steps. If pupils are accessing this in the classroom, think about free topic writing once a week then this could be used as cold tasks to show progression.

As an introduction to cognition and learning: following are alternative curriculums that can be built into a setting's curriculum offer, which will help to form stepping stones to the National Curriculum. These are pupil led, dependent on which stage of development and engagement the pupil is at. These are also used in Special School settings.

Curriculums Can Include

Dingley's Promise - Early Years
Equals Curriculum
Interoception Curriculum - Kelly Mahler
Sensory Curriculum - Flo Longhorn
PSHE Association Planning Framework for Pupils with SEND (including teaching children safeguarding)

Assessment Can Include

Engagement Model
Pre-Key Stage Standards
Personal Targets
MAPP (Mapping and Assessing Personal Progress)
Quest for Learning
Branch Maps

The example below references all types of learners.

	PMLD Learner (complex profound, multiple learning difficulties). Earliest Stages of Learning.	Semi-Formal Learner (complex learning needs). Flexible and Holistic Approach.	Subject Specific Learner (moderate learning difficulties). Qualifications and Developing Skills.
Curriculum	Interoception Sensory Reading Intervention Framework: Reading for All PSHE Planning framework for pupils with SEND	Equals Interoception Reading Intervention Framework: Reading for All Writing Progression Programme White Rose Maths/ Numicon Breaking Barriers PSHE Planning framework for pupils with SEND Older pupils: OCR Life and Living Skills City and Guilds Pre-Functional skills: Maths and English skills ASDAN AQA TITAN (Travel training) Duke of Edinburgh	Equals Reading Intervention Framework: Reading for All Writing Progression Programme White Rose Maths PSHE Planning Framework for Pupils with SEND Older pupils: Functional Skills ASDAN AQA OCR Life and Living Skills City and Guilds TITAN (Travel Training) Duke of Edinburgh
Assessment	Engagement Model Personal Targets (EHCPs) Quest for learning	Choosing from: Personal Targets (EHCPs) Engagement Model Pre Key Stage Standards Standardised Tests Older pupils: ASDAN AQA Maths and English Skills Life and Living Skills	Choosing from: Personal Targets (EHCPs) Engagement Model Pre Key Stage Standards Standardised Tests Older pupils: ASDAN AQA Functional Skills

The following chapters will explain more in depth the Reading and Writing programmes that have been listed. The first chapter discusses the crucial role that working memory plays in the classroom.

5 Understanding How Children Learn

The Crucial Role of Working Memory in the Classroom

Chapter Introduction

I feel that one of the key factors in teaching is to understand how children learn. Teaching for me isn't just about teaching a curriculum but it is more about delivering something to someone so that they can absorb and apply it. Emma Adcock- Principal Teaching and Learning Consultant @ VNET Education who shares the same passion wrote this chapter dedicated to understanding how children learn with a focus on working memory.

Working Memory

As educators, we often find ourselves puzzled by the seemingly contradictory behaviours of children in our classrooms.

> *Points of Reflection: How can a child who brilliantly explained a concept yesterday struggle to recall it today? Why might a pupil who can solve multi-step mathematics problems in one context become overwhelmed by similar problems presented differently?*

Working memory isn't just another educational buzzword; it's a fundamental cognitive system that profoundly shapes how children engage with learning tasks daily in our classrooms. There is a growing recognition that working memory plays a pivotal role in shaping what children can understand and remember.

For educators, understanding how children learn is essential for making informed decisions about curriculum, pedagogy and assessment. While many factors influence learning – motivation, environment, relationships and prior knowledge – cognitive psychology offers compelling insights into the processes that drive how children think, process and retain information.

This chapter explores working memory, how it develops and, most importantly, how understanding it can transform our teaching practice. By recognising the power and limitations of children's working memory, we can create learning environments that work with, rather than against, the natural cognitive processes of our pupils.

What Is Working Memory?

Working memory enables learners to hold and manipulate information long enough to complete a task and understand a concept. Recognising the power and limits of working memory is key to effective learning.

DOI: 10.4324/9781003596820-9

Working memory is the system in the brain that allows us to *hold* information briefly while we *manipulate* it. Unlike long-term memory, which stores knowledge across time, working memory is a temporary storage system that enables us to keep small amounts of information in mind while using it. It's sometimes described as the brain's 'Post-it note' or 'whiteboard' – an area where thinking happens, ideas are compared, problems are solved and new knowledge is constructed.

Children are not born with a fully developed working memory capacity. This cognitive system develops over the years. Working memory undergoes significant development throughout childhood and adolescence. Children aged 3–5 typically demonstrate limited working memory capacity and often struggle following multi-step instructions. Between the ages of 6 and 10, steady improvements occur as children gradually develop the ability to handle increasingly complex tasks and simultaneously hold more information in mind. By ages 11–15, working memory capacity approaches adult-like levels, though efficiency continues to improve. Working memory undergoes continued refinement during adolescence and into early adulthood, with notable improvements in processing efficiency and strategic manipulation of information in the mental workspace.

However, development varies considerably between children and working memory capacity.

The variation in working memory development became apparent to me while teaching a group of Year 2 children all the same age. For example, during instruction for a simple craft activity involving four sequential steps, I observed striking differences in their ability to retain and follow directions. Pupil A could hold all four steps in mind and proceeded independently, while Pupil B needed to return to the visual instructions after each step. Interestingly, Pupil B outperformed many peers in a different activity involving visual patterns. This reinforced that working memory development isn't simply a matter of 'good' or 'poor' memory, but a complex picture of different strengths and challenges that vary from child to child, even among those of identical age.

Working memory is a system with boundaries even in adulthood. For children, it is under constant pressure in a learning environment.

It is not that children with lower working memory cannot learn – it is that they often need information presented and processed in more structured, supported ways. Crucially, if working memory is overwhelmed, information usually doesn't become long-term storage.

Research suggests that younger learners can only hold three to five information elements simultaneously. Once that threshold is exceeded, information is deemed lost, muddled or incomplete. This is a significant cause of errors in learning, not because children have forgotten what they have learned, but because their mental workspace becomes overloaded or the retrieval strength of that memory is low.

In contrast to long-term memory, which stores knowledge over time, working memory is short-lived and limited in capacity. This capacity is typically lower for children than for adults.

Common Misconceptions about Working Memory

One persistent misconception is confusing working memory difficulties with attention or motivation problems. For example, Pupil C's inability to complete multi-step tasks was viewed as defiant or disinterest. Only after observing that they consistently completed the first step correctly before going off-track was it recognised that it was a working memory challenge underlying their behaviour. They needed external memory support rather than behaviour management strategies – a visual checklist which then transformed their classroom experience and engagement.

Another misconception is the belief that working memory capacity can be substantially increased through training. For those pupils with identified working memory difficulties, commercial 'brain training' showed little transfer to classroom tasks. What proved more effective was teaching these children compensatory strategies – note-taking skills, visualisation techniques and self-monitoring approaches – that worked around their working memory limitations rather than attempting to 'fix' them.

Finally, many assume that memory challenges are consistent across domains. Working memory isn't a uniform capacity but a complex profile of strengths and challenges that varies between individuals and across different types of information.

The Importance of Working Memory in Learning

Working memory plays a central role in many learning tasks.

> ### Example of impact: Working memory and reading.
>
> Year 1 Phonics: When introducing the digraph 'sh', I noticed a pupil could successfully sound out each letter in 'ship' as 's-h-i-p' but struggled to blend these sounds into the complete word. Their working memory was fully occupied with holding each sound, leaving insufficient capacity to perform the mental manipulation required to blend them. I reduced the working memory load by introducing a sliding motion with my finger under the word while gradually elongating the sounds. Within two weeks of this approach, the pupil successfully blended three- and four-sound words independently. This demonstrated how a seemingly simple reading task significantly demands a young child's working memory.

From the Present Moment to Lasting Knowledge

Children's learning must pass through working memory before it becomes part of their more permanent understanding. In this sense, working memory functions as a gateway: information must pass through to become part of a learner's long-term memory.

Although working memory is transient, it plays a crucial role in building more permanent knowledge. Learning involves moving information from the working space of the present moment into the long-term store, where it can be retrieved and reapplied in future contexts. Transferring information from short-term use into long-term knowledge is where learning either sticks or slips away.

If a pupil has to concentrate hard to decode a word in a sentence, they have less capacity to consider the meaning of that sentence. In other words, the more we can *lighten* the working memory load, the more we create room for *thinking*. Professor Rob Coe (2013) stated, 'Learning happens when people have to think hard.'

Spotting Working Memory Challenges

In his influential book, *Why Learning Fails (and What to Do About It)*, Alex Quigley (2024) makes the compelling observation that 'patchy prior knowledge is more the norm than the exception'. This insight highlights a fundamental challenge for working memory in the classroom. When pupils attempt to learn new material with gaps in their foundational knowledge, their working memory becomes overwhelmed trying to fill these gaps while processing new information simultaneously.

Children struggling with working memory demands may not always be obvious. Common signs include:

- Forget what they've been asked to do partway through a task.
- Struggle to follow verbal instructions.
- Complete part of a task correctly but omit key elements.
- Abandon a multi-step process midway through.
- Appear distracted or off-task when they're cognitively overwhelmed.

These behaviours are often misunderstood. What looks like forgotten learning may be cognitive overload. Understanding working memory helps educators tailor their support accordingly.

For some pupils, despite understanding the concept when we discussed it, they would still calculate the first operation correctly but then stop, seemingly forgetting the remainder of the task. The updated report from the EEF (2025), 'The Effective Deployment of Teaching Assistants Guidance Report', recommends a self-scaffolding framework so that pupils can self-scaffold their learning using process success criteria to complete tasks with the greatest amount of independence, while providing support when it is required.

Example of Impact: Using Visuals.

While teaching in Reception, I noticed that working memory overload often manifested during task initiation. After introducing an activity where children needed to create patterns with coloured blocks, I observed several children wandering or becoming distracted. The following day, I provided a simple visual task card with three pictures showing the steps: 1) collect blocks, 2) create a pattern, 3) draw your pattern. The improvement was immediate – children who had previously struggled to begin the task could follow the visual sequence independently. One pupil, who often needed one-to-one support, pointed to each picture on his card as they completed each step, effectively using it as an external working memory aid. This simple adaptation reduced the cognitive load of remembering multiple instructions while supporting independence.

> *Points of Reflection: One common theme that comes through in most areas is using visuals. They are used to support communication, anxiety, working memory and behaviour regulation.*

Cognitive Load Theory (CLT) and Its Practical Use

The relationship between working memory and learning has been formalised in the Cognitive Load Theory (CLT). This theory suggests that the cognitive effort involved in any learning task is made up of three types of load:

1. Intrinsic load: The inherent complexity of the content.
2. Extraneous load: How the content is presented can be helpful or unhelpful.
3. Germane load: The effort in processing, understanding, and building mental models.

> ### Example of Impact: Managing Extraneous Load.
>
> I witnessed the impact of extraneous load first hand during a history lesson with a Year 5 class. Initially, I presented a timeline of Tudor monarchs with decorative borders, colourful backgrounds and various font styles I thought would make it visually appealing. My pupils struggled to extract the key information. I redesigned the content the following week with a clean, consistent layout, uniform fonts and strategic highlighting of key dates. The difference in comprehension was remarkable – one pupil who had been overwhelmed by the previous version accurately recalled the sequence of monarchs and key events. This experience made concrete for me how presentation choices can either support or hinder learning, regardless of the inherent complexity of the content itself.

A Possible Solution?

- How classroom tasks are introduced and scaffolded can either support or hinder learning. Poorly presented tasks can strain working memory unnecessarily, crowding out the mental space needed to understand and retain new content.
- Good teaching manages these loads. For example, when a teacher presents a clear diagram alongside an explanation, they reduce extraneous load and increase germane load. When instructions are cluttered or overly complex, the reverse happens – pupils expend effort decoding the task rather than learning from it.
- The goal is not to eliminate challenge – struggle is part of learning – but to ensure that mental effort is focussed on *learning*, not *coping* with poor design.
- Working memory is less taxed when new content aligns with learners' knowledge. For example, a pupil who understands the concept of multiplication will find it easier to understand area models because they can draw on an existing understanding structure. This prior knowledge lightens the cognitive load, freeing up space in working memory to take on new ideas.

Building Memory-friendly Teaching Practices

- Repetition and retrieval practice are powerful tools that strengthen memory, making information more accessible and reducing working memory demands over time.
- Making explicit connections to prior knowledge effectively reduces cognitive load by allowing pupils to attach new concepts to existing mental frameworks rather than processing them in isolation.

> **Example of Impact: Connecting New Learning to Existing Learning. Making Everyday Connections.**
>
> While teaching a science unit on the water cycle to my Year 3 class, I discovered the profound impact of connecting new learning to existing knowledge. Rather than presenting evaporation, condensation and precipitation as abstract scientific terms, we discussed everyday experiences – watching puddles disappear after rain, seeing steam from a kettle and observing water droplets on a cold window. When I later introduced the formal vocabulary, I noticed a pupil, who typically struggled with scientific terminology, making confident connections. 'Oh, evaporation is like when my wet football boots dry up in the sunshine!' he exclaimed. Three weeks later, when assessing understanding, even students who typically found recall challenging could explain the water cycle by referring to their reference points before articulating the scientific principles.

- We also know that explicit, chunked instruction that breaks complex tasks into manageable parts helps avoid overloading pupils' limited mental bandwidth, preventing the working memory bottlenecks that lead to confusion and frustration.

> **Example of Impact: Teaching Explicitly and Managing Working Memory.**
>
> With my older Key Stage 2 pupils, I shifted toward teaching explicit strategies for managing working memory load. We discussed 'chunking' techniques for remembering multi-digit numbers or spelling patterns. I taught note-taking strategies using mind-maps and abbreviations. These approaches acknowledged developing metacognitive abilities while still providing necessary support. In a particularly successful lesson, Year 6 pupils analysed their learning strategies, identifying when their working memory became overwhelmed and selecting appropriate supports. One pupil, who had previously hidden his struggles, shared with the class that he used 'mental files' to organise information during lessons – a strategy we then explored together.

- A well-sequenced curriculum gradually scaffolds new concepts, ensuring that foundational knowledge is secure before introducing more complex ideas. This allows working memory resources to focus on new learning rather than struggling with prerequisites.
- Pre-teaching key vocabulary ensures children understand the language of a unit before encountering it in context. This proactive approach reduces intrinsic cognitive load during lessons, as pupils won't need to process unfamiliar terms while grasping new concepts simultaneously.

> ### Example of Impact: Pre-Teaching Vocabulary.
>
> The impact of pre-teaching vocabulary became clear during our Year 2 Great Fire of London topic. Before our main lesson sequence, I spent 15 minutes introducing key terms like 'bakery', 'flammable' and 'spread' through pictures, actions and simple definitions. During subsequent lessons, I observed one pupil, who typically struggled with content retention, actively participating using these key terms correctly. When I later compared the written work of this class with my previous year's class (where I had introduced vocabulary within the lessons themselves), the difference was striking. By ensuring children were familiar with key terminology before encountering it in context, they could focus their working memory on understanding historical concepts rather than simultaneously decoding unfamiliar vocabulary.

- Pairing language with visuals creates powerful memory support through dual-coding principles. When teachers combine spoken or written words with pictures, symbols or gestures, they provide multiple pathways for information processing and reduce cognitive load. Using dual-coding principles aids the retention of essential concepts, creating visual hooks for verbal information that might otherwise be difficult to maintain in working memory.

> ### Example of Impact: Dual Coding.
>
> In my Year 2 class, I observed how dual coding transformed our teaching of animal habitats during science lessons. Rather than simply explaining that polar bears live in the Arctic, I displayed an image of a polar bear on an ice floe while simultaneously describing its habitat. As children learned each new animal-habitat pairing, they would see the visual (the animal in its environment), hear the verbal explanation and perform a simple gesture we created together (like shivering for Arctic animals or stretching tall for giraffes in savannas).
>
> When one of my pupils, who typically struggled with retaining science vocabulary, was asked the following week to recall where polar bears lived, I noticed

her making a slight shivering motion before confidently answering 'the Arctic'. She later explained, 'I remembered the picture in my head and my body remembered the cold feeling'. Combining visual images, verbal information and physical gestures creates multiple pathways for encoding information. Three weeks later, during our assessment activity where children matched animals to habitats, the same pupil and many others who previously struggled with recall could make connections with minimal prompting, often mimicking the gestures as they searched their memory. This approach was particularly effective for children with working memory challenges, as it reduced the cognitive load of remembering information through a single channel.

- Repetition and rehearsal of key information strengthen memory traces and support retention. Effective teachers build low-stakes recall activities such as quick quizzes, review sessions or lesson 'flashbacks' into their regular teaching routine. These opportunities for retrieval practice help transfer information into long-term memory, gradually reducing working memory demands as concepts become more familiar and automatic.

Example of Impact: Repetition and Retrieval.

In my Year 1 geography lessons, I discovered the power of repetition and retrieval through our 'Around the World' topic. Rather than simply teaching the continents once and moving on, I implemented a simple 'continent song' with corresponding movements that we sang for just two minutes at the start of each lesson – Africa (reaching up high like a giraffe), Antarctica (hugging ourselves and shivering) and so on. Initially, many children struggled to remember even one continent name without the song prompt. After three weeks of this consistent, playful retrieval practice, I observed a remarkable transformation during our map activity. Lily, who had previously found it difficult to recall any continent names, confidently placed all seven continent labels on our classroom floor map. When I asked how she remembered, she spontaneously performed the little dance moves we had practiced. What struck me most was that even my pupils with language and memory challenges could participate successfully – the combination of music, movement and regular repetition had created multiple pathways for remembering what would otherwise have been abstract geographical knowledge. This simple routine transformed what could have been forgettable information into knowledge that children could readily access and apply.

- Worked examples and modelled practice provide crucial scaffolding for complex tasks. By showing children what success looks like before expecting independent work, teachers allow pupils to focus on understanding processes without the additional burden of managing multiple unfamiliar steps simultaneously. This gradual release Model (I do, we do, you do) approach prevents working memory overload and builds confidence through structured support.
- Creating environments with reduced clutter and distraction helps protect precious working memory resources. Clean, well-organised layouts direct attention to essential information and minimise cognitive interference that can disrupt learning.

> **Example of Impact: Environmental Design.**
>
> The influence of environmental design on working memory became evident when I redesigned my Year 3 classroom displays mid-year. I replaced our busy, colourful 'word wall' (which contained hundreds of vocabulary words in various fonts and colours) with a simpler, categorised display with consistent formatting and ample white space. I was sceptical about whether this would make a difference, but I observed children frequently referencing the wall for vocabulary help during independent writing tasks. Christopher, who rarely used classroom resources, explained: 'I can actually find the words now'. This experience showed me that visual clutter competes for children's attention and working memory resources – even well-intentioned educational displays can create cognitive overload if not thoughtfully designed.

Curriculum Design

Beyond classroom strategies, curriculum design has a significant role to play. A well-sequenced curriculum does more than introduce content – it supports memory development over time. A curriculum that thoughtfully revisits key concepts over time, builds gradually from foundational knowledge and makes deliberate connections between ideas can significantly reduce cognitive strain on learners. Strategies that strengthen long-term learning and reduce cognitive load include:

- Spaced retrieval, which strengthens memory traces by revisiting content at strategic intervals rather than cramming.
- Cumulative knowledge-building so that prior content is systematically revisited, deepened and explicitly connected to new ideas to create robust schemas.
- Interleaved practice mixes topics or question types to foster flexible thinking and strengthen retrieval pathways. It requires pupils to identify appropriate strategies rather than repeatedly applying the same approach.

Example of Impact: Spaced Retrieval.

Thinking back to my classroom practice, I learned about the power of spaced retrieval. Instead of the traditional 'times table of the week' approach I had used in previous years, I implemented a systematic review system with my Year 4 class. Monday introduced new multiplication facts, but Tuesday through Friday began with quick recalls of previously learned tables. I created a simple rotation where 6, 7 and 8 times tables were constantly revisited in short, varied formats. After six weeks, I was astonished by the difference in retention compared to my previous classes. One pupil, who had historically struggled with maths facts retention, proudly announced he could 'actually remember them this time'. The distributed practice approach proved far more effective than the massed practice I had relied on previously.

Example of Impact: PE Lessons.

Physical education presents unique working memory challenges that are often overlooked. Teaching a new dance routine to my Year 3 class demonstrated how movement sequences tax working memory differently than academic tasks – breaking the routine into clear 'chunks' of 3–4 movements, giving each section a memorable name, and using visual position markers on the floor dramatically improved retention. One pupil, who struggled with sequential instructions in classroom settings, showed unexpected aptitude when movements were structured this way.

Points of Reflection: A curriculum that supports memory isn't simply about covering content – it's about returning to it, revisiting it and strengthening it over time.

Working Memory Profiles in SEND

Different neurodevelopmental conditions often present distinct working memory profiles.

Various neurodevelopmental conditions display distinct working memory profiles that inform effective support strategies. Pupils with ADHD typically struggle with the central executive component of working memory, affecting their attention control and task management. However, their visual working memory may remain relatively preserved compared to verbal working memory.

Teachers can implement strengths-based approaches that leverage working memory components while supporting areas of difficulty. For example, they can use visual supports for pupils with verbal working memory challenges or provide verbal explanations for those who struggle with visual processing.

Assistive technology plays a crucial role in externalising working memory demands. Tools like text-to-speech, speech-to-text and organisational software reduce cognitive load and allow pupils to focus on learning content rather than managing information.

Inclusive classrooms are often those that explicitly manage cognitive demands:

- *Use visual timetables and cue cards* to reduce daily memory demands.
- *Give thinking time* before asking for answers.
- *Support task initiation* with prompts, checklists and worked examples.
- *Allow rehearsal aloud*, especially in writing tasks.
- *Reduce clutter* in slides, worksheets, and instructions to focus attention on essentials.

Beyond Memory: Emotional Safety

While working memory is a key factor in learning, it is not the only one. Emotional safety, classroom relationships, self-regulation and motivation all influence a child's learning capacity. That's why understanding working memory must be paired with strong relationships, responsive teaching and emotionally literate classrooms. When children feel safe, seen and supported, they are better able to make full use of their cognitive resources.

Working memory doesn't operate in an emotional vacuum – it's profoundly influenced by children's sense of safety, belonging and emotional regulation.

> ### Example of Impact: Mindfulness Practices.
>
> I witnessed this connection most powerfully during SATs preparation with my Year 6 class. Despite thorough content knowledge, several pupils experienced what appeared to be working memory failures during practice tests – forgetting previously mastered concepts or becoming overwhelmed by multi-step problems. I observed remarkable improvements after implementing daily mindfulness practices and explicitly discussing stress responses. Molly, who had frozen completely during a previous assessment, later explained, 'When I feel worried, it's like my brain gets too full to think properly.'
>
> This experience prompted me to integrate emotional regulation support alongside cognitive strategies across all year groups. In my Year 3 class, we developed a 'brain space' metaphor, visualising how difficult feelings could 'take up room' needed for learning. We practiced simple breathing techniques when cognitive demands were high. The impact was particularly noticeable for one pupil, who would become tearful when confronting challenging tasks. After learning to recognise and manage her emotional response, she developed greater persistence, explaining, 'I'm making space in my brain for the hard stuff.'

Children who felt secure in taking risks demonstrated greater cognitive capacity than those preoccupied with social concerns or fear of failure. Creating classroom environments where mistakes were normalised and celebrated as learning opportunities visibly reduced cognitive load for many pupils.

This interconnection between emotion and cognition reinforced that supporting working memory isn't simply about cognitive strategies – it requires holistic attention to children's emotional needs. Some of the most effective 'working memory interventions' aren't necessarily memory strategies but approaches that helped children feel safe, valued and emotionally regulated.

> **Chapter Summary**
>
> The key takeaway from this chapter is understanding how children learn, which means paying close attention to how they think. That begins with working memory. Recognising its role and limits can create more inclusive and effective learning experiences. When we recognise working memory and its central role – as the workspace where new learning happens – we gain powerful insights into supporting every child's educational journey. Understanding working memory isn't just about addressing difficulties; it's about optimising learning for all pupils in our care.
>
> Things that may have appeared as attention problems, lack of motivation or inconsistent learning has often revealed itself as working memory limitations that can be addressed with thoughtful support.
>
> Ultimately, when we support working memory, we support *all* learners, not just those with identified needs, but every child striving to hold on to a new idea, connect it to what they know and use it to build something new. That is the essence of learning, and it begins in memory.

Further Reading

What Makes Great Teaching Report - Professor Rob Coe (2014)
Improving Education: A Triumph of Hope Over Experience - Professor Rob Coe (2013)
The Effective Deployment of Teaching Assistants Guidance Report, EEF, March 2025: https://educationendowmentfoundation.org.uk/education-evidence/guidance-reports/teaching-assistants
Working Memory and Learning: A Practical Guide for Teachers - Susan E. Gathercole and Tracy Packiam Alloway (2008)
Improving Working Memory: Supporting Students' Learning - Tracy Packiam Alloway (2011)
Memory at Work in the Classroom: Strategies to Help Underachieving Students - Francis Bailey and Ken Pransky (2014)
Why Don't Students Like School? - Daniel T. Willingham (2021, 2nd Edition)
Visible Learning and the Science of How We Learn - John Hattie and Gregory Yates (2013)
How Do We Learn - Hector Ruiz Martin (2024)
Why Learning Fails and What to Do About It - Alex Quigley (2024)
Understanding How We Learn (A visual guide) - Yana Weinstein, Megan Sumeracki, with Oliver Caviglioli (2018)

6 Interventions: Pre-Programme and Reading

Chapter Introduction

This chapter is dedicated to reading. It is based upon an intervention framework that I have named Reading for All because the aim behind it was to create something that as many pupils as possible could access. I researched many different reading programmes and interventions, putting them into different categories based upon Uta Frith's (1985) Model of Reading Acquisition. The Framework incorporates a progression in stages that includes pre-programmes to reading through to later stages when children have gained that 'automaticity' of reading. In this chapter, each part of the Framework will be broken down with a brief explanation of each approach.

How the Framework works is to identify a pupil's starting point so we can build their curriculum and create their journey. For some learners their journey requires pre-learning stages and for other learners this becomes their main curriculum. Assessment will be explored later on; however, it is important to highlight here the importance of identifying starting points by determining what the pupil can do and how they do it.

The Intent behind the Reading Framework was to build something that could be accessed by every pupil including those with the most complex of needs, which is in reference to Scarborough's (2001) Reading Rope. I believe that those with needs can be seen as learners that do not always have complete ropes: they are either frayed, incomplete, cut off, loop back or not there. Therefore, when researching strategies and programmes the aim was to repair as many of these ropes as possible; hopefully opening up access to Reading for All as well as opening up the definition of reading. The Simple View of Reading (Gough and Tunmer, 1986) and The Dual Route Cascaded Model are two theories that were used to also inform the Intervention Framework and are worth exploring. There is a lot of focus on the Simple View of Reading; however, the Dual Cascade Model helped to identify pupils that could read – they just couldn't read out loud. These models both highlight the amount involved in reading as well as routes and pathways used to process.

Uta Frith's (1985) three-stage reading acquisition is the basis of the Intervention Framework purely because it showed three very clear stages of reading, enabling teachers to place most students in one of three areas. The addition of the Pre-reading stage enabled Profound and Multiple Learning Disability (PMLD)/pre-formal and semi-formal learners to access the model and assessment, which is often difficult to achieve.

DOI: 10.4324/9781003596820-10

Reading Intervention Framework: Reading for All			
Pre-Programme	Stage 1	Stage 2 - Phonics	Stage 3
-Rhythm -Rhyming -Nursery Rhymes -Multi-sensory -Curiosity Programme -Attention Autism -Sensology -TACPAC -Objects of Reference -Tactile and Noisy Books -Story Massage -Braille -Signalong -Makaton -Resonance Board -Decoding the Environment -Circle Time Activities e.g. Days of the Week	-Rhythm -Rhyming -Nursery Rhymes -Continuous Provision of Early Reading -Exploration of Words and Initial Sounds -Whole-Word Approach -Precision Teaching -Progression of Skills (Look Match, Name, Select) -Word sets -Personalised Word Banks -Core Words of the Week -Language Experience Books -Story Massage -Signalong -Makaton -Activities Relating to the Curriculum Topic -Decoding the Environment -Circle Time Activities e.g. Days of the Week -See and Learn Programme	-Initial Sounds -Phonics for Pupils with Complex SEND (SSP) -Whole-Word Approach -Precision Teaching -Progression of Skills -Word Sets -Personalised Word Banks -Carousel Teaching and Guided Reading -Signalong -Circle Time Activities, e.g. Days of the Week Interventions could include: -Bob Books -Pictophonics -Toe by Toe -Word Aware	-Comprehension Skills – Reading for Meaning -Complex Sounds -Chunking/Syllables for More Complex Sounds and/or Longer Words -Vocabulary Building through Word Study/Maps -Guided Reading Sessions -VIPERS -Carousel of Reading Activities
- Use of AAC - Sensory Stories - Sensory Drama - Storytime (skills sessions) - Blank Level Questioning - Visual Aids - Talking Mats			

Copyright material from Darleen Matoe Grimsby (2026),
Developing Educational Plans for Learners with SEND, Routledge

The idea is that you assess a pupil either through a standardised test or through observation and knowledge of what and how the pupils access learning and then place them in a stage. The pupil then accesses what is in that stage moving through programmes and possibly moving through stages. However, they do not have to work down each programme in that stage. The idea is that you use programmes listed in that stage to build their curriculum.

For example:

- Assessment: Unable to access Standardised Test. Using a pre-reading tracker from Phonics for Pupils with Special Educational Needs (PPSEN), it highlighted that Pupil A is working on Stage 1. Therefore, their programme of study for reading is:

Stage 1	-Use of AAC
-Rhythm	-Sensory Stories
-Rhyming	-Sensory Drama
-Nursery Rhymes	-Storytime (skills sessions)
-Continuous Provision of Early Reading	
-Exploration of Words and Initial Sounds	-Blank Level Questioning
-Whole-Word Approach	
-Precision Teaching	-Visual Aids
-Progression of Skills (Look, Match, Name, Select)	-Talking Mats
-Word Sets	
-Personalised Word Banks	
-Core Words of the Week	
-Language Experience Books	
-Story Massage	
-Signalong	
-Activities Relating to Topic	
-Decoding the Environment	
-See and Learn Programme	
-Circle Time Activities e.g. Days of the Week	

- This is what it may look like in a classroom. To highlight, it is not all aimed at just one pupil as it has to be manageable (this is explored further in the chapter):

Whole Class	Small Group	Individual
-Rhythm -Rhyming -Nursery Rhymes -Continuous Provision of Early Reading -Sensory Stories -Sensory Drama -Continuous Provision of Early Reading -Core Words of the Week -Story Massage -Circle Time Activities e.g. Days of the Week		-Personalised Word Banks -Language Experience Books -Use of AAC
	-Exploration of Words and Initial Sounds -Whole-Word Approach -Precision Teaching -Progression of Skills (Look, Match, Name, Select) -Word Sets -See and Learn Programme -Blank Level Questioning -Visual Aids -Talking Mats -Use of AAC	

The remainder of the chapter is dedicated to the three stages of reading and explaining the approaches in each of the three stages. The aim is that you can take away information on 'what' and 'how' to use each approach, starting with the Pre-Programme stage.

Pre-Programme

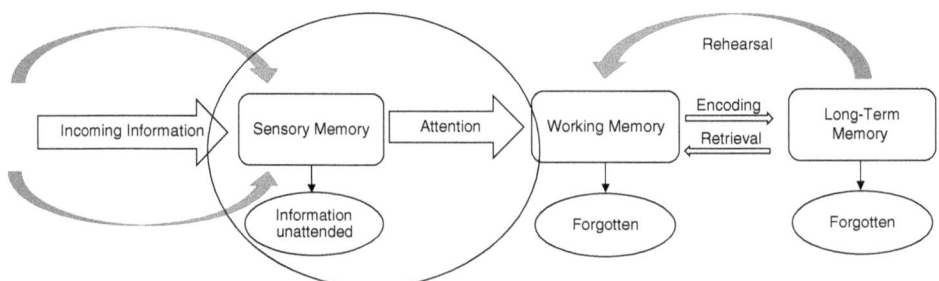

In naming this stage of the Framework, I contemplated many different options, which included pre-phonics, pre-programme, pre-learning and so on, but I decided on using pre-programme as it is a pre-programme of study to the more formal stages of reading.

The Pre-Programme stage focusses on using sensory input to gain attention, make links, process and maintain that for periods of time. Listed below are brief descriptions and helpful links for further reading and research.

Curiosity Programme

This programme is for those working with or supporting any very young child or children showing some early differences with communication and social interaction.

This programme can work as an excellent preparation for children who might go on and work through the Attention Autism 4 stage programme but need a more individualised start (Attention Autism, 2024).

Attention Autism

Attention Autism is a learning approach that aims to develop natural and spontaneous communications skills for autistic children through visually based and highly motivating activities (Attention Autism, 2024). Attention is in most educational plans, therefore something to highlight here is to ensure that those delivering this intervention have had sufficient training. If the training has been cascaded, ensure that it is of the programme including the aims, and not only one of the stages. There are Attention Autism groups that you can join that share lots and lots of ideas. Another idea is to have a bank of shared resources in your setting so that people are not spending lots of money going out and buying things for their class.

More information on both The Curiosity Programme and Attention Autism can be found at: https://attentionautism.co.uk/

Sensology

The aim of Sensology is to wake up the basic five senses and movement related sensory systems. Created by Flo Longhorn, more information can be found on the following blog: https://www.twinkl.co.uk/blog/sensology-what-is-sensology-and-how-do-i-run-a-sensology-workout-session

Days of the Week

Written by Kerry Goldsmith.

Learning the days of the week using the senses.
Introduction songs: https://www.youtube.com/watch?v=3txOrvuXIRg https://www.youtube.com/watch?v=8GKmCQOy88Y https://www.youtube.com/watch?v=mXMofxtDPUQ

Colour of the objects match the colour of the day. Below are some ideas of what you could use for each box.		Monday – Red Tuesday – orange Wednesday – yellow Thursday – green		Friday – Blue Saturday – purple Sunday – pink
Touch/skin	Taste/tongue	See/ eyes	Smell/ nose	Hear/ears
Feathers Pinecone Pebble Fur, silk leather Cord Chains Fidget toys Slime Water spray Paint, felt pens, pencils or chalk Tough Tray to write the days	Strawberries Orange jelly Lemon juice Mints Blueberry jam Tomato Carrot Banana Green pepper Blueberries Some sweets such as: Popping candy and blue spray	Fairy lights Coloured plastic Shiny objects Mirror Torch Puppets Coloured toys Slinkey Wind-up toys Pop-up toys Balloon Bubbles Ceiling lights/ strobes	Perfume Bath bombs Lavender, rose, rock, leather. peppermint Essential oils – violet eucalyptus etc. Toast Paprika Ginger Clove Coconut Apple Marmite Peanut butter Biscotti	Monday – jazz Tuesday – pop Wednesday – Disney Thursday – heavy metal Friday – classical Small musical instruments: bells, symbols, horn and drums Musical or popping toys Whistles Clapping hands Stamping feet Clicking fingers Party poppers Crunching paper/ emergency blanket
Warning some pupils can have allergies, specific dietary requirements such as halal or some sweets can cause hyperactivity and you may need to **check care plans and with parents/carers** before adding foods, e.g. containing E numbers, milk, nuts or containing vanilla essence. Using strobe lighting or flashing lights be aware of pupils with light sensitive epilepsy.				
Aims: To know how many days in a week. To explore day and night.		To sequence events in a day. To understand language tomorrow, yesterday, today, weekend and next week.		To be able to tell the time. To know the months of the year. To know the order of months in the year. To use a calendar.

Start listening to one of the YouTube songs, sign the days of the week during songs, encourage pupil participation (use symbols or switches if required).

Place all the boxes mixed up in front of pupils. Choose pupil to help organise boxes.

Optional – sing days of the week song to support pupil participation. (Eye gaze and symbols PMLD support.)

Questions: 'What day is it today?', 'What day was yesterday?', 'What day will it be tomorrow?'. Extend by asking, 'What days do you attend school?' and so on.

Each day has a box with symbol and objects related to a colour: Monday – red, Tuesday – orange, Wednesday – yellow, Thursday – green, Friday – blue, Saturday – purple and Sunday – pink.

Option: Sign each colour and day when delivering the lesson.

Explore all objects in the box allowing pupils the opportunity to participate. Encourage peer on peer interactions, for example Pass the toy to . . ., can you give the object to . . ., can you find your friend . . ., can you throw the ball to . . . etc.

Each box will contain or have a sound, smell, touch, taste and see element that will be consistently used so the association will be made with that particular day.

Saturday and Sunday boxes can be used to support pupils at home. This will help understanding of the passing of time and also further children's knowledge to know what will happen next. It can be included in teaching weekend, tomorrow and the next day.

Use symbols and class display to show what day, date and month it is.

Option: Could go through visual timetable of what activities and daily routines will be happening that day.

Differentiate for pupils needs this could include the other senses.

Example Activities:

Vestibular (balance) activities: skipping, trampette, bounce on Pilates ball.

Proprioception (movement) activities: stand on one leg, walk along board, pick up heavy items, moving heavy items from one place to another, dribble a ball through cones.

Interoception (internal) activities: squeezing muscles, (body breaks) feeling something hot or cold, breathing techniques (figure of eight, breathing through a straw, fast breathing) spinning on spin chair or board or running fast to increase heart rate.

End session with

Emotions: for example, Zones of Regulation – How do you feel?

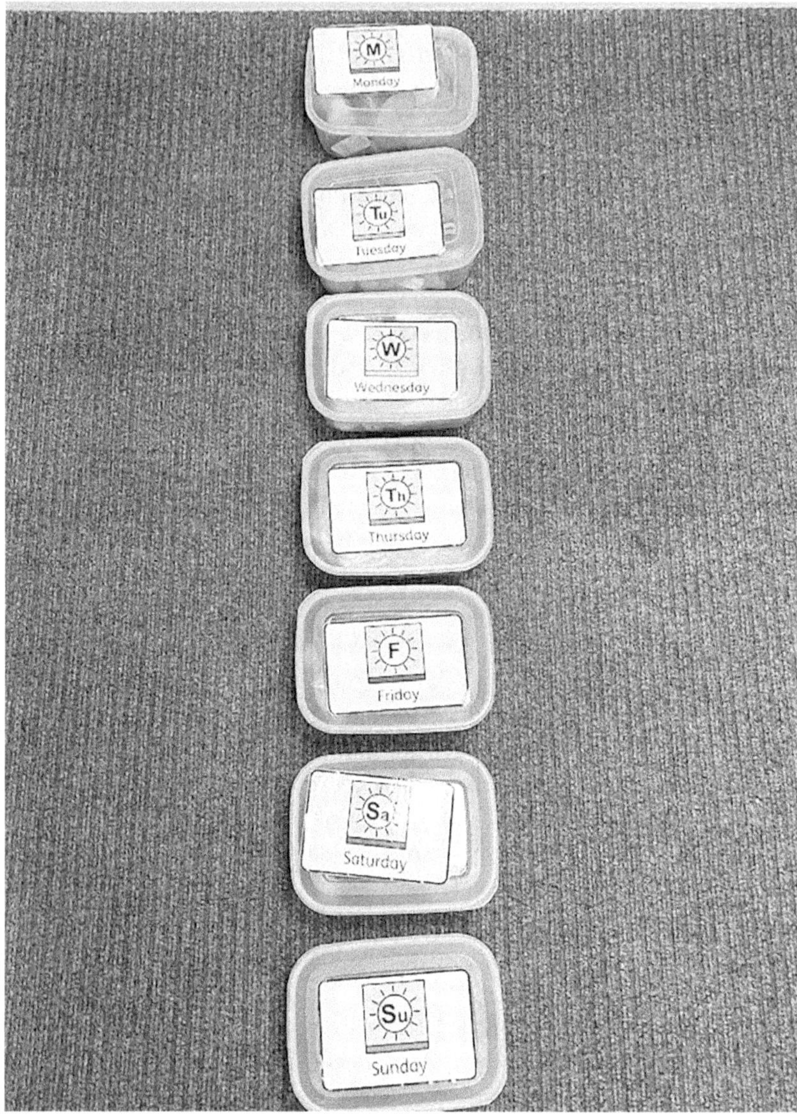
M
Monday
Tu
Tuesday
W
Wednesday
Th
Thursday
F
Friday
Sa
Saturday
Su
Sunday

Interventions: Pre-Programme and Reading 103

104 *Developing Educational Plans for Learners with SEND*

Interventions: Pre-Programme and Reading 105

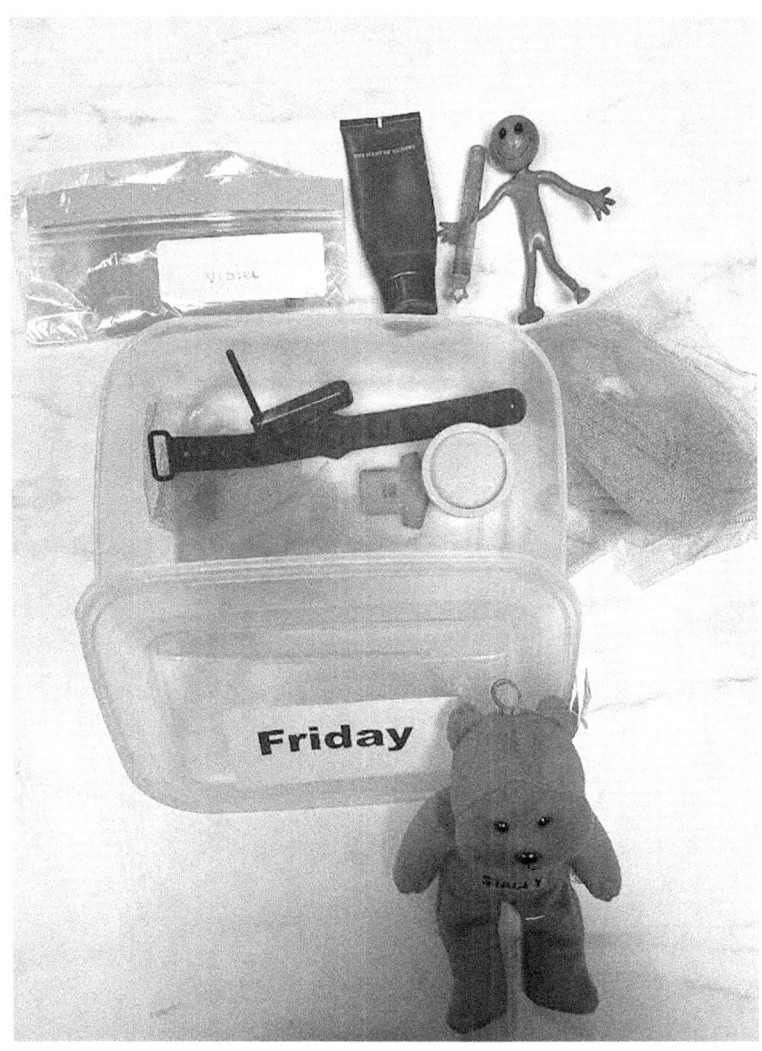

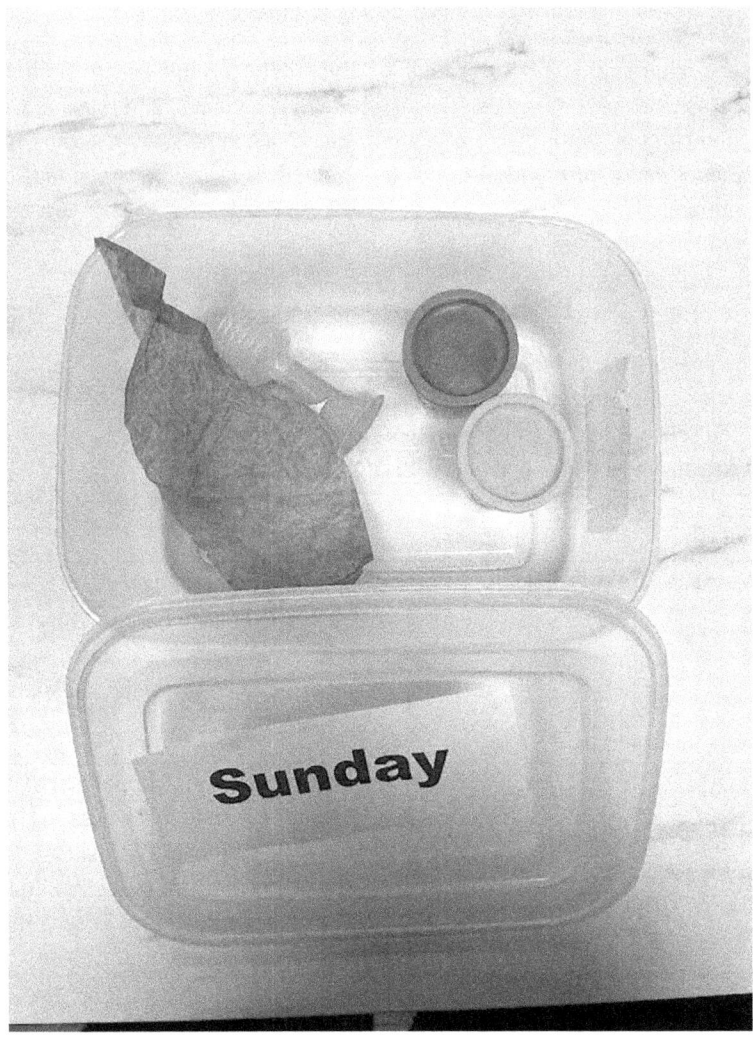

TACPAC

TACPAC is a structured tool that brings together touch and music creating sensory communication between two people. TACPAC links together what you see, feel and hear at the same time; preparing the pupil for letters (what they see) and sounds (what they hear). TACPAC helps people with sensory impairment, development delay, complex learning difficulties, tactile defensiveness and limited or pre-speaking levels of communication (TACPAC 2024). More information can be found at: https://tacpac.co.uk/

Story Massage

Story massage is an approach to storytelling, which uses positive touch through ten easy massage strokes suitable for all ages. It is an interactive, engaging and relaxing way of sharing stories. You can use story, rhyme or song or personalise the story massage to meet the needs of the pupil. More information can be found at: https://www.storymassage.co.uk/

Always remember:
Ask permission to touch.
Say 'thank you' at the end.
Watch/listen/respond to feedback during the massage story.

Using the strokes during the Story Massage:
Vary the speed, size and direction to suit the words.
Respect the sensory needs and preferences of the individual.
The instructions can be easily adapted for any part of the body.

Story Massage Stroke	Action on back and shoulders.
The Calm	Rest the flats of both hands gently on your partner's back, shoulders and arms. Hold for as long as feels comfortable.
The Squeeze	Place both hands on your partner's shoulders. Now gently squeeze and release. Repeat this gentle 'squeezing' movement several times working down the arms. Ensure that the pressure feels comfortable.
The Circle	Rest one hand on your partner's shoulder. With the flat of the other hand, make a circular movement on the back.
The Wave	Rest one hand on your partner's shoulder. With the flat of the other hand, make a wave-like, zig-zag movement on your partner's back.

© storymassage.co.uk

Resonance Board

A resonance board is a board that you can sit or stand on and feel vibrations of sounds. These can be purchased or made and used in different ways. It can be such a powerful sensory tool for some pupils. More information can be found at: https://www.sense.org.uk/activities/resonance-boards/

Decoding the Environment

This is an important skill and most of us do it already: this just puts a name on it and brings a little more attention to it. Decoding the environment includes decoding symbols, objects of reference, key transition indicators, risk assessing and most importantly decoding what is around us. An example of when we can teach this is through transitions, that is, when this happens then we will do this. For example, when it is sensory story time, the lights go on and off twice then pupils would decode that as story time; make their way to the carpet and form a circle ready for the story. This can also be assessed and tracked to show progress.

This is the end of the Pre-Programme stage; once you have gained the pupil's attention, made links between senses and met their sensory need, then we can move on to introducing letters and their sounds. We can expose, encourage and explore further making those letter and sound connections (what we see and hear) with pupils.

Stage 1 – Logographical Stage

This stage is where children recognise whole words through their salient graphic features. For example, when you drive past McDonalds and the child says, 'Look Mc Donalds', this is typically recognised by the M logo. The first section focusses on the 'what' can be implemented followed by the 'how'.

What

Word Sets

These sets are the teaching of words and meaning with the purpose of communication. It incorporates topics, words and assessment.

	Clothes Identification	Body Part Identification	Snack Identification	Weather Identification
Set 1	coat, hat, gloves, shoes	head, arm, leg	biscuit, cracker, cereal, bread (toast)	sunny, raining, snowy
Set 2	jumper, T-shirt, trousers, skirt	foot, hand, tummy	water, squash, crisp, raisins, drink	windy, cloudy, frosty

Copyright material from Darleen Matoe Grimsby (2026),
Developing Educational Plans for Learners with SEND, Routledge

Set 3	cardigan, leggings, dress, scarf	eyes, mouth, nose	apple, orange, breadstick, milk	stormy, hailing, hot, cold
Set 4	knickers/pants, socks, vest	knee, back, ears	orange squash, blackcurrant squash, water	
Set 5	pyjamas, nightdress, dressing gown			

Mastery Criteria:

For the word sets: When the student correctly names the item four times without any errors on five consecutive days, move onto the next step.

Steps: Once Set 1 and 2 are mastered, repeat both sets together and meet mastery criteria for example:

Set 1
Set 2
Set 1 and 2
Set 3
Set 1, 2 and 3 and so on

Recording of Individualised Words

Recording uses a simple tally sheet to record mastery:

Name: _____

_____ **Identification**

Sets used: _____

Date	Tally	Total Correct	Incorrect (Identify)

Copyright material from Darleen Matoe Grimsby (2026),
Developing Educational Plans for Learners with SEND, Routledge

Personalised Word Banks

In addition to the word sets, these are pupil specific. They can come from what is in their communication books and/or what is needed for that specific pupil to access their environment. You could also create a bank of words labelled: Words I need at school, then pick from that bank for individual pupils.

These could consist of:

> Pupil's name
> Adults they work with
> More
> Finished
> Help
> Stop
> Go
> Toilet
> Places specific to the pupil e.g. Sensory Room
> Talking Mat: good/bad

Or

(Communication) At school I need:			At school I need (child specific):		
I want	Waiting	Hot	Name	Snack	Colour
Help	Now	Cold	Class	(snack ID	(colour ID
More	Next	Sitting	team	sheet)	sheet)
Finish	Then	Choosing		Set 1	Set 1
Toilet	First	Eat		Set 2	Set 2
Stop	I am	walk/		Set 3	Set 3
		walking		Set 4	Set 4
(Communication) In the community I need:			(Communication) At home I need:		
Play	Danger				
Out	In				
No	Out				
In	Like				
Want, look, on	Don't like				
Go					
Get					

Or

Monday: Snack	Response when shown object/symbol	Other response
toast		
cereal		
cup		
plate		
finished		
chocolate bun (Photo)		

Tuesday: Share a book Snowman	
Student will focus fleetingly on illustrations or objects related to the book.	
Student will reach out to illustration, book or object related to the book.	
Student will explore the book and resources related to the book using their senses.	
Students will show enjoyment during a 'reading' session.	
Other reaction:	
Other comments:	

Show the flashcard (symbols), give time to either verbalise or repeat, then give the symbol and asked to 'find the same' (match).

Wednesday: Timetable	Response when shown object/symbol	Other response
Circle		
Activity		
TACPAC		
Attention Autism Stage 1		
Dough Disco		
Music		

Thursday: Transition		
Toilet		
Bus		
Swimming pool		
Soft play		

Friday: Staff and classmates Photos	Response when shown card	Other response
(name)		
(name)		
(name)		
(name)		

Reaction to story – sensory story/massage		
Student will focus fleetingly on illustrations or objects related to the book.		
Student will reach out to illustration, book or object related to the book.		
Student will explore the book and resources related to the book using their senses.		
Student will show enjoyment during a 'reading' session.		
Other reaction: Repeating words		
Other comments: E.g., Pupil showed a strong preference for the 'touch items' – particularly items they could squeeze. Pupil refused all the 'taste items'.		

N.B. Some pupils respond to and use the Makaton sign for please, this is then used for any request along with taking the adult to the place or to the item then signing please.

The following is a key that can be used to make recording and assessment easy and efficient. Progress can be tracked through the accumulation of sheets.

EC: Eye Contact; **LA**: Looked away; **PA**: Pushed away; **NR**: No reaction; **M**: Matched; **V**: Verbalised; **R**: Repeated verbally; **D**: Distracted

How

In the Moment

These can be taught in real time in the moment; making it purposeful. Teach and model when these approaches can be used and how. Examples include:

- During snack time when the snack is finished, refer to the card and say, 'Finished'. The pupil will then pair the two together. This is done in isolation so the pupil does not need to process anything else just those two things.
- Every time the child goes to the toilet show them the card.
- When a child is laughing, pull out the happy card and say (name) is laughing, (name) looks happy. The same can be done for calm, angry and sad. If a child is crying say (name) is crying. (name) looks sad. Does (name) want . . . . .

Whole-word Approach and Precision Teaching

There is some debate around whole-word teaching and phonics; what I have found to be most effective is using both. The whole-word approach through precision teaching, highlights that the student can read and incorporating phonics, gives the pupil motivation and belief that they can achieve it. Use this as a gateway to phonics for those that can potentially move on.

It is important to add in here, sight word teaching to give this a little more context. The Dolch sight word lists were created by Dr Edward William Dolch. He created a list of the most frequently used words in children's books in that era so children could access text in a quick and easy way while formal phonics begins.

This stage of the Framework is meant more as a way of teaching pupils words they can then use in their communication and interaction. The selection of words is based on the pupils' needs. As a professional, you need to decide what that looks like, reflecting and building their reading path along the way. Some pupils will move on to access phonics and text, while others may progress through environmental words but still enjoying stories led by you. However, it can also be used to teach words while phonics is being introduced if pupils are on that path. It is not restricting but rather figuring out how it can best be used for pupils in their reading journey.

Teaching the whole word will boost pupils' confidence and get them started into reading. It is important to think about not only teaching the whole word but also what the word means. For example, whole-word 'toilet'. This is what it looks like, this is what it says. Now let us go and find it in school so we know what it is. Brilliant! You found the 'toilet sign'. You are reading!

See and Learn Programme

A language programme created for Down syndrome children, which can also be used for pupils with special educational needs. This programme teaches language combining specific photographs, progression of skills and assessment. An effective tool for those pupils pre-speaking. As pupils respond to this, you could add in photographs of the classroom environment, so that pupils can start to make further requests alongside their visuals. More information can be found at: https://www.seeandlearn.org/en-gb/

> *Points of Reflection: When teaching language, think about the pupil, their capabilities and what they need. Think about a progression from a vocabulary-based programme then moving through to a sentence building programme. For example, the See and Learn Programme has a vocabulary programme and a phrases programme. For those pupils starting out speaking, think about vocabulary before moving onto something like colourful semantics as they may not be able to learn words for the first time and build them into a sentence at the same time.*

Progression of Skills: Look, Match, Name, Select

Commonly used progression of skills, which can be transferred to many different types of activities. Pupils can access from any point in the progression, making it accessible to most learners. It is used in the See and Learn Programme. It begins with the pupil just looking at the card, gaining that attention. Then moves on to matching cards together with the same picture. Next, pupils are naming the card (for those speaking pupils) and last is when the adult names and the pupil selects.

Following are other approaches that are incorporated into Stage 1.

Core Words

These are books designed to support teaching students specific core words. It has a range of lesson plans and resources for introducing and teaching core vocabulary weekly. More information can be found at: https://www.tobiidynavox.com/products/core-first-lessons?fbclid=IwAR05krPS5CRX6ZYE-EGkLV-J48AhOwKbE9_keTy2bizWfebakF_XJQrWZkE

Core Words of the Week

Core words of the week by Mrs Speechie P. This particular resource has a core word in the middle surrounded by various ways in which you can teach the meaning of the word, for example through play, toys/light, modelling, transitions, routines and actions. The words used are often those that can be quite difficult to teach, for example the words 'make' and 'want'.

Language Experience Books

Although these have been given a title, they are books that are personal to the pupil. These can be used in two ways:

- Simple: Books that follow the same language pattern on each page. They have a picture at the top with a simple sentence underneath. For example, at the start of the year the book could contain a picture of the pupil with the sentence (caption) it represents: 'It is (name of pupil)'. The next page could have a picture of the teacher with the sentence, 'It

is (name of adult)'. The other pages could contain pictures and names of all the adults that work with that pupil. The next book could be about the pupil. For example, the picture could be of the pupil sitting on a chair, with the sentence '(name of pupil) is sitting'. The following pages would follow the pattern of the picture doing an action.
- Led by the pupil: For those pupils that cannot write but can tell a story, have a picture of that pupil doing an activity or on a family holiday and encourage the pupil to tell you all about it. The adult can scribe the story and, in this way, the pupil can access the story as it was their retelling (the writing chapter will have writing links to this).

This is especially effective for those pupils who have no interest in books and/or stories. This is about them; and they will see themselves in the book, which brings curiosity and purpose.

Those are the strategies for Stage 1 leading into Stage 2 where we enter the more 'formal' part of teaching reading with a heavier focus on phonics. Most of this section's focus is on a phonics programme aimed at pupils that struggle to access mainstream teaching of phonics.

Stage 2 – The Alphabetic Stage

This is letter-sound by letter-sound analysis, which is a strictly sequential putting together sounds to make a word. Each letter is important and so is the order it is in (Frith, 1986). It is here that the child obtains explicit knowledge of letters, sounds and how to merge these into words.

Phonics for Pupils with Special Educational Needs (PPSEN)

This is a phonics programme designed for pupils who cannot access a mainstream style phonics programme. In addition, it has a pre-programme stage and a companion booklet for learners with complex SEND. The programme still has the same features as mainstream designed programmes; however, it breaks areas down and identifies specifically where gaps in processing are. It works through books with planning tools, activities, assessment points and tracking documents. PPSEN has been extremely successful in reaching pupils that could not access phonics previously. Numerous case studies have supplied data, which evidences the effectiveness of the programme. More information can be found at: https://www.phonicsforpupilswithspecialeducationalneeds.com/. This can be accessed by older pupils; however, there is also this programme: That Reading Thing. More information can be found at: https://thatreadingthing.com/

Example of Impact: Year 7 Pupil Accessing a Formal Curriculum at a Complex Special Needs School.

This pupil was unable to read and knew three to five letters and their corresponding sounds. They only picked up a pencil to draw pictures to show specific adults how they were feeling. They couldn't and wouldn't engage in any writing or reading related activities and for a few years, showed challenging and dismissive behaviour. The aim was to engage this pupil into something reading related, which was fun while his peers accessed guided reading and carousel teaching sessions. While trying to think of different activities we used a Where's Wally type of approach (shared later in the chapter). The pupil responded positively, so much so that this activity became the gateway to slowly becoming interested and engaged in the phonics programme PPSEN. The pupil is now reading text and writing sentences and there has been no recording of any behaviours that challenge. Following are their reading assessment results. First is their starting point and then their assessment 6 months later.

January
Blending: 0
Segmenting: 0
Grapheme to sound: 5/25
Sound to grapheme: 3/25
Reading basic core high frequency words: 2/46
Spelling basic core high frequency words 0/46

After using the PPSEN programme, the pupil was assessed again in July. Following were the results:

July
Blending: 19/20
Segmenting: 20/20
Grapheme to sound: 25/25
Sound to grapheme: 25/25
Reading basic core high frequency words: 46/46
Spelling basic core high frequency words 46/46

The best thing to come out of this, was that the pupil said, 'I can read now, I don't have to be naughty, I could even get a job and have a life'.

Points of Reflection: Are there pupils in your setting that have been taught phonics for a significant period of time without making progress in their reading?

Bob Books

The best thing about these books is they do exactly as they say. The very beginning books use only select sounds, which are shown on the first pages of the book. Whereas other books include words pupils do not yet know which throws them because they cannot sound them out. Or they use words the pupils have not yet been introduced to such as 'and' and 'was'. Therefore, it gives time for pupils to segment and blend and then get their heads around 'sight' words. This is a very effective way of allowing pupils to apply sounds they are learning and make all of the connections without any other clutter.

Whole-Word Approach and Precision Teaching

This approach can be used to access the National Curriculum and teach high frequency words as a possible gateway to phonics. Below are two separate case studies: one accessing National Curriculum words and the other accessing words relating to their interests. Especially for older pupils, this can be a good way to start as it is hard to find high-level interest and low-level text for older pupils. So, this and PPSEN can be an effective combination.

> **Example of Impact: Year 6 Pupil in Mainstream Education and Alternative Provision.**
>
> This pupil was unable to read so the adult decided to teach high frequency words using the whole-word approach. In a period of three months, the pupil now has a bank of words that they can read. The teacher uses these words to type up stories that the pupil reads. This feeds into their writing as the pupil has their bank of words that they put next to them to support writing their own stories.
>
> By teaching individual words, this helped the pupil better understand how letters make words as a whole and by leaving gaps, words make sentences. Most recently, the pupil has started to recall some phonics they had been taught previously, which has provided that bridge for the adult to then re-introduce phonics.

> **Case Study: Year 5 pupil in a complex needs special school setting.**
>
> A Down syndrome child that was in Year 5 was not able to read anything except for his name when prompted. They loved shopping and anything related and therefore to begin with, their sight word list was around shopping, for example Tesco, McDonalds, Sainsburys, and, the, me, Mum, etc. Over a period of eight months, the pupil and the adult built up and accessed a bank of words. His teacher wrote stories incorporating these words, which he started to read. Throughout that time, once he became motivated then the teacher added in phonics using PPSEN.

> *Points of Reflection: For those pupils accessing whole-word teaching do you also teach the meaning of the word? Do we incorporate the words they read into a text so the pupil has a chance to apply by reading those words in sentences or do they just practise those words in isolation?*

Based upon those case studies, following is a plan that could be used to teach a combination of words and phonics.

> 1. Whole-word approach
> Activity 1 -Flashcarding: Functional words – exit, toilet, stop, I, pupil's name
> Activity 2 – Word map: Complete the word map for exit
> Activity 3 – Find the word exit in the classroom, around school or in a picture
> 2. Initial sounds
> This week's sounds (including first letter of their name) + PPSEN activities
> 3. Application of whole word
> Always include a reading element:
> Storytime: Sharing books/language experience books

Carousel Teaching and Guided Reading

This is an effective way of differentiated teaching especially if you have pupils placed in every stage of reading. It identifies what you are going to teach, who to and how, all on one plan.
This example uses only one adult in the room.

Monday	Tuesday	Wednesday	Thursday	Friday
Group 1 1 – Phonics/word sets (A) 2 – Grab bag activities (I)	Group 1 1 – Where am I? 2 – Phonics/word sets (A)	Group 1 1 – Where am I? 2 – Phonics/word sets (I)	Group 1 1 – Where am I? 2 – Phonics/word sets (A)	Group 1 1 – Share Where am I books (A) 2 – iPads
Group 2 1 – Reading comp (I) 2 – Phonics (A)	Group 2 1 – Answer reading comp (A) 2 – Reading activity – clay characters	Group 2 1 –Mark reading comp (A) 2 – Phonics	Group 2 1 – Phonics 2 – Reading activity – clay characters	Group 2 1 – Free choice reading activities 2 – Phonics (A)
Group 3 1 – News round iPads 2 – News round videos	Group 3 1 – Reading comp 2 – Vocabulary mats with partners	Group 3 1 – Reading comp 2 – Answer questions (A)	Group 3 1 – Mark reading comp (A) 2 – Decide clay character. Draw plan.	Group 3 1 – Clay characters 2 – Clay characters

Below explains what is included in the example plan followed by how you can implement into the classroom.

What

- Groups 1, 2 and 3: These are the names of the differentiated groups. In this case, Group 1 are accessing a combination of Phonics Set 1 and word sets using the whole-word approach. Group 2 are accessing phonics and simple text and Group 3 are readers.
- 1 and 2 are the two parts included in each session, which is around 15 minutes each.

A = adult working with pupils and I = independent working

- Activities:

Grab bag activities are specific to the pupil. They can be accessed by the pupil and can be specific to their targets. These can include: puzzles, instruction colouring sheets, colouring, task boards, Lego, blocks, gross and fine motor skill activities and Fizzy Hands activities.

- Reading Comprehension Sheets:

There are so many of these from all different sites. One set of comprehension activities are Evan-Moor Daily Reading Comprehension, these books have simple text and multiple choice. Therefore, pupils that have specific learning difficulties can still access by identifying the multiple choice letter rather than writing out the answer in sentences thus opening up reading comprehension activities to a wider range of pupils.

Use these sheets throughout the week. For example, with Group 3:

Monday

Using iPads to access News Round activity to retell the news and make videos. These can then be shared with the rest of the class, sharing weekend news.

Tuesday

Read the text.

Highlight unknown vocabulary.

Use vocabulary mats to explore unknown words.

Wednesday

Read the text again. Read questions. Underline answers in the text. Answer questions. Read with a partner and check answers.

Thursday

Mark the reading activity with an adult. Discuss unknown vocabulary.

Introduce and plan for the next activity.

Friday

Fun activity related to the reading comprehension or topic of study.

- Fun activities – Where am I? This activity uses the concept similar to Where's Wally. Pupils make books, putting a picture of their faces into a scene that they want to for others to be able to find them. This idea came from the previously shared case study, which highlights the effectiveness of finding fun activities that show the other side of reading, taking away that chore-like feeling.

How

In the beginning, to set this up can take some time as do all routines; however, it works on its own once you have set it up. What can be helpful is when you are setting it up, use visuals to support understanding. These visuals could include:

Dedicating a whiteboard, screen or working wall to house the schedule showing that day's plan for both adults and pupils to follow. You can add photos of pupils to each group.

Using 1st and 2nd followed by What and Who information for each session.

1st	2nd
What: Phonics/word sets	What: Grab bag activities
Who: Mrs Grimsby and you	Who: Yourself

Have resources for each group in an easily accessible place, for example: labelled trays containing resources put underneath the whiteboard at the front of the class.

For specific pupils, using task boards can support instruction especially for independent activities.

| Choose word | cut | glue | Write sentence |

Now and then boards for those students that need it.

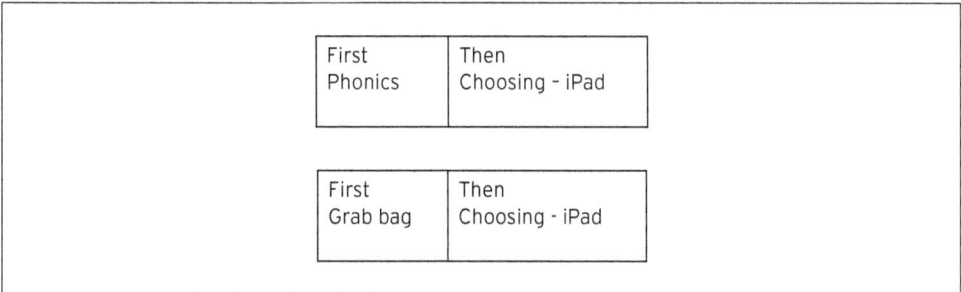

This concludes Stage 2. The pupils would then move to becoming automatic readers. The next stage focusses on complex sounds and automaticity, coming away from reliance on segmenting and blending and more toward using those skills automatically to recognise and read the word.

Stage 3 - Orthographic Stage

This is when you can read words automatically (automaticity of reading) without needing to sound out the word on a regular basis only when unfamiliar. You can instantly access the word and the meaning.

Therefore, when pupils are at this stage, the focus is on ensuring the pupil builds vocabulary and meaning especially if the pupil is hyperlexic: reading words but with very little comprehension of what they are reading. Their brain just wants to absorb letters. Vocabulary word mats are an effective way of teaching vocabulary. Use the approaches in this stage, which are already common practices.

All Stages

Following are approaches that can be used in every stage when working in any dynamic whether it is whole class, small group or one-to-one.

Storytime - Skill Sessions

This is the time where we read a story and incorporate specific skills. Examples of some of those key early skills:

Understanding how books work, this includes the right way up and turning the page, matching, identifying, selecting and retelling.

Incorporating Blank Level Questioning

This is how blank levels can be incorporated into reading and everyday activities as well as interventions for specific pupils. They can be incorporated into the early years as part of your setting's offer especially through continuous provision and play.

Assess pupils to identify the level they are working in, then have blank level questions accessible while working with pupils. This could be during structured and unstructured times, for example: when pupils are playing or while in a guided reading or reading session.

Sensory Stories

There is so much information on the internet about sensory stories. These are a great way to bring stories to life and engage the senses. Making those links between what you see, hear and feel, these are enjoyable and engaging ways to open access to stories for all pupils.

Example of a sensory story:

The Gruffalo Sensory Story
Created by Hannah Nicholas

This sensory story is based on the book *The Gruffalo* and has been adapted to include multi-sensory elements.

- When the story states, 'A mouse took a walk in the deep dark woods', the sensory element for pupils is:

Touch: Handle bark, sticks, or soft moss-like materials to represent the forest environment. This will be repeated every time the mouse walks in the woods.

- Each time the story describes the Gruffalo, the sensory element for pupils is:

Sight: Use a Gruffalo puppet and encourage pupils to focus on the specific areas of the Gruffalo described in that section.

- When the story mentions 'roasted fox', the sensory element for pupils is:

Smell: Roasting scent – present a smoky aroma using safe, food-related scents such as barbecue-flavoured crisps or toasted marshmallows.

- When the story mentions the owl, the sensory element for pupils is:

Taste: Mini scoops of real or dairy-free ice cream.

- When the story mentions 'scrambled snake', the sensory element for pupils is:

Proprioception: Snake grasping and movement – use a soft, flexible snake toy or prop. Encourage children to hold, twist and manipulate the toy to mimic the snake's slithering or coiling movements.

- When the mouse meets the Gruffalo for the first time, the sensory element for pupils is:

Vestibular: Switch with mouse sounds (e.g., squeak) and assist pupils in crossing their midline to reach the switch.

- When the mouse says, 'Just walk behind me and soon you'll see', the sensory element for pupils is:

Proprioception: Walking/Stomping – model walking or stomping and support students in moving their feet or tapping the bottoms of their feet/shoes to feel the sensation.

- When the mouse and the Gruffalo hear a hiss and meet the snake, the sensory element for pupils is:

Touch: Snake's texture – allow students to touch a snake toy or prop, feeling its slippery, smooth surface, or introduce textures to simulate a snake's scales.

- When the mouse and the Gruffalo hear a hoot and meet the owl, the sensory element for pupils is:

Touch: A small fan – allow students to feel the cool air on their faces, arms, or hands, mimicking the sensation of the owl flying away into the sky.

- When the mouse and the Gruffalo hear feet and meet the fox, the sensory element for pupils is:

Touch: Fox's fur – allow students to touch the fox's soft fur.

- When the mouse says that their tummy is rumbling, the sensory element for pupils is:

> **Interoception**: Tummy rub for hunger – an adult gently rubs the student's tummy, providing a calming, mindful touch that encourages the student to focus on the sensations within their body.
> - When the mouse finds a nut, the sensory element for pupils is:
>
> **Smell**: The scent of a nut.

Sensory Drama

This brings together storytelling and multi-sensory approaches, which as motivating, engaging and captivating and also involves pupils. Again, it allows everyone to get swept away in a story and have fun with it. These approaches are especially engaging for those pupils who like to recite their favourite stories that they watch on YouTube, or those that struggle to read books for themselves. More information can be found here: https://www.nationaldrama.org.uk/sensory-dramas/

Additional Ideas

- Pictophonics is a method, which uses characters to represent sounds. The characters are used as a guide and sit above the letters that make a sound in the word.
- Word Aware is a whole-school approach to teaching vocabulary. There are three books in the set and these include teaching vocabulary across the curriculum, teaching vocabulary in the early years and small group teaching as an intervention.
- Reading activities. These could include:
- Making capes with old T-shirts
- Clay, plasticine, dough characters
- Following instructions, for example have the pupils follow instructions to make the playdough
- Scenes built by Lego, construction materials, for example cardboard
- Real life scenarios – reading bus timetables, reporting back weekend football scores
- The internet is full of Guided Reading Activities especially on places like Pinterest.
- Call Scotland not only has resources for communication but also for reading and learners with dyslexia. The following resource and many others can be found at: https://www.callscotland.org.uk/downloads/posters-and-leaflets/

Chapter Summary

To end this chapter, following is 'Reading on a Page'. This document gives a clear outline of the Reading Intervention: Reading for All, helping staff know what is expected for a pupil depending on what stage they are placed in. It can double-up as a moderation tool using the key questions at the bottom of the template, using a RAG rate system termly to track and highlight the journey of the provision for that class.

Intent of reading. What it looks like	Implementation /teaching methods/ scaffolding	Interventions available	Use of IT	Impact -Assessment (Choose which is relevant)
Pre-Reading	Rhythm -Rhyming -Nursery Rhymes -Sensory Stories -AAC -Multi-sensory -Thermoforms -Tactile Image Printing -Decoding the Environment -Tactile and Noisy Books -Story Massage	-Sensology -TACPAC -Objects of Reference -Braille -Signalong -Makaton -Resonance Board -Attention Autism	-Talking Mats -Sensory Stories -Interactive Books -Living Paintings -Access to Books	-PPSEN Pre-Programme Stage Tracker -Communication Tracking Sheet
Stage 1 - The first phase can be considered a pictorial stage, when the child's brain photographs words and visually adjusts to the shape of the alphabet's letters.	-Rhythm -Rhyming -Nursery Rhymes -Sensory Stories -Storytime -Exploration of Words and Initial Sounds -Activities Relating to Topics -Look, Match, Name, Select Activities -AAC -Decoding the Environment -Language Experience Books -Story Massage	-Whole-Word Approach -Precision Teaching -Progression of Skills -Personalised Student Word Banks -Language Experience Books -See and Learn Programme -Signalong	-Talking Mat -Sensory Stories -Interactive Books -Living Paintings -Access to Books	-PPSEN Pre-Programme Stage Tracker -Communication Tracking Sheet -Word Set Assessment Sheets -Standardised Tests -TALC Assessment (Blank Level) -Interventions: Own Assessments

Stage 2 - The second phase is the phonological stage, when the brain begins to decode the letters (graphemes) into sounds (phonemes).	-Phonics for Pupils with SEN (PPSEN) -Guided Reading -Carousel Activities	-Visual Phonics -Pictophonics -Interventions (Brooks' What works for literacy difficulties) -Precision Teaching -Progression of Skills -Word Sets Personalised student Word Banks -Word Aware -Signalong	-Interactive Books -Nessy	-PPSEN Tracker/ Assessments -Communication Tracking Sheet -Word Set Assessment Sheets -Standardised Tests -TALC Assessment (Blank Level) -Interventions: Own Assessments -Book Band Progressions -Comprehension Record Sheets
Stage 3 - The third phase is the orthographic stage, when the child is able to recognise words quickly and accurately.	-Comprehension Skills (Reading for meaning) -Complex Sounds; -Chunking/ Syllables (for more complex sounds and or longer words) -Vocabulary Building (through word study/ maps) -Guided Reading Sessions -VIPERS -Carousel of Reading Activities		-Kindles	-PPSEN Tracker/ Assessments -Standardised Tests -Interventions: Own Assessments -Year Group/ Guided Reading Sheets -Book Band Progressions -Comprehension Record Sheets
Intent What it looks like in your class:	**Implementation** Teaching methods/ scaffolding approaches that are in place in your class:	**Interventions** being delivered in your class	**Use of IT**	**Impact** What progress is being/ beginning to be made?

Copyright material from Darleen Matoe Grimsby (2026),
Developing Educational Plans for Learners with SEND, Routledge

Interventions: Pre-Programme and Reading

The next chapter will focus on writing; as pupils acquire letters and sounds the idea is that they would then implement these into their writing making those key links.

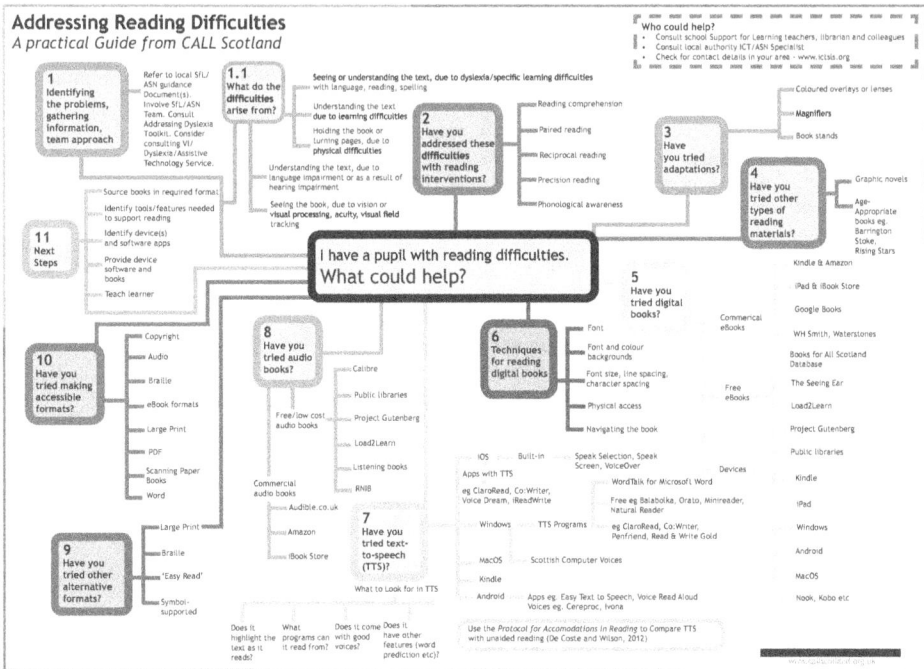

Credit: Call Scotland: https://www.callscotland.org.uk/

Further Reading

- What Works for Literacy Difficulties? - Greg Brooks (2020)
- Beneath the surface of developmental dyslexia - Frith (in Surface Dyslexia: Neuropsychological and Cognitive Studies of Phonological Reading-M. Coltheart, K. Patterson and J.C. Marshall (1985))
- Scarborough's Reading Rope from Connecting early language and literacy to later reading (dis) abilities: Evidence, theory, and practice (in Handbook of Early Literacy Research - S.B. Neuman and D.K. Dickinson (2001))
- Dual Route Cascade Model of Reading (in Psychological Review - M. Coltheart et al. (2001))
- The Simple View of Reading - P.B. Gough and W.E. Tumner (1986)
- Reciprocal Teaching: https://www.readingrockets.org/classroom/classroom-strategies/reciprocal-teaching
- Power of Reading: https://clpe.org.uk/books/power-of-reading/about
- Free multi-sensory stories that have different levels of complexity: https://inclusiveteach.com/sensory-story-collection/
- Fred's Fluency: https://www.fredsteaching.com/
- See and Learn Programme: https://www.seeandlearn.org/en-gb/
- Bob Books: https://bobbooks.com/about/
- Attention Autism, 2025: https://attentionautism.co.uk/attention-autism-programme/

7 Writing and Maths Interventions

Chapter Introduction

You would have noticed that this chapter includes both Writing and Maths Interventions and the reason for this is because both are not as extensive as reading and therefore would be short chapters but as the interventions are effective and worth sharing, I wanted to still include them in some way in the book.

The writing section of the chapter focusses on a specific 'bridging programme' and the maths section focusses on concrete, pictorial and abstract methods of teaching. These sections are again ideas that you can take and use as a basis to mould around the pupil.

Writing

Like reading, there is also a writing rope, which highlights all of the different aspects involved in writing. Writing can be a challenge because of what is involved, not only the technical side of manipulating a pencil on to paper but recalling phonics to spell words, holding your ideas and sentences so you do not forget what you wanted to write, sentence structure and punctuation so that it makes sense and so on.

To understand this better and see it from a visual point of view, you can refer to Joan Sedita's Writing Rope. It is important for us to understand the amount involved in writing, so we can understand how challenging it can be for pupils, especially those that cannot process all those things together. The following programme is aimed at those pupils who struggle to make the step from mark-making, overwriting and copying to independently writing a sentence. Therefore, this intervention is a stepping stone from those skills to being able to understand and write sentences. It breaks the different elements into separate steps, minimising what is involved in each step, rather than everything all at once. The programme provides clarity on what the pupil needs to do at each step when there is multiple processing.

Writing on a Page

To begin with, the following 'Writing on a Page' document outlines what writing looks like built into a curriculum. The document is split into five stages with the first stages being around mark-making but the main focus for this chapter is on Stages 2 and 3 where you would implement the Writing Progression programme. The latter stages incorporate Talk 4 Writing.

Stage of writing - what it looks like	Pre Key stage standard	Teaching methods and scaffolding	Interventions available	Use of I.T.
Stage 0 - Makes marks with no meaning, exploring, uses fingers and handprints, may use some mark-making tools. Exploring or experimenting with the marks different objects can make. May use a palmer grip or other grip.		Continuous provision indoor and outdoor. Toolboxes (indoor and outdoor). Trace patterns and shapes. Adult-led: Mark-making with hands, fingers, feet and bodies. Different surfaces: chalkboards, lightboxes, sand, pathways.		Use of iPad to mark-making, e.g. draw and tell app. Light boards. Table top computer with drawing app.
Stage 1 - Holds tools, makes marks and gives narrative or story to marks (usually pictures). Understand the concept that squiggles have meaning. wavy lines could be left to right or letters shapes and drawings that represent writing. Scribbling that represents writing or objects.	**Standard 1.**	Indoor and outdoor writing provision. Initial Sound letter exploration: PPSEN Modelling: -Mark-making, role play e.g. taking orders in a café, writing a shopping list, taking the register, making cards. Writing name on work (over writing). Ask pupils to talk to you about what they have drawn. -Exploring texts/book point to the words as reading. -Matching letter card to letter card. -Matching word cards to word cards. Provide real life context: -Adult modelling drawing and writing Collaborative writing: -Write Dance -Toolboxes containing things that can make marks. Examples: -Outdoor toolboxes Expectation: To be able to hold a pencil in preparation for writing. Begin name writing.	Fizzy Hands Therapeutic Putty Dough Disco Pencil Grips and Toppers Write dance Pegs to Paper	Using a stylus to draw on a touch screen.

	Standard 2	Writing Progression Expectation: Pupil can write their name. Beginning to write words.	PEGS to Paper. Write from the start. Handwriting without tears. Use yellow lines to highlight line spacing.	Use and recognise letter on a keyboard or iPad. Wet Dry Try for letter formation. Using a touch screen.
Stage 2 – 'write' from left to right, display pencil control, can join vertical lines, circle, replicate patterns, pictures begin to look like the object they represent. Emergent writing: beginning to see some letter shapes. Pupils can say out loud what they want to write, groups some shapes or letters into separate 'words'.				
Stage 3 – pupil can form letters (in line with phonics phase), uses finger spaces (understand concept of a single word), can write a simple sentence, e.g. I+watch TV. Uses capital letter and full stop. Can use 'and' as a conjunction, e.g. I+watch TV and play Xbox. Uses suffixes; es, s, ed.	Standard 3/4	Writing Progression Sound out words together. Modelling writing: -shared writing, guided writing, overwriting (letter formation only). -Word mats/ sound mats. -Writing checklists and visual/reminder, e.g. finger spacer.	Nelson handwriting scheme Tri line paper	Clicker 7/ Symwriter Using keyboard. Wet Dry Try

Copyright material from Darleen Matoe Grimsby (2026),
Developing Educational Plans for Learners with SEND, Routledge

	Standard 5	Talk 4 Writing: -Questioning to extend writing -Teacher modelling of writing -Story cubes -Word banks -Story maps or Text maps -Story mountain/ text planning sheets -Writing frames -Diary writing	
Stage 4 - pupils handwriting matures in line with fine motor skills, know appropriate size for upper case and lower case, can expand a sentence (expanded noun phrase) the **black** dog sat on the **rough** mat, uses conjunctions, because, but uses speech marks, capital letter, full stop,!, comma for lists, apostrophe for contractions and possession, uses suffixes -ing, er, est, ment, ful, less, ly.			
	Standard 6	Writing frames or planning tools for writing, dictionaries, Thesaurus	
Stage 5 - uses a dictionary, writes in paragraphs, identifies and selects correct homophone, uses prefixes, can use alternative conjunctions (however, whereas, although). Develop their own style of handwriting.			

The Writing Progression Programme: Teaching Progression

Stages 0 and 1 focus on mark-making.

Stage 2 into Stage 3: Writing sentences. The Writing Progression programme is outlined below using seven steps. The seven steps are teaching instructions for the adult and clear expectations and outcomes for the pupil, therefore, explaining what the adult does and what the pupil produces.

Whole class/small groups

Model writing/Speaking and listening

Step 1 – Adult has picture (same as pupils have) on flip chart or board.

Step 2 – Ask pupils to talk about the picture. The adult writes down their sentences (modelling basics of sentence writing capital letter and full stop).

Highlight and model punctuation/grammar/spelling.

Step 3 – Adult to ask pupils questions to facilitate communication.

Refer to Blank Levels of Questioning

Step 4 – Continue to write down sentences to label/caption the picture.

Step 5 – For those beginners, use the sentence starter: *It is* . . . . This is because *It is* is very simple and uses beginnings of phonics and only one curvy letter.

For those more able pupils choose a sentence that they are going to write. Make a list of 'help words' that pupils can copy, and hide away anything else.

Modelling:

Step 6 – Work through the following: The adult writes the sentence on a whiteboard. *It is* . . . . Rehearse sentence several times. Each time, erase a word but leave the line, until the sentence is not there, only lines. Pupils now have a 'holding sentence' in their mind. Keep 'help' words either on the lines or in a separate 'help words' box. (Use teacher judgement when they can begin to write these on their own.)

Step 7 – Pupils then go and write their sentences.

Independent writers – have lines marked in book already, eventually take away individual word lines.

134 Developing Educational Plans for Learners with SEND

For example:

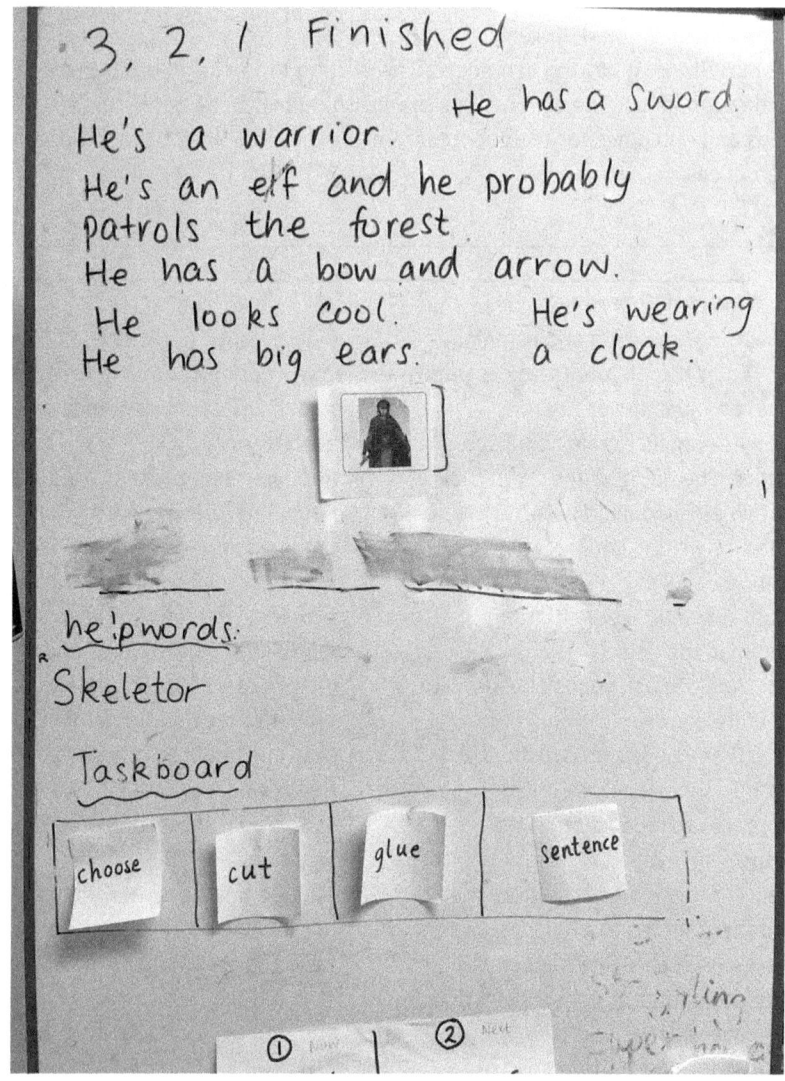

This picture shows Steps 1-4, encouraging pupils to share their sentences and ideas whether they can write them or not. The focus is on speaking and listening. Otherwise, some pupils may not contribute because they think the expectation is that they will also have to write it. They may think that if they cannot write it then they will not say it, possibly limiting their contributions.

For this example pupils decided to call the character Skeletor. The simple sentence was: *It is Skeletor.*

- *Skeletor* stayed on the board as the help word under the sub-heading.
- One of the four pupils chose to write his own sentences about Skeletor and what he looked like.
- The other three pupils wrote the simple sentence concentrating on capital letters. They used the checklist to check work and tick off.

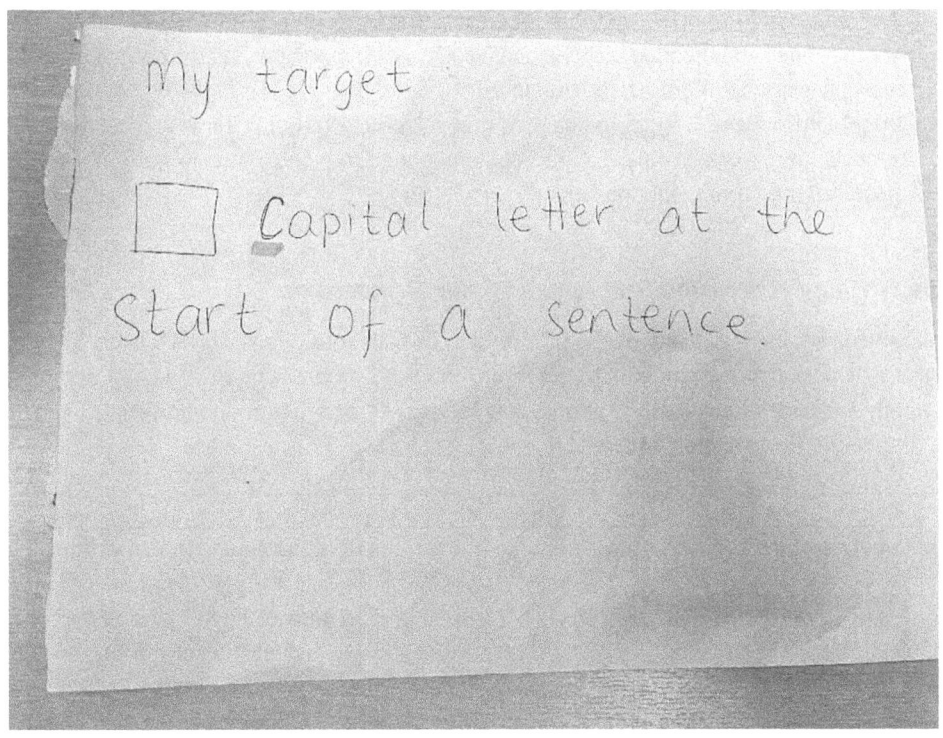

- These photos also highlight the use of visual aids such as 3, 2, 1, finished, checklists and taskboards and also how these can be used together and how they don't need to be made really fancy.
- For those that want to write more sentences, then they can. Keep it on the same topic though so that it naturally becomes a paragraph; when you move onto paragraphs or sections under a heading then they have already been doing it.
- Step 6 is to model writing for pupils so that they can see what is expected. This step also rehearses the sentence so that pupils can hold it in their minds before picking up a pencil and writing the sentence themselves, which leads into Step 7.
- Progression through sentences:

It is . . . .
It is . . . . . . and . . . .
This is . . . .
This is . . . . It is . . . . It is . . . . And . . . .

- The reason 'It is' is chosen is because no matter what phonics programme you use, these letters are always in the first set. These letters mostly use straight lines; only the 's' uses a curve. Remember that the aim is to try and ease the load when starting out writing thus taking away the chore like difficult feeling and replacing it with confidence and self-esteem building.
- Using checklists (tickable targets) supports embedding that learning. Keep checklists minimal to keep that simple and small step nature. Once the pupil is consistently using

the Target, for example capital letters, then that is mastered and can be taken away. Another one can be added. Let the pupil lead on how many targets they are able to successfully work on at a time, for example:

- Target 1 introduced. Target 1 embedded then introduce Target 2. Target 1 mastered then remove it and work on Target 2. Target 2 embedded then introduce Target 3. Target 2 mastered then remove it and so on.

The Writing Progression Programme: Skills Progression

Following is a table that outlines the progression of skills that pupils work through. The programme is designed for students to enter into the skills progression at any point and move through. Assess the pupil first through a cold task to see where they should enter.

Step 1: Cut, Paste, Match and Read

Label a picture.  Pre Key Stage Standard (PKSS): Standard 1	Cut, paste and match word cards. These could be topic based, e.g. at the start of the year, class staff. It could be their own name. e.g. It is Emily. Encourage mark-making underneath.

Step 2: Trace

Label a picture.  Additional challenge: Words on individual cards (post it notes), pupils sequence cards first to make the sentence, then trace. PKSS: Standard 1	Trace the sentence: e.g. It is Emily. Speaking: If pupil shares any additional information, the adult writes it. Therefore, the pupil will still feel as though they can share ideas even if they cannot write them all down. (Double up as a language experience book.)

Copyright material from Darleen Matoe Grimsby (2026),
Developing Educational Plans for Learners with SEND, Routledge

Step 3: Copy

Label a picture. 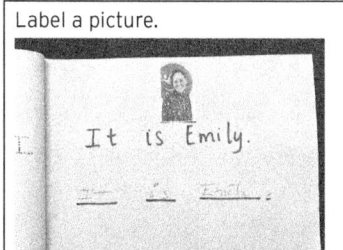 PKSS: Standard 2	Draw the corresponding lines underneath each word. Pupils copy the sentence using the lines: e.g. It is Emily. __ __ ___. Modelling: Teacher to model copying the sentence (adult has their own).

Step 4: Fill in the blank

Label a picture. 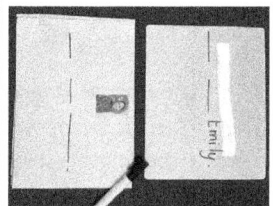 PKSS: Standard 3 Progress to PKSS: Standard 4	Draw corresponding lines. Pupil to only have the 'help' word. e.g. Emily. ___ ___ ___. Modelling: Adult to write *It is Emily* on whiteboard. Say It is Emily then erase *It* and put a line in its place. Say sentence again then erase *is* and put line in its place. Say sentence again but leave out *Emily*. Then pupil writes *It is* in their book and copies *Emily* (*Emily* is known as the 'help word'). Alternative: Pupils type instead of write

Copyright material from Darleen Matoe Grimsby (2026), *Developing Educational Plans for Learners with SEND*, Routledge

Remember that this is for beginner writers who have not been able to bridge that gap yet; however, it has been used to support those pupils who need a confidence boost and/or a short period of lower demand. A time where they may need to gain some confidence back and then re-join their peers. Pupils as they 'get it' and become more confident will start to progress and add more in on their own. This programme can be flexible and, for example, the use of computers can be built in as well.

Although typically people would think to use this programme with younger pupils, following is a case study which gives you an example of when this was used for an older pupil and the impact that it had.

Example of Impact: Year 7 Pupil Went from a Mainstream Setting to Complex Needs School.

This pupil joined the class from a mainstream setting in Year 7. When joining the class, he presented as an anxious individual with a fear of failure when attempting any tasks within the classroom, including picking up a pencil or even talking confidently to adults and peers. He has a speech and language barrier, making it difficult for him to pronounce some letter sounds, which resulted in difficulty understanding what he was saying, unless adults and peers knew him well.

First, the sentence starter writing approach was delivered to a small group of four pupils, including this pupil. We introduced talking through the sentence, first enabling pupils to get involved without even picking up a pencil. From this we then broke the sentence down further into sounding out and spelling the sentence starter, in this case 'It is' as a group. We repeated this for a few weeks before introducing writing this sentence starter into books. At first, we wrote this together and then this pupil would copy the sentence starter and ending help word. He soon built up confidence to write this sentence starter completely independently, resulting in writing a dictated sentence. He then confidently used a word mat to support finding his help word instead of copying from an adult. This enabled a completely independent sentence to be written and read back. As the lesson progressed, this pupil grew in confidence very quickly and was the first to get involved with any group sounding out. He then learnt another sentence starter and could use these sentence starters to form two independent sentences about a picture linked to the story with the aid of a word mat for his ending help words. He quickly became confident with capital letters and full stops as this learning was repeated and rehearsed. During the next annual review for this pupil, parents' feedback was positive, and this pupil told their parents that English and writing was now their favourite part about school. All staff within the team working with this pupil recognised the fast progress and more importantly the growth in the pupil's own self-esteem and pride in their writing achievements.

Writing and Maths Interventions 139

> Points of Reflection: For those pupils that are still overwriting beyond Year 2, what do you put in place to support them? How do you move them from only practicing their name?

Following is a picture example of using this programme with an autistic learner who is able to write and spell words but needed a structured programme to coherently write sentences.

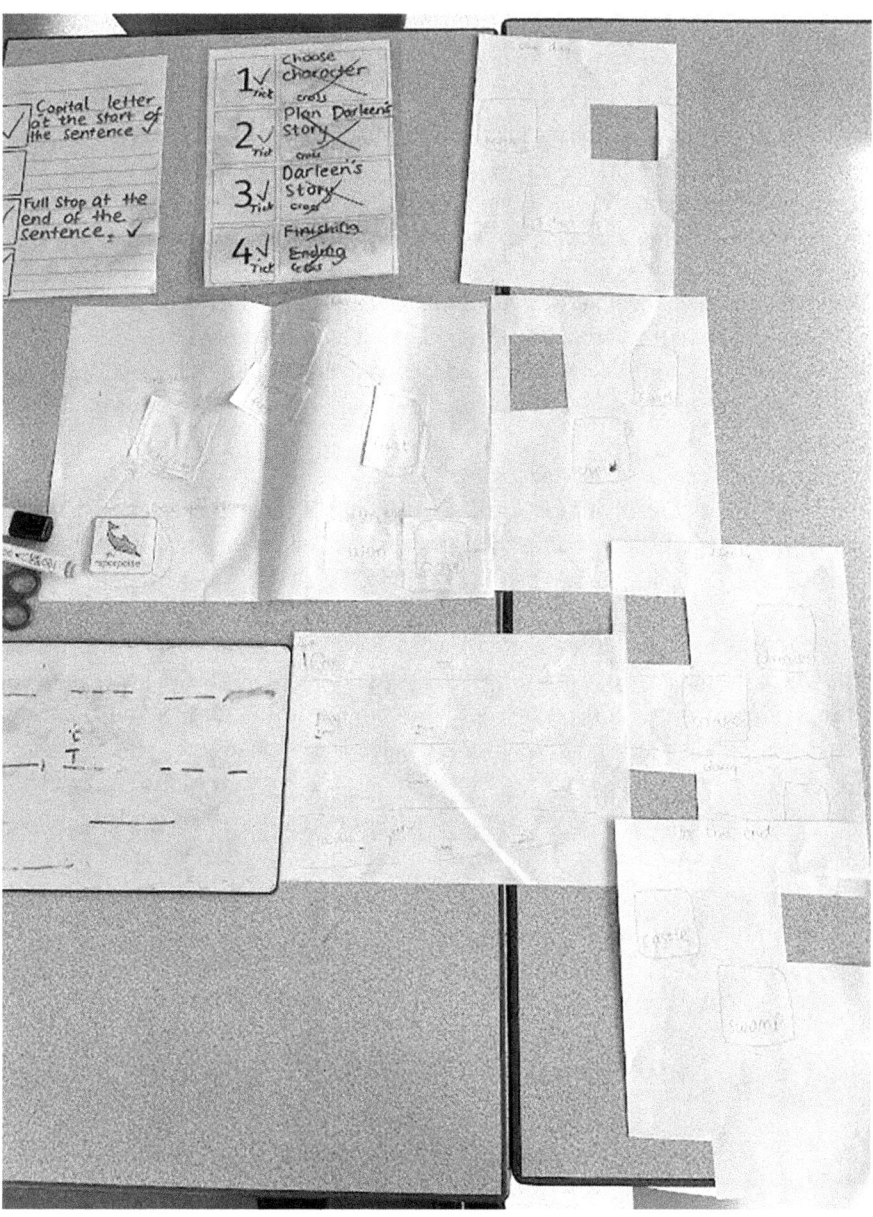

140 *Developing Educational Plans for Learners with SEND*

This example used the following:

- A story plan using a five-sentence story approach. Each sentence accompanied with the choice of three options.
- Teaching progression to write out the first sentence.
- Step 4 of the skills progression.
- Think for Pink and Yay for Yellow marking approach.
- Task board of what they needed to do in the lesson from the start to the end.
- Checklist of what the pupil needed to include in their writing.

Assessment Cycle

This is the assessment cycle, which allows you to review their progress at intervals and continue setting targets and markers for yourself and also the pupil to work towards creating that progression through provision. Again, highlighting those core themes of the book: enabling environments linking to confidence, self-esteem and managing anxieties.

1. Start with an Independent Task: Pupils complete piece of work independently with no adult support at all (no verbal prompts except initial instructions).
2. Analysis of task: Use Pre-Key Stage Standards and create targets for pupils to focus on and achieve. For example, if a child uses a lowercase i for *I went to the park*, then make this a target.
3. Targets are incorporated into teaching activities.
4. Independent task: End of unit/phase of teaching, pupils complete piece of work independently with no adult support at all (no verbal prompts except initial instructions).
5. Analysis task: Compare the two pieces of writing.

This can also be used with fiction, for example, alongside a Talk 4 Writing approach. Adaptations would be where the pupil is up to in their writing skills progression. This example shows a mixture of copying 'help' words and independently writing words (the teacher knows they are up to trying or can write), creating that balance and maintaining confidence in themselves.

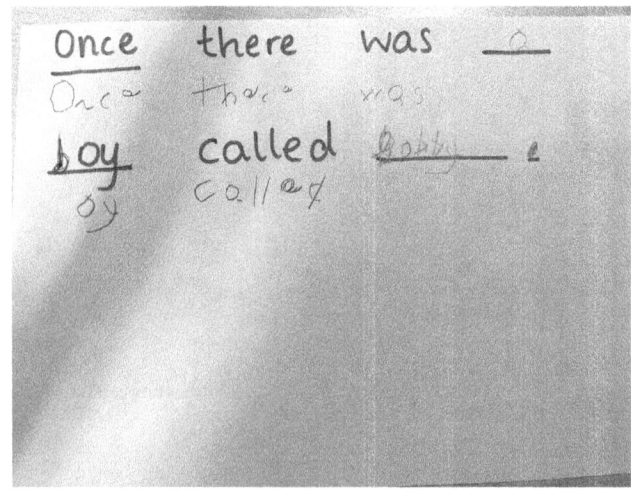

Writing Summary

In summary, the key takeaway is reflecting upon and thinking about what is in place for learners who are struggling to make that connection and write simple coherent sentences. Asking yourself those questions: *Are you at a place where things are not 'clicking' for that pupil and now you are not sure what will work? If this is the case then think about the teaching that is taking place and the progression of skills. Have you broken it down far enough? Are there too many things all at once for the pupil to process?* The aim of this chapter was to provide you with some ideas and tools that could contribute to answering some if not all of those questions.

Maths

Maths is one of those subjects where some learners can thrive because it is very 'black and white'. You calculate and find an answer; however, for pupils to be able to make progress it is important to embed key skills that are taught early on.

Some of the most important early maths skills are:

- Number recognition: Learning to identify numbers and count forwards and backwards.
- Sorting: Learning to group objects into categories.
- Measurement: Learning to measure quantities like length, area, and volume.
- Estimation: Learning to make a good guess about the size or amount of something.
- Pattern recognition: Learning to identify patterns in numbers, visuals or words.
- Critical thinking: Learning to identify relationships, make connections and apply reasoning.
- Problem solving: Learning to solve equations, understand ratios and recognise patterns.

These skills help children build a foundation for more advanced math concepts like addition, subtraction, multiplication and division.

- Number sense: Understanding the relationship between numbers.
- Pattern recognition: Enables pupils to see the relationships between numbers and objects.
- Critical thinking: Develops logical reasoning skills.
- Problem solving: Develops creative approaches to tackling problems and then further complex problems.

For some pupils, embedding these skills take a little longer or gaps can appear, creating that spikey profile. Following are some interventions and strategies that can be used for those pupils that fall into these categories.

White Rose Maths

White Rose Maths has become very popular and is used in so many schools throughout the UK. More information can be found at: https://whiteroseeducation.com/resources

Numicon Breaking Barriers

This is specifically designed for teaching children who experience particular difficulties learning maths, including those with special educational needs and disabilities. This programme goes right back to the beginning stages of maths and everything that you need is in the easy to use and easy to follow pack. Pupils can start at the beginning or join throughout the book depending on where they are up to. This has been used with pupils of all ages including those PMLD pupils in Key Stage 3. It supports pupils in filling in gaps by revisiting and embedding those key early maths skills and knowledge.

Concrete, Pictorial and Abstract Approach: Pictorial Step (CPA)

This section will specifically focus on the pictorial step.

Pictorial is the 'seeing' stage. Here, visual representations of concrete objects are used to model problems. This stage encourages children to make a mental connection between the physical object they just handled and the abstract pictures, diagrams or models that represent the objects from the problem.

Building or drawing a model makes it easier for children to grasp difficult abstract concepts (for example, fractions). Simply put, it helps students visualise abstract problems and make them more accessible (Maths No problem, 2025).

Think about drawing and drawing out the stages of thought. An easy example to help explain this is teaching column addition and subtraction. Column addition and subtraction is an easy and quick way to record and solve problems. Drawing it out teaches the understanding.

For example:

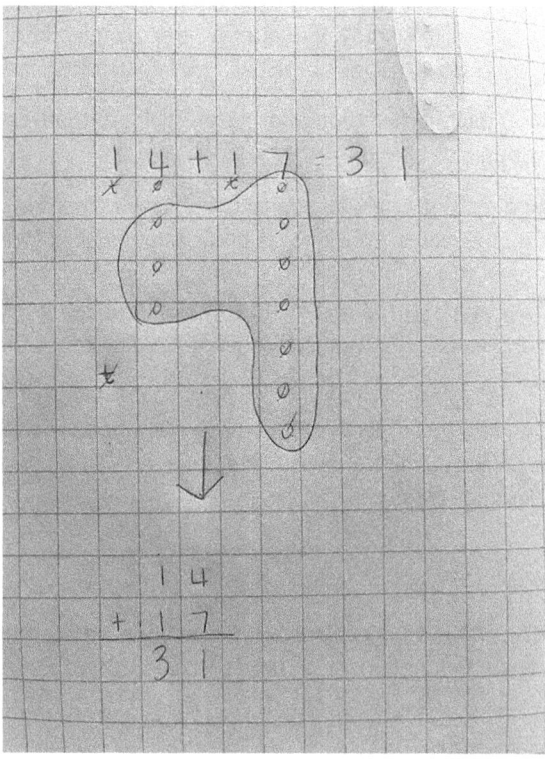

Drawing it out teaches the visual representation which shows what the recording of it means. Therefore, that one important step in the process that can be often missed out.

In the example above, the pupil draws seven ones and one ten, then four ones and one ten representing the numbers 17 and 14. They then add up the ones until they make a ten and then group these to show that they have now made a ten. Then they write a new ten. Count any remaining ones and that becomes the ones. Then count the tens and that becomes the tens answer. The example shows it recorded as a column addition to highlight the importance of the steps from pictorial to abstract.

Maths Summary

Although only a short section in the book, it is not meant to undervalue or give any less emphasis to this area. Instead, pre-programme strategies and visual aids can all contribute to the teaching of maths just the same as with reading and writing. Instead of repeating those approaches again here in maths, I have listed some specific interventions for maths and then the idea is that you would take other 'in the moment' strategies to incorporate into regulating the pupils so that they can make progress through an intervention like Breaking Barriers or White Rose Maths. One important point to add before the chapter ends, if pupils are not accessing White Rose at the age of their peers, then what are they accessing? Ask yourself: can they still engage in the same topic but access a lower year level? For example, a Year 5 student is working at Year 2 therefore they access the Year 2 topic plan instead of Year 5. By using the anticipate and plan approach to adaptive teaching rather than after-thought, the philosophy 'maths for all' is incorporated fully into the classroom.

Chapter Summary

Although this chapter is not as in-depth as other chapters, the key takeaways are to reflect upon:

How are you assessing where pupil's gaps are?

For those pupils where they are not yet able to access the National Curriculum, what are those bridges of support that you are putting in place?

The aim of this chapter was to provide some of those adaptations and bridging support when it comes to writing and maths and how we first need to identify what they can do and where the gaps in learning are. Then with this information you can then use variations of curriculums and interventions to bridge gaps.

Further Reading

The Writing Rope: A Framework for Explicit Writing Instruction in All Subjects – Joan Sedita (2022)

8 Assessment and Tracking

Chapter Introduction

This chapter touches on different types of assessment for different subjects and areas; it includes a section on the Engagement Model with accompanying resources.

Assessment informs planning, teaching and learning, which informs assessment and so on. So, the first assessment is to identify that starting point and then use that information to create a curriculum path; building in interventions and strategies. Next, assessment is to measure the progress made through that provision. Not only to assess the pupil's progress but to ask the question: are the provisions and interventions having an impact? Putting in place the assess, plan, do review approach.

This helps to reduce workload as you have that data rather than guesswork; again reiterating that anticipate and plan approach. Then you can anticipate barriers and plan to address them (Aubin, 2024) through scaffolding, reasonable adjustments, subtle changes or an intervention. You can plan when and how you will implement these.

Assessing pupils will help you to unpick quicker and put in place the right scaffolds especially when sometimes all that is required is a subtle addition to access the curriculum rather than a six-week intervention.

Assessing Reading

Linking back to the previous chapter, which focussed on reading, here it talks about finding out where pupils are so that you can identify the reading stage they are working at. Following are assessments that can identify and provide that information. There are many different tests that you can access that will give you a reading age. For example:

Salford Sentence Reading Test
Hertfordshire Reading Age Test

When you have that reading age score, it provides us with a 'What'. That 'What' identifies the gap between their age and their reading age. We can see what age they are typically reading at, which will identify their starting point. Next, it is also important to have a 'How'. Therefore when you are delivering these tests it is important to take notes on how the pupil reads. Do they read by sight? Do they sound out unfamiliar words or do they just guess? Do they apply phonics to their reading? As well as this test also complete a phonics test with pupils so you know how they read and possibly where the gaps are. All of this will help to create a picture of their reading starting point and place them in a reading stage. The pupil can do this with this, so we will start here and use this programme and these strategies. The reading intervention model was designed to help identify programmes of study and strategies to support, creating a path.

Assessing Writing

Independent writing tasks are effective ways of assessing writing.

> *Points of Reflection: Independent writing: If the adult left the room and came back, would it have been the same piece of work? Sometimes, people do not realise that they have helped in some little way even though they say the pupil did it.*

Independent writing tasks can be either fiction, non-fiction and/or name writing.

- Fiction: have a picture of interest on a page and ask the pupil to write a story or a paragraph about that character. Non-fiction – diary task (this takes away any imagining) ask the pupil to write about their weekend or what did they did at school. For other pupils it could be as simple as writing their name. We want to identify their starting point. Do not forget to think about phonics included in their writing. If the pupil struggles to segment, then they may struggle to segment the word to then write it. Use phonics to inform analysis of both reading and writing. Take the phonics assessment and cross-reference it with the independent task.
- Analyse letter formation: which letters are formed correctly? Which are not? Are there any patterns? Build the information you gather from this area into their curriculum. For example, incorporate activities to practice lines that make up the letters they find difficult.
- Analyse name writing: observe a pupil writing their name, really watch how they do it. Think about these aspects separately to unpick any specific barriers:
  - Hand and pencil
  - Pencil to paper
  - Weight of pencil on the paper.
  - Manipulation to create the letters.
  - Does the pupil lose focus? Can you identify at which point they do this?
- Analyse sentences: Use this sentence to identify where you would place the pupil using Pre-Key stage standards.

Again, you want to create a starting point for their writing. What are their strengths that you will incorporate into their writing first, to build confidence? Where can I put practice activities into their timetable to target their gaps, for example as a morning task?

Assessing Maths

Sandwell Numeracy Test

This particular test covers all areas of maths and year groups. The assessment record will identify any gaps in pupils learning, corresponding year groups and their strengths. The idea is the same as the other subjects: to build a picture of the pupil's maths ability. One useful part of the assessment is the notes section as when you are delivering the test you can write down how they arrived at the answer. Ask yourself: did they guess? Did they use their fingers? How are they getting to an answer? As this assessment starts from an early age you will also be able to identify if those key early maths skills are in place and if not, which ones are not. Sandwell will clearly show what the pupil needs to develop by revisiting or using specific interventions.

Assessing Interventions

Evidence Based Practice Unit (EBPU) Logic Model will help to gain clarity on the logic that underpins an intervention. It will help you to unpack, choose and moderate an intervention. More information can be found at: https://www.annafreud.org/get-involved/networks/evidence-based-practice-unit/

Tracking Communication and Pre-Learning Skills

This tracker was created to track pupils that access Pre-Programme and Communication based learning.

Name:

Year Group: R   1   2   3   4   5   6   7   8   9   10   11

Activity	Level						
	L1	L2	L3	L4	L5	L6	L7
Learning to Communicate							
Object of Reference							
Intensive Interaction							
Attention Autism							
Communication Skills							
Blank Level							
Information Carrying Words							
Reading Stage (Working in)	Pre-Reading	Stage 1	Stage 2	Stage 3			

Copyright material from Darleen Matoe Grimsby (2026),
Developing Educational Plans for Learners with SEND, Routledge

Criteria

Activity	Level 1	Level 2	Level 3	Level 4	Level 5	Level 6	Level 7
Learning to Communicate	Pre-intentional Responds to events- smiles gurgles	Anticipatory Anticipates what will happen – moves body/ looks in direction	Intentional Clearly indicates what wants – eye gaze, sounds, gesture	Words and ideas Uses words/ signs/symbols to tell what wants/doesn't want	Joining words and Ideas Talks about things can see/do, using signs, symbols, words	Abstract words and reasoning Uses language to plan, question, predict negotiate and reason	
Object of Reference	Pupil given the OoR and is taken to activity	Pupil given OoR and will go to the activity with prompting- physical, gesture, verbal	Pupil given OoR and goes to/ looks at activity/ understands event without prompting	Pupil will select OoR from a range and make a choice and go to chosen activity	Pupil selects appropriate OoR independently, goes to the activity or uses it to make request-		
Intensive Interaction	Encounter –	Awareness	Attention & response	Engagement-	Participation	Involvement	Pupil initiated interaction
Attention Autism	Capturing attention	Extending engagement	Turn Taking	Having a go			
Communication Skills	Choice between two items	Choice between four items	Begin to combine two words; more.../I want.....	Demonstrate intent to communicate	Initiates communication	Demonstrate awareness of listeners needs	Understands purpose of communi- cation aid

Copyright material from Darleen Matoe Grimsby (2026),
Developing Educational Plans for Learners with SEND, Routledge

Blank Level	Matching Perception – naming things	Selective analysis of perception – answering who, what, where	Reordering perception talking about stories and events	Solve complex and abstract verbal problems – answering why
Information Carrying Words (ICW)	1 ICW Understands 'Pass me the **scissors**' when there is a choice of scissors, pencil, paper	2 ICW Understands 'Put **teddy** on the **chair**' When there is a choice of teddy, dolly and chair, table	3 ICW Understands 'Put **big cat** in the **car**' when there is a choice of a big cat, a small cat, a big dog and a small dog, a car and a boat	4 ICW Understands 'Give **Alice** the **big red brick**' with a choice of Alice or Matthew, and red/blue/ yellow bricks and cars which are big and small

Copyright material from Darleen Matoe Grimsby (2026),
Developing Educational Plans for Learners with SEND, Routledge

The Engagement Model

> *Points of Reflection: For those pupils not accessing the National Curriculum, what are they accessing and how are they being assessed? What do you do for those pupils that are working well below expected, term after term?*

People I have spoken to regarding the Engagement Model always say that they 'overthink' it. Quite simply: the Engagement Model assesses how much the pupil engages in an activity. If they are engaged then they are learning and if they are not, then you need to make changes to the activity so they are engaged. That is what the Engagement Model does: tells you if they are engaged or if they are not. Then, it can be used to assess the effectiveness of the curriculum you have in place, ensuring pupils can meet the targets that they are set through that provision. There are five areas that are used to measure engagement: Initiation, Persistence, Exploration, Anticipation and Realisation.

There are several training videos on the Engagement Model. https://www.wholeschoolsend.org.uk/resources/webinar-using-engagement-model-mainstream Following are ideas how the Engagement Model can be implemented, which uses the mentioned training as a guide.

Implementation of the Engagement Model

This is an Engagement Model APDR cycle.

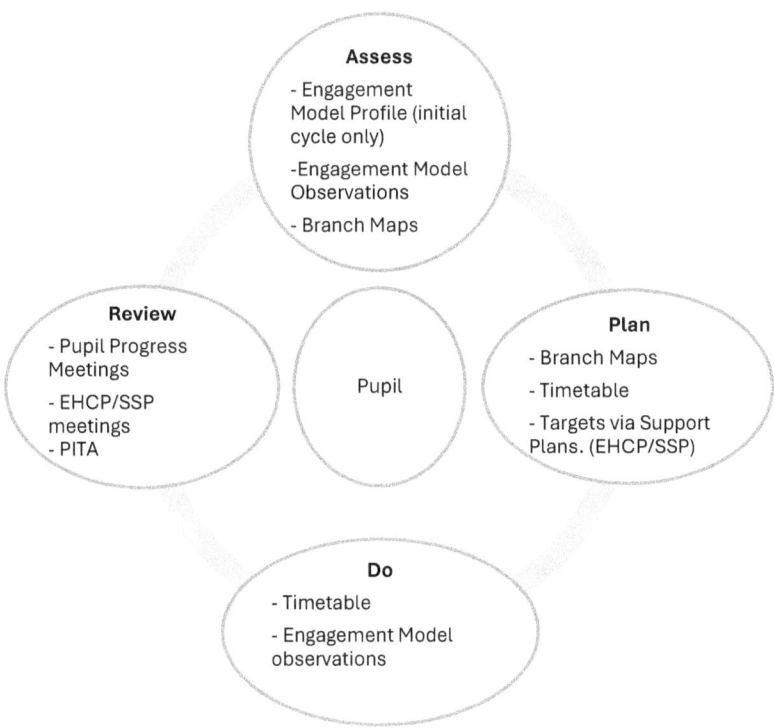

The website Engagement 4 Learning is where I found the most useful templates and engagement definitions: https://engagement4learning.com/e4l-engagement-model-resource/

1. Initial Observation

Initial observation: use the Engagement Model definition questions to complete an Engagement Model Profile. This will help to create the pupil's starting point and learn about the pupil's level of engagement, strengths, weaknesses, likes and dislikes. Following is a simple template for you to refer to.

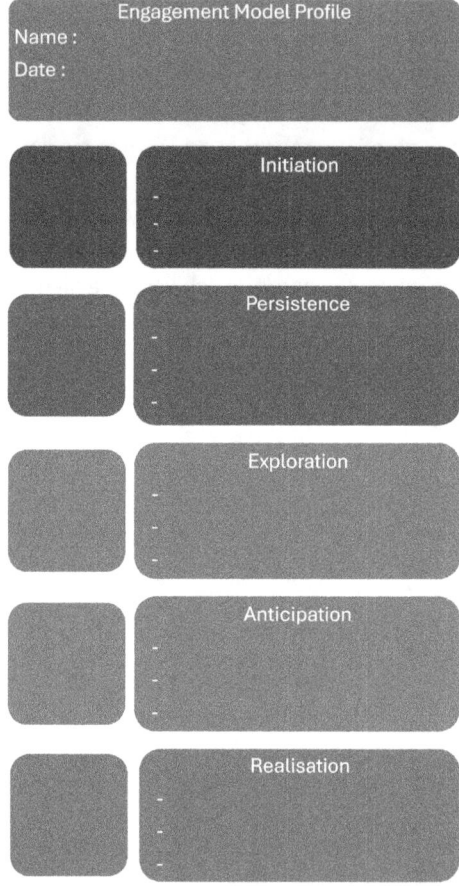

The left-hand side could be for symbols representing the five areas or photographs of the pupil engaging in an activity. The five exploration boxes are where the observation notes would go. There are many different templates that are available via a Google search that have accompanying examples and example questions to help complete the observation and fill in the boxes. There are two sites in the further reading section that are helpful with providing guidance for what would go in the boxes.

2. Plan

Use what you have found in the assessment to help plan the curriculum and provision for that pupil again making links to the anticipate and plan approach. For example:

Pupil A

Anticipation

- The pupil does not anticipate in any activities until after they have started and will not anticipate their end.
- The pupil will join the activity and will anticipate after 3-4 times of repetition, for example playing Boo, after the 3rd time, the pupil will show anticipation by their facial expressions and body movement by jerking forward and backwards. When the game finished, using a verbal cue, the pupil stayed seated.

Plan for Pupil A

Target:

The pupil will look at, attend to, and follow a series of 2-3 visual prompts that indicate an upcoming activity, showing a clear indication of anticipation (such as pausing current activity, redirecting attention, or preparing for the next task).

Timetable/Plan:

Attention Autism is scheduled in the pupil's timetable already. Add in a targeted teaching activity (engagement activity) before this.

Implement following visuals:

Now and Next Board

Timer and 3, 2, 1, Go and 3, 2, 1, finished

3. Do

Use the board to show the pupil it is time for 'Boo' game then Bucket. Say 3, 2, 1 go (showing the visual) then play Boo. Have the timer on for 2 minutes. When the timer beeps. Say 3, 2, 1, finished (showing the visual). Cross out Boo on the Now and Next board and say Bucket time. Have a dedicated space for Bucket time so eventually the pupil will move to that space showing that anticipation.

4. Observations

It is up to you as a team to decide when to do these, for example at the beginning, mid-way point and at the end. They would then be shared during pupil progress meetings as evidence of their engagement in their curriculum activities. Again, there are many different templates out there that you can use. Engagement 4 Learning has an Areas of Engagement Scale that incorporates a really effective scale. Then, the documents together show the pupil's journey beginning with their starting point.

5. Review

After you do it, you review it. Is what we are doing having an impact? The observation sheets will help you to answer this. They will highlight any of the five areas that show lack of engagement, therefore prompting you to think about how you can provide more opportunities to see more of the other engagement areas.

In this stage ask the questions: is the child working towards or away from their target? Are the provisions that are in place having an impact? Is the pupil engaging in the provisions? Again, these would be found in the observation sheets. Reading these will identify themes and inform your analysis of the impact of the provision. The Engagement Model should measure if the pupil is accessing (engaging) in the activities you are planning and if not, why not. If the pupil does not engage then will they make progress? This is what the Engagement Model measures the engagement the pupil has in the activity.

This can be shared and moderated through pupil progress meetings, dip dives, deep dives and point in time assessments. The observation sheets will also inform EHCP and SEN support plan meetings.

Following are key points for you to take away and think about regarding The Engagement Model.

- When using the Engagement Model, get used to the language of the five areas: use it, embed it in your targets, SEN support and EHC plans.
- The model's observation sheets will highlight any of the five areas that are not being covered and which areas are being covered a lot. Reflect upon providing activities that incorporate more of those 'lacking' areas.
- If there is lack of engagement from the pupil, then make those changes to provide opportunities for engagement in an activity. For example, add in a gestural prompt or a visual aid.
- Reporting: include in the report (observation sheet) a section where you can write what can be changed to provide more opportunities. For example, the pupil was unable to show perseverance and determination during sensory circuits because the sensory circuit bench was too thin for them to walk across and therefore gave up. Next time, I will use a wider bench.
- How do we know if the pupil is making progress? There is no data or no graph. This is where we can use the communication tracker to show progress through their curriculum. There will also be assessments depending on what you are doing, for example Phonics for Pupils with Special Educational Needs has a pre-programme section on the tracking document. These will run alongside the Engagement Model. The Engagement Model assesses the engagement in those curriculum activities and their own assessments will show progress they are making. If they have the engagement then logically they should be able to make progress through the provision.
- In moving forward think about this: if the pupil is now engaged, what is next? What can be reduced or changed? What skills can be transferred to other activities?

Chapter Summary

Assessment is key in identifying a starting point. Without starting points pupils can become an after-thought; the activities that we provide for them can lack in a systematic approach. With a starting point, we can anticipate and plan in a structured way building on skills and knowledge. We will then be able to show their journey through their provision. When we have the provision right for the pupil this contributes to that emotional regulating environment.

 **Further Reading**

Early Maths Skills

- Early maths skills 0-3 years: https://www.zerotothree.org/resource/help-your-child-develop-early-math-skills/
- Maths Skills by Age: https://www.beginlearning.com/parent-resources/math-skills-concepts
- 7 Key Maths Skills Primary students must learn: https://icodeschool.com.au/7-key-maths-skills-prep-and-primary-students-must-learn
- Mini Maths Enrichment: https://www.theoldstationnursery.co.uk/journal/mini-maths-enrichment-encouraging-maths-in-the-early-years

Interventions

- Number Stacks
- Twinkl. Same Day maths interventions and Small Step planning tools.
- White Rose Maths
- Catch Up Numeracy
- The Mathematics Shed

Writing

- The Writing Rope: The Strands that are woven into Skilled Writing – Joan Sedita. Reading Rockets (2025): https://www.readingrockets.org/topics/writing/articles/writing-rope-strands-are-woven-skilled-writing
- National Literacy Trust: Targeted Interventions for Reading, Writing and Language Development: https://literacytrust.org.uk/programmes/interventions/
- Twinkl: Writing Interventions Pack
- Top Tips for writing and Grammar Interventions: https://www.risingstars-uk.com/writing-and-grammar-intervention
- Improving Literacy in Secondary Schools: https://educationendowmentfoundation.org.uk/education-evidence/guidance-reports/literacy-ks3-ks4
- Talk 4 writing: https://www.talk4writing.com/
- Pobble 365: https://www.pobble.com/
- Literacy Shed: https://www.literacyshed.com/

Assessment

- The Engagement Model Guidance: https://www.gov.uk/government/publications/the-engagement-model/the-engagement-model
- The Engagement Model information and resources: https://engagement4learning.com/e4l-engagement-model-resource/
- Cherry Garden Branch Maps: https://www.cherrygardenschool.co.uk/branch-maps/#branchmaps
- Mapping and Assessing Personal Progress (MAPP): https://equals.co.uk/mapp-semi-formal-mapping-and-assessing-personal-progress/
- Quest *for learning* is a guidance and assessment resource to support teachers and classroom assistants of learners with PMLD, providing ideas for and pathways to learning: https://ccea.org.uk/learning-resources/quest-learning
- Equals Curriculum. Curriculum schemes of work for pupils with Profound & Multiple Learning Difficulties (PMLD), Complex Learning Difficulties (CLD), Severe Learning Difficulties (SLD), Moderate Learning Difficulties (MLD) and Global Learning Difficulties (GLD): https://equals.co.uk/curriculum/
- Phonics for Pupils with Special Educational Needs: https://www.phonicsforpupilswithspecialeducationalneeds.com/

Part III
Physical and Sensory

Preface

The Physical and Sensory section of the book comes before Social, Emotional and Mental Health. I wanted to highlight how the senses and Interoception play a key role in emotional and behavioural regulation. This part of the book will go into detail about the senses and how they affect our responses and regulation; it will also list sensory regulation tools and ends with a chapter on sensory impairments and physical needs. The Social, Emotional and Mental Health section will dive into emotions and emotional regulation tools.

> *Points of Reflection: I ask that you keep in mind all of the 'what' and 'how' information that has been shared already throughout the book. The 'how' especially will continue to be relevant as more approaches and strategies are shared. You may be asking the question: how am I going to fit it all in? To help answer this, refer back to the section on timetabling and finding those 'pockets' of time. These 'pockets' can be around 3-4 minutes several times a day which works with the 'little and often' approach. It does not have to be a big intervention: think more along the lines of 'grab bag' approach.*

Remember that universal approaches as part of quality first teaching can benefit all pupils and do not always need a separate intervention. Examples can include movement breaks, yoga and fine and gross motor skills integrated into P.E. Some can come in the form of adjustments (anticipate and plan), for example specific scissors, writing slopes, overlays or weighted pencil grips.

> *Points of Reflection: In relation to a sensory need or avoidance, try to figure out what is the pupil seeking or avoiding? What feedback are they looking for or moving away from? What is making them feel good or feel bad? If you are able to identify this, then it is easier to try and meet the need the most appropriate way. When you can give time, give it to 'unpicking' behaviour responses that you can anticipate and plan, which in turn can help to manage anxiety and avoid escalation.*

9 Sensory Processing and Regulation

Chapter Introduction

This chapter begins by briefly defining some key words that relate to sensory processing. If you would like to look further into these, websites with more information are provided in the further reading section. Following the brief definitions the chapter introduces sensory interventions and strategies aimed at:

- Exploring and learning about emotions, responses and regulation through our senses.
- Regulation: either in the moment or as part of a curriculum through the day.
- Feeling good: giving feedback to the body, which feels good, which means pupils will continue to seek.
- Not feeling good: avoiding feedback, which means pupils will have a flight response to.
- Communication: linking to communication so pupils can then use communication tools to make a request.
- Meet a need: giving feedback to the body for 2-3 hours, therefore the pupil doesn't feel the need to try and seek it and/or communicate this in a different way.

All of these aims link together to meet the pupil's body's needs, regulating the pupil and helping with managing anxiety.

Key Definitions

What is Sensory Processing?

The term sensory processing refers to how the body receives and interprets incoming stimuli through our senses. It is our brain's way of understanding the world around us, what is happening inside us and whether to react to or ignore that information. Basically, our brain takes in information from our senses, organises it and then responds appropriately.

Sensory integration and processing is important in everything we need to do daily, such as getting dressed, eating, moving around, socialising, learning and working. Each sensory system has its own unique role and together they inform our brain how to react and interact with our environment. This process helps us to maintain a sense of position, level of alertness in different surroundings and our ability to move.

DOI: 10.4324/9781003596820-15

Everybody has different sensory preferences and sensations that we do not like. We only require support and intervention if our sensory processing is stopping us from doing what we want and need to do in our daily lives.

'For example, it may be that a child strongly prefers some fabric textures, but cannot tolerate others and this becomes a problem because they are unable to tolerate their school uniform' (Connect, Humber, NHS, 2024).

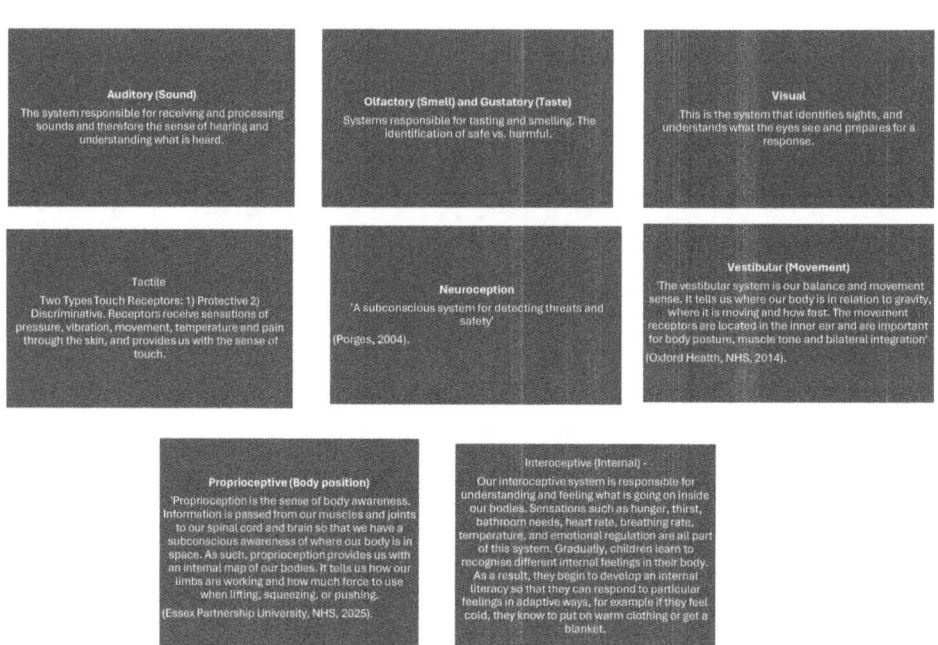

Our Senses

Sensory Processing Difficulties

Sensory processing difficulties are issues with processing information that comes in through the senses. As we have already established, the nervous system processes this information and generates a response or reaction to what is happening around the child in their environment. However, for some people, sensory processing does not develop as efficiently as it should which can make it difficult to generate an appropriate response to environments and everyday situations. This can affect daily living, education and social interactions. It can also result in a wide range of confusing and sometimes negative behaviours.

Some pupils may have difficulty receiving and responding to information from their senses. Those with sensory processing difficulties may experience difficulties figuring out what is going on inside and outside of their bodies. Some behaviours that may indicate sensory processing needs, which if persistent, will have an impact on accessing daily life, which may include:

- An aversion to anything that triggers their senses, such as light, sound, touch, taste, or smell.
- Running out of busy places when there are lots of visuals and/or sounds present.
- Difficulty coping with processing so many different things at one time.
- Seeking lots of physical movement through the day.
- Someone who needs more information into their muscle and movement systems, to tell them where they are in space.
- Sensitivity to light touch.
- Sensitivity to unexpected or light touch and have an anxious response to it.
- Seeking heavy touch and hugs.
- Seeking lots of heavy touch, through hugs for example, to get more input to their touch system. This can be calming for them.
- Difficulty with posture and co-ordination.
- Difficulty concentrating. (Essex Partnership University, 2025)

Sensory processing difficulties include: hyper-sensitive (over) which typically means those who are easily stimulated; hypo-sensitive (under) which typically means those who are not so easily stimulated; and sensory craving which typically means those seeking out things that provide particular stimulations.

Hyper-sensitivity

For those with hyper-sensitivity they typically tend to respond too much too soon or for too long to sensory stimuli that most people would find tolerable. These individuals may have:

- A dislike or avoidance of touch and texture experiences for example; messy play and physical contact.
- A dislike of loud sudden noises.
- A dislike of bright lights.
- Avoidance of playground equipment (e.g. swings and slides).
- Avoidance of certain foods and food texture, colours, temperatures, etc.
- A dislike or avoidance of certain smells. (Essex Partnership University, 2025)

Pupils can be observed avoiding times throughout the day, which may be a response to over-stimulation. They are taking in more information from their senses than their brain can process. If they are struggling to suppress and process the information coming in then they go into overload. This overload can cause stress, frustration and anxiety, which can then be observed in their behaviour. Overwhelmed by all the input, the brain responds to the situation by going into fight, flight, freeze, fawn or flop mode.

So, responses in pupil's behaviour can include:

- A low pain threshold
- Clumsy, uncoordinated movements
- Discomfort and confusion
- Covering of eyes or ears frequently

- Picky food preferences
- Showing aggression, impulsive or defiant behaviour when they are overwhelmed. The body is reacting to being overwhelmed. Or sometimes, because they are constantly seeking that stimulus for example, some pupils seek out food to eat or water to be in and want that all of the time.
- Avoiding sensations, as they have possibly anticipated that it will be too much, so they will avoid being over-stimulated. For example, some individuals will avoid water because of the sensation. They can also become cautious and afraid of things because they are worried about the impact it will have on their bodies. This also feeds into anxiety.
- This can have an impact on forming relationships as individuals can be unsociable, especially if they are hyper-sensitive to noise.
- Upset by transitions or unexpected change, not knowing what is coming next and the impact that that might have.

Hypo-sensitivity

For those individuals with hypo-sensitivity, they typically tend to be unaware of sensory stimuli. This may mean that they have a 'delay before responding and that their responses may be muted or with less intensity compared to others, so a lack of response to things like pain or extreme hot or cold' (Oxford Health, NHS, 2014). These individuals may:

- Have no fear or do not feel pain.
- Seek movement or touch opportunities (fidgets, rocks, jumps, leans on peers).
- Mouth or chew things.
- Poor attention/unresponsive to the environment or people around them.
- Distractible.
- Lack of energy. (Essex Partnership University, 2025)

Therefore, it can look different and quite contrasting for these pupils. They can crave interaction with the world around them, trying to gain some sensory feedback, trying something, realising the feeling and then wanting more. Looking like they are hyperactive when they are just trying to make their sense more engaged. These pupils 'need' this feedback so that they can feel 'just right'. On the other hand, they can appear inattentive because they are not receiving enough input: the senses aren't feeding back that information. Therefore, they are not involved and engaged in activities in their environment, there is nothing sustaining and holding their attention.

Their response behaviour may look like:

- Passive, quiet and withdrawn
- Difficult to engage in conversation or other social interactions
- Easily lost in own fantasy world
- Apathetic and easily exhausted
- Excessively slow to respond to directions or complete assignments
- Poor inner drive, uninterested in exploring. (Oxford Health, NHS, 2014)
- A high pain threshold.

- Bumping into walls.
- Touching things.
- Putting things into their mouth.
- Giving bear hugs.
- Crashing into other people or things. (Essex Partnership University, 2025)

> **Example of Impact: Year 7 Pupil, Attended a Complex Special Needs School since Reception.**
>
> The peaks in sensory stimulation were not evident and obvious until the pupil was in Year 4. This particular pupil would look inattentive a lot of the time, they enjoyed just laying on a beanbag in their own world, displaying a low inner drive.
>
> When we would go on a piece of trim trail equipment the pupil would then become hyperactive. They would suddenly show huge excitement with no fear. They wouldn't risk assess, instead they would use the equipment incorrectly to get more stimulation. Once we had finished on the equipment, they would then return to the beanbag and back to their own world.
>
> This also happened when someone would run their nails along the inside of the pupil's arm. The pupil's face would light up, they would make lots of loud noises while constantly putting their arm out for you to repeat it. Each time their face would show surprise and you could see the pupil processing the feedback information that was being sent to the brain.
>
> Sometimes they would sit down cross-legged, push themselves up off the ground and slam their bottom back on the ground, showing no signs of pain or discomfort.
>
> For this pupil the team put in place a sensory regulation programme for him to engage in throughout the day, which gave a balance of input to all of their senses. This included:
>
> Sensory Circuits in the morning and afternoon
> TACPAC
> Trim Trails circuits
> Massage
> Sensology: One sense a day
> Heavy work activities
>
> Once this was in place then we saw a decrease in sudden highs during particular activities and then lows. This pupil became more engaged throughout the day in all activities.

Sensory Craving

'These individuals are driven to obtain sensory stimulation and are often referred to as sensory seekers. However, when they do get that stimulation and feedback it can result it disorganisation as they don't know what to do as the drive might not be there anymore, or it did not satisfy the need and there is a drive for more' (Oxford Health, NHS, 2014). Hence times when adults will question: 'I am not sure what the pupil wants, they asked for water and now not sure if they want it'.

The responses that pupils may show include:

- Constantly wanting control over every situation.
- Does not wait for their turn, constantly interrupts.
- Angry or explosive when needs to sit still or stop activity.
- Intense, demanding, hard to calm.
- 'Prone to create situations others perceive as "bad", "dangerous" or "disruptive"' (Oxford Health, NHS, 2014).
- Jumping off high places.
- Smelling objects.
- Repetitive movements.
- Unusually agile.

> *Points of Reflection: At this point, you may have made some links between sensory related behaviours and other diagnoses. I believe that we use the pupil's behaviours and then implement strategies to encourage positive behavioural responses.*

Dip Dive: Sensory Seeking and Avoiding: Fleeing Without Regard to Safety.

A large number of families do share worries that their child will run off and has no knowledge of danger, stranger danger; essentially any regard to safety. First of all, I am not saying that this is the main reason why this behaviour may happen, I am just sharing another possibility.

When things are overwhelming, the child enters into 'flight mode'. They want to run away from what is going on in their environment as a response. The urge to react is the urge to run without any regard for anything else around them. The aim is to run away not to risk assess.

One of the reasons for being overwhelmed could be that the child is sensory seeking, they like the inner feeling that something gives them and then they are drawn to it. If they see that 'thing' then they are intrinsically motivated to go and get it and receive that feedback that makes them feel good. Alternatively, the child is sensory avoiding. They are trying to get away from it.

When parents share that their child has no idea of danger and they like to run off, take into account the possibility that the child may be sensory avoiding or sensory seeking.

If this could be the case then naturally the next step is to try and figure out what it is that they are seeking or avoiding. This can be done through observations and/or providing the pupil with different experiences and seeing what their responses are. Try including sensory experiences into their day through tough tray activities, oral sensory and texture exploring. For example, I sang to a child while playing and they covered their ears and tried to move away (might have been my singing!) . . . that indicates they don't like that sound. You can use antecedent, behaviour and consequence charts or just chatting and reflecting among staff and families to share experiences and responses.

Interoception and Emotions: Interoception is Step 1 in Teaching Emotional Regulation

Moving into this section it is important to keep in mind the brief definitions regarding the senses as it will help you to make sense of the role interoception specifically plays with feeding information back to the brain, seeking or responding to an urge and the link to our emotions. Interoception receptors are located all throughout your body, in your heart, lungs, stomach, bladder, skin and muscles. The job of the receptors is to pull in information about how your body is feeling and then send it your brain. Your brain can then use this information as clues to your emotions.

For example, the receptors in the lining of your stomach are pulling in information about how your stomach is feeling. What is the condition of your stomach? Your stomach is growly and empty, that information is sent to your brain, and your brain uses that as a clue that you are hungry then you are feeling hunger. Or maybe the receptors in the lining of your stomach are pulling in information that your stomach has that butterfly, tingly feeling in it. Your brain uses that as a clue that you are feeling anxious or nervous. So, there is a very tight body-emotion connection (Mahler, 2020). Then, that feeling urges us to act.

When the brain uses those clues, it then attaches it to an emotion and this is where we link up with vocabulary: a label. The emotion is then described/labelled by a word. Typically, we would say, 'We are hungry'. *This is a great example, which highlights how our body uses all development areas to respond to a need or a want. The sensations start (sensory/physical) which sends information to the brain (cognition and learning), queuing an emotion (SEMH), labelling and communicating (communication and interaction) that feeling and meeting that need.* I understand it as creating a chain of events:

Receptor → Brain → Process, Label and Respond

166 *Developing Educational Plans for Learners with SEND*

Based upon this, Interoception is where we need to start. It is our body signals that are clues to identifying our emotions, then we can regulate those. Interoception is Step 1 in that process. We need to notice our body signals, so that we can connect them to a meaning, to an emotion. For example, we need to notice the tingling in the stomach to identify we are feeling nervous.

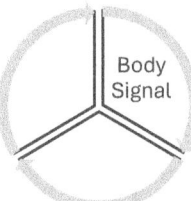

The next step in making that tight connection between our body signals and their meaning is to be aware of what emotions we are experiencing in order to find what will meet that need and manage that feeling. Our body signals give meaning to emotions. By learning those signals, we can explore and learn about our emotions.

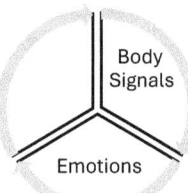

Next, we explore and learn what strategies are effective in meeting and managing those emotions. When we have these sensations, feelings and emotions, our bodies are urged to act and regulate. Therefore, the subsequent step is to choose a way to effectively regulate and manage our emotions. For example, you are feeling nervous, then you need to pick out what strategy will help manage that. When we are feeling hungry, request food (using a 'food' symbol card located in communication books). Or when you are feeling angry, instead of hitting, choose something which is more of an effective strategy. As our bodies urge us to react, we need to choose the most appropriate response that will meet that need and manage that emotion. Part of that is meeting a need and what feedback the body gets. For example, a pupil that can feel they are getting angry can ask for 'ice' to regulate and crunch out that surge in their body.

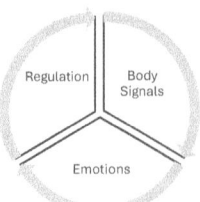

Once we are aware of how we feel, then we are able to understand how other people feel. It is not until we are able to recreate our own experiences that we can use those to then recognise how others may feel and 'walk in someone else's shoes'.

Points of Reflection: If we stop and think about it, the information we get through our senses can link to and significantly impact on the social, emotional and mental health of our pupils. Therefore is there a possibility that at times, pupils are communicating to us that they are overwhelmed or underwhelmed due to stimulation and sensitivity to something in their environment, and in turn, telling us key information about themselves?

Chapter Summary

The key message in this chapter is the important role that our senses and sensory processing play and the link they have to everything in and around us. What this chapter highlights is the importance of including these factors when you are unpicking behaviours. Instead of saying 'There was no trigger', keep the senses, processing and the environment in mind. For example, could a sensory experience have triggered that behaviour response, could it have been a memory, a smell that they didn't like? Instead of telling you that they did not like it, it was communicated through as a hit or a bite.

In summary, this chapter focussed on the 'what', whereas the next chapter will look at the 'how' we can support those with sensory needs to regulate, offering strategies that can be used both in the moment and as part of a daily curriculum.

Further Reading

- Sensory Processing: https://www.oxfordhealth.nhs.uk/wp-content/uploads/2014/05/Sensory-Processing-presentation-February-2014.pdf
- Connect. Children's Services and Adult Learning Disability Services: https://connect.humber.nhs.uk/service/humber-sensory-processing-hub/what-is-sensory-processing/
- https://eput.nhs.uk/media/b2sdvcsb/sensory-processing-disorder-information-leaflet-for-parents.pdf
- https://eput.nhs.uk/patient-carer-and-visitor/children-and-young-people-experiencing-sensory-processing-needs/explore-our-senses/introceptive/
- https://www.kelly-mahler.com/resources/blog/what-is-emotional-intelligence-and-how-does-interoception-come-into-play/
- https://bridgewater.nhs.uk/wp-content/uploads/2021/12/Warrington-Childrens-Occupational-Therapy-A-Guide-To-Sensory-Circuits-advice-sheet.pdf
- https://eput.nhs.uk/patient-carer-and-visitor/children-and-young-people-experiencing-sensory-processing-needs/sensory-useful-resources/

10 Sensory Integration Interventions

Chapter Introduction

This chapter aims to provide you with specific programmes, strategies and/or activities that have been created to support pupils with sensory processing difficulties. These are presented as a list and accompanied with a brief outline. I do encourage further reading and training so that you are able to implement these effectively. Sometimes these strategies are met with: 'I tried it, it didn't work'. This can sometimes be due to the implementation of the strategy or intervention not being as intended because of a lack in understanding and training. These strategies are designed to be built-in as opposed to bolt-on, therefore including them in a daily timetable or in the moment as an adaptative approach.

> *Points of Reflection:* In a training session, I would have shared information from the following chapter; this is usually the point I get to where everyone is excited, wanting to know what they can do. So, I continue with: 'I don't have a magic wand, this won't happen overnight, here are some strategies that you can use'. Then, boom! I have lost all the adults in the room; the enthusiasm has gone and it is now a room of deflation echoing, 'I have heard it before'. However, I have worked in some situations where a request board or sensory activities put into a daily timetable were magic wands. Where the strategies do not happen overnight, for those adults that keep going with it, it does happen! I ask that you go into this chapter with an open and reflective mindset.

I want to highlight that some strategies are mentioned several times but under different sub-headings for example, fidget toys feature in sensory diet and sensory tools. This is done on purpose as I wanted to incorporate all activities under their heading even if they had been mentioned already under another category.

Following are a list of headings and sub-headings that include approaches that you can use to support pupils to regulate their sensory needs. It begins with the broader sensitivities, environments and toolboxes and finishes with specific interventions or strategies.

Hypersensitivity

- Provide regular short bursts of gross motor play throughout the day.
- Ideally provide 'open doors' access to the outdoor area so that children have the space and freedom to move around as they need it. This can also provide a safe environment for 'flight mode'. Possibly have an 'outside' symbol card so the pupil can take it to indicate they need the outdoor area, promoting independent communication and regulation.
- Provide frequent movement breaks between focussed activities, any 'too much too soon' energy then has a release rather than an outburst.
- Taking the child's socks and shoes off and placing a cushion under their feet when they are sitting, will help them to feel grounded and calm.
- Provide lots of fun fine motor activities.

Hyposensitivity

- Encourage short periods of time with small group work to support desensitising the pupil to play activities.
- Allow the pupil to play with low key activities alongside a busier group for short periods.
- Allow the pupil to be a spectator of more active play, with no pressure to join in but offer invitations to play when they feel ready.
- Place the occasional obstacle in the pupil's way. Support the pupil in recognising this item and learning how to move safely around this.
- Try sitting the pupil on a beanbag. As the bean bag wraps around the pupil's body, it provides proprioceptive feedback.

Sensory Processing Activities

- Bouncing on a trampoline.
- Space hopper or playing 'jumping beans' games.
- Playing lots of ball games; these can include target throwing.
- Walking.
- Dancing and moving to music.
- Yoga: CosmicKids and/or Yogabugs.
- Pulling, pushing or carrying heavy objects for example, digging in wet sand and soil, kneading dough, pushing a wheelbarrow, sweeping.
- Gardening, having an outdoor garden that pupils could support growing and maintaining.
- 'Row, row your boat' song with a partner (adult).
- Obstacle courses. Where possible include tunnels and/ or blankets to crawl under as well as obstacles to climb over, which are already quite common in EYFS outdoor areas (minus the blankets).
- Different textured surfaces for the pupil to walk across with bare feet, for example bubble

wrap, textured stepping stones, sand, grass, and so on.
- Finger rhymes and songs.
- Bubble blowing, blowing feathers across the floor.

Sensory Circuits

> *Points of Reflection: As an adult, what do you do when you come into school in the morning? I mess about a bit, get a coffee, put my stuff out on my desk, and so on. Then start work. That is my transition from home to school. How about for pupils? When they come in, sometimes they are excited, anxious or worried and are expected to come in sit down and start a task of some sort. Would it be more beneficial for pupils that struggle with that transition to participate in a sensory circuit and have that time to work through the motions and then be ready to enter the classroom with more focus?*

Sensory circuits are an effective way to achieve a positive transition from home to school or even after lunchtime play back to the classroom.

What Is a Sensory Circuit?

A circuit is a session where each pupil performs a series of activities to develop sensory motor sensory skills. Activities are split into three groups: Alerting, Organising and Calming that are completed in that order.

A key element that is often lost is that Sensory Circuits are about feedback to the body, feedback to your senses. Circuits help with learning, tracking and will feed the body and the senses.

I do urge that you consult an occupational therapist to train and support your setting with Sensory Circuits to ensure that they are used effectively.

Sensory Diet

Implementing a sensory diet is an effective way to support pupils to regulate and de-escalate challenging behaviours. A sensory diet is a personalised plan of activities and strategies that provide the necessary sensory input to help regulate the pupil's nervous system. For example, a pupil may benefit from swinging, jumping on a trampoline or playing with tactile materials during breaks throughout the day. An occupational therapist can help to develop a sensory diet that is tailored to the pupil's needs. Resources can include sensory play kits, indoor swings, and tactile toys.

Sensory tools	Fidget toys, weighted vests, kick bands or tactile objects to help them regulate their sensory input.
Sensory activities	Incorporate sensory activities such as swinging, jumping, or crawling into the pupil's daily routine to provide sensory input.
Sensory breaks	Provide pupils with scheduled sensory breaks to take a break from academic tasks and engage in sensory activities to regulate their sensory input.
Sensory rooms	Create a sensory room or designated sensory space for pupils to access when they need a break or require additional sensory input. These don't have to be expensive and could include: dark den pop up tent, head, hand and feet massage tools, visual aids, for example like/ok/dislike, stretch bands.
Sensory-friendly materials	Use sensory-friendly materials such as noise-cancelling headphones, adjustable lighting, or comfortable seating to create a sensory-friendly environment.
Sensory snacks	Provide pupils with sensory snacks such as crunchy or chewy foods to help regulate their sensory input. Also see Oral Processing.
Sensory stories	Use sensory stories to help pupils understand and regulate their emotions and behaviours. This was covered in Chapter 6.
Sensory integration therapy	Provide pupils with sensory integration therapy to help regulate their sensory input. This can be provided or guided by an occupational therapist.
Sensory breaks	Provide pupils with scheduled sensory breaks to take a break from academic tasks and engage in sensory activities to regulate their sensory input.
Sensory play	Pupils to engage in sensory play activities such as playing with sand, water or slime to regulate their sensory input.
Sensory walks	Sensory walks: Take pupils on sensory walks where they can engage with their environment through their senses and regulate their sensory input.
Sensory bins (tough trays)	Provide pupils with sensory bins filled with materials such as rice, beans or sand.
Sensory-based art	Art activities such as finger painting.
Sensory-based calming activities	Such as deep breathing or progressive muscle relaxation to help pupils regulate their emotions and behaviour.

Sensory Toolkit

A sensory toolkit is a collection of items that can be used to help individuals regulate their sensory needs and manage stress or anxiety. It can be customised to suit the pupil's specific sensory needs. For example, a pupil who seeks tactile input may benefit from a fidget toy or textured sensory ball. A pupil who is easily overstimulated by noise may benefit from noise-cancelling headphones or a white noise machine.

In some settings, we have also had a 'classroom toolkit' for any pupil to use, rather than borrow from a pupil specific box. The classroom kit can be available to use in the moment.

Here are some examples of items that could be included in any sensory toolkit, which have been separated into different senses:

Auditory

- Noise-cancelling headphones or earplugs

Smell

- Essential oils on tissues in small freezer zip lock bags
- Lavender in small bags
- Scratch and sniff stickers

Oral

- Chewable necklaces or bracelets
- Ice
- Blowing bubbles
- Ice poles
- Snacks with different textures e.g. crunchy carrots, chewy foods

Visual

- A visual schedule or checklist (if this is a trigger then move and use it for your reference)
- A sensory bottle or glitter jar
- A small fan or personal cooling device
- Eye mask
- A light-up bubble tube or fibre optic lamp
- A sensory storybook or visual social story
- Light up toys
- Torch flashlight
- Snow globe

Busy hands

- Fidget toys or stress balls
- Pickstones
- Putty (scented) or playdough
- A tactile discrimination kit with items such as different textures of fabric or materials
- Stress ball
- Bubble wrap
- Spinning top

Proprioceptive

- Weighted lap pads or blankets
- A vibrating pillow or massager
- Weighted vest or vest
- Massaging brush
- Foam roller or massage ball
- Body sock
- Tunnel

Brain breaks

- Diamond Art
- Colouring book
- Puzzles
- Favourite books to read
- Whiteboard and pen
- Etch sketch
- Activity books
- Worry book

Movement

- Stretchy kick bands for chairs
- A mini-trampoline or exercise ball
- A sensory swing or hammock
- A balance board or wobble cushion
- Yoga poses

It is important to consult with an occupational therapist or other qualified professionals to determine which items may be most helpful for each individual. These can be expensive when purchasing from specific websites when sometimes cheaper substitutes can be made, for example fairy lights in a salad spinner.

Sensory-Friendly Environment

A sensory-friendly environment is designed to meet the specific sensory needs of pupils, providing them with a safe and comfortable space to learn and play. The list below provides examples. The idea is for you to pick and choose what you can realistically implement. If you are setting up a specialist provision, you may be able to implement more of these than those that are in a mainstream class. Here are some strategies for creating a sensory-friendly environment:

Reduce noise levels	Noise can be overwhelming. Consider using noise-cancelling headphones or white noise machines to reduce noise levels in the environment. You may also consider creating quiet areas or using sound-absorbing materials to help reduce noise levels.
Control lighting	Bright or flickering lights can be overstimulating. Consider using dimmer switches or lampshades to control lighting levels. You may also consider using natural lighting sources such as windows or skylights.
Provide sensory tools and equipment	Sensory tools and equipment such as weighted blankets, sensory toys or fidgets can help pre-verbal autistic pupils regulate their sensory needs. Consider providing a variety of sensory tools and equipment in your environment.
Consider the temperature	Temperature can be an important factor in creating a comfortable environment for pre-verbal autistic pupils. Consider the temperature in the environment and adjust it as necessary. You may also consider using fans, air conditioning or heaters to help regulate the temperature.
Create designated calm-down area	Designated calm-down areas provide pre-verbal autistic pupils with a safe and comfortable space to calm down and regulate their emotions. Consider creating a designated calm-down area in your environment, with comfortable seating, calming lighting and sensory tools and equipment.
Reduce clutter	Clutter can be distracting and overwhelming for pre-verbal autistic pupils. Consider reducing clutter in the environment by organising materials and using storage containers.
Use visual supports	Visual supports such as picture schedules or visual rules and expectations can help pre-verbal autistic pupils understand what is expected of them and reduce anxiety in the environment.

Heavy Work

What Is Heavy Work?

Heavy work is activity that requires effort from our muscles and these tasks usually involve activation of the muscles and joints of the body through the proprioceptive system by movements such as pushing, pulling or lifting. The movement activities create resistance input to the muscles and this feedback is ultimately what calms and regulates the sensory system. (Beck, 2024)

According to Beck (2024), heavy work may include any activity that involves:

Pushing
Pulling
Lifting
Carrying
Chewing
Jumping
Squeezing

Climbing
Pinching
Brushing
Any other actions that use the muscles and joints with weight of the body or object.

Examples of Heavy Work Activities That a Pupil Can Do in School

Pushing or pulling a cart or trolley:	Carrying objects:	Resistance exercises:
Pupils can be asked to push or pull a cart or trolley. This can be incorporated into activities such as moving classroom materials, carrying books, or transporting equipment.	Pupils can be asked to carry objects such as books, equipment, or boxes. This can be incorporated into tasks such as moving materials between classrooms or helping with setting up for activities or events.	Pupils can do resistance exercises such as wall push-ups or chair dips. These activities involve pushing or pulling against a stable object.
Climbing stairs:	**Jumping or bouncing on a therapy ball:**	**Using resistance bands:**
Pupils can be encouraged to climb stairs as part of their daily routine. This activity provides resistance and requires the use of multiple muscle groups, providing proprioceptive input to the body.	Pupils can be asked to jump or bounce on a therapy ball, which provides proprioceptive input to the body. This activity can be incorporated into activities such as spelling or math drills.	Resistance bands can be used to provide resistance during stretching or exercise activities. The resistance from the bands provides proprioceptive input to the muscles and joints.

These activities can be used as both 'in the moment' strategies or put into the pupil's daily timetable. A great tool for when you see a pupil is needing redirecting, had enough of an activity or starting to 'fizz' then this is a good time to go with this type of activity.

Tactile Touch

I am going to separate tactile touch into two categories:

- Physical tactile touch: This is from another adult applying pressure through physical touch, for example massage or squeeze side hug.
- Exploration tactile touch: This is everyday experiences through touch of different food textures, textured objects for example: sand, different materials for example: fabric, experiencing pain and different temperatures.

Exploration can be achieved through sensory boxes. Allowing pupils to explore different textures while taking note or using 'like/ok/don't like' to better understand pupil preferences.
The remainder of this section will focus on physical touch.
First of all, you must seek consent from parents and pupils. Physical tactile touch can be a powerful tool that adults can use to support pupils. It involves providing appropriate, non-restrictive and soothing touch to support a pupil's sensory needs. Using this type of touch can help a pupil re-regulate and relax when they are experiencing a dysregulated state. Physical tactile touch provides proprioceptive input to the muscles and joints, which can help regulate the nervous system. This improves body awareness and promotes emotional regulation, which can help to reduce feelings of anxiety, stress, and dysregulation. It also enhances sense of safety.

> **Case Study: Year 7 Autistic Pupil Attending a Complex Needs Special School.**
>
> When this pupil was distressed, upset and/or anxious, he would typically communicate this through swearing or hitting out. I would often be asked to come and provide 'in the moment' support. The first time I did this, I wanted to see if the pupil would respond to tactile touch, so I asked if I could try a head massage (I already had a positive relationship with the pupil) and they said yes. He responded well: instantly calming. I asked him if this helps and he responded with 'Yes'. So it became part of his behaviour support plan. Whenever I was asked to support the pupil, I would respond using this approach as part of his plan. He would often push his head into my hand. I would use the words 'hard' or 'soft' and he would respond indicating the type of pressure he wanted. This was the only communication at this point. I would stop and say the words 'more' or 'finished' and he would respond with 'more'. This would continue until he would then tell me what was bothering him. Then instead of hitting out, he would walk out of the classroom and come and find me. The next step was for him to tell an adult to call for me and then eventually transferring the process to other adults that he trusted.
>
> The second pupil was similar; however, they were non-speaking. I would ask the pupil if they would like a massage (pointing to a massage symbol card) they would sign yes. Then I would ask them to sit down and if I could touch his feet. He would nod and take his shoes and socks off. I would massage his feet. Next to him would be more and finished symbol cards, hard and soft symbol cards. I would ask the same questions as in the case study above and this pupil would communicate their preferences through pointing to the cards. This strategy was used both in the moment and put into their daily timetable particularly after any transitions.

Safe and Appropriate

The point these case studies highlight is that this type of touch can regulate pupils with sensory needs. For some adults they may feel uncomfortable doing this and some pupils may not respond to this. Therefore, tactile touch is defined as massage, slight pressure, light touch along arms or on the back of pupils, a side hug with a slight squeeze. It is always safe and non-restrictive. Ensure that if you are using this it should be on plans that are shared, explained, demonstrated and signed by parents. To ensure that touch is safely and appropriately implemented to support pupils, here are some guidelines for using tactile touch:

- Respect personal boundaries: It is essential to respect a pupil's personal boundaries and not touch them in a way that makes them uncomfortable or distressed.
- If a pupil does not like it or wants it to stop, they may communicate this through kicking or hitting you. You need to be aware of your body especially head positioning, that is, don't lean your face over the pupil's feet and legs.

- Tactile touch should be appropriate and non-restrictive.
- Be aware of cultural differences: adults should be aware of cultural differences and norms around touch and adjust their approach accordingly.
- Obtain consent: adults should always obtain consent before touching a pupil, especially if the touch is new or unfamiliar.

Examples of physical tactile touch can be in the form of a head, hand or foot massage, a side hug 'squeeze' and/or deep pressure on a pupil's shoulders.

Tense and Release (Progressive Muscle Relaxation)

> *Points of Reflection: If you are sat reading this book, try clenching your fists and then releasing the tension. Most of you will feel some kind of release or sensation in your body.*

Tense and release is basically a two-step process where you tense particular muscle groups in your body and then release the tension. You would use one muscle group at a time. This is a great exercise for pupils as well as yourself. The following example is using your left hand:

Step 1 – Make a tight fist with your left hand and squeeze as hard as you can for about five seconds. You can also inhale at this point.

Step 2 – Open your hand and release the tension: your muscles should become relaxed. You can exhale at this point.

The following tense and release exercises that you can do with different muscle groups:

> Forehead: raise your eyebrows
> Mouth: open your mouth wide and stretch out your jaw
> Eyes: shut your eyelids tightly
> Neck and shoulders: lift your shoulder up toward your head
> Chest: take a deep breath in
> Hand: clench your fist
> Arms: form a muscle by clenching your fist, bend your elbow and raise your fist toward your head.
> Stomach: suck your stomach in
> Bottom: clench tightly
> Legs: raise your leg, pull your toes towards you
> Feet: point your toes downwards

Oral Processing

Those pupils that have difficulties with oral processing might drool and/or mouth non-food items to gain that oral feedback. If we provide time for them to 'work-out' the muscles in their mouth this will help to regulate the need for that type of input.

Oral sensory processing information and activities can be found at:

- https://www.griffinot.com/child-oral-sensory-seeking/
- https://sensorysid.com/10-strategies-for-oral-sensory-seeking/
- https://www.oxfordhealth.nhs.uk/wp-content/uploads/2014/05/Sensory-Oral-Skill-Development.pdf

Another point to consider here is that some pupils have 'electrical' type sensations and feelings in their body and in their mouths. This is when you see pupils trying to put sharp objects in their mouths or wanting to snap or crunch things. First of all, take note on what they are putting in their mouths and then find foods to substitute that, for example ice or frozen carrots to crunch on or soggy rice crispies for a spongy texture.

Chapter Summary

The intention of this chapter is to provide the reader with practical approaches that can be used in the moment or implemented into a pupil's daily curriculum to meet sensory needs. They are just stepping stones introducing you to what is available. Remember that if we provide these strategies for pupils, we also need to provide ways to communicate with the pupil what we are doing, keeping those all-important links between regulation and communication to ensure that we continue to reduce anxiety and emotional distress. A good place to start any further reading would be: https://www.andnextcomesl.com. This is a website that has effective resources to support in all areas including sensory processing.

11 Sensory Impairments and/or Physical Needs

Chapter Introduction

> Many children and young people with vision impairment (VI), hearing impairment (HI) or a multi-sensory impairment (MSI) will require specialist support and/or equipment to access their learning, or habilitation support.' 'Some children and young people with a physical disability (PD) require additional ongoing support and equipment to access all the opportunities available to their peers (Department for Education, 2014).

This is a very specialised area and therefore this chapter required specialist knowledge. I co-authored this chapter with Hannah Nicholas who leads provision for all pupils who have multi-sensory impairment and physical disabilities. Through her extensive research and what she provides in her own classroom and throughout the school, we have put together this chapter. This is where you will find lists of equipment, support and resources for you to use if you are teaching pupils with sensory impairments and/or physical disabilities and difficulties.

Hearing Impairment (HI)

Pupils with HI should have access to a specialist teacher, Teacher of the Deaf (TOD) and staff should follow their expert advice. Specialist Deaf curriculum framework:

https://www.batod.org.uk/resources-category/specialist-deaf-curriculum-framework/

Pupils with hearing impairments may use a variety of assistive devices, including bone-conduction hearing aids, traditional hearing aids and cochlear implants. Additionally, some may rely on assistive listening devices, such as FM systems, or other supportive technologies to enhance their hearing experience.

Hearing Impairment and Speech Development

Children or young people with hearing impairments often experience difficulties with their speech. This is because they may be unable to hear certain sounds, which affects their ability to develop those speech sounds. It is therefore essential to have access to their audiogram, as this will show which sounds they are missing.

By referring to the speech banana on the audiogram, you can identify the phonetic sounds they are unable to hear. When a child cannot hear certain sounds, it becomes much harder for them to develop those speech patterns. This is why visual support is crucial when communicating with a student with both hearing and vision impairments. For example, if a child cannot hear specific sounds in a spoken instruction –such as 'sit down' – they may not fully understand what is being asked of them. By using visual cues alongside verbal instructions, you can help ensure they comprehend and follow directions. Understanding their audiogram and using visuals will also provide insight into why they may struggle with pronouncing certain words.

Ensuring Access to Hearing Aids and Assistive Technology

To support children and young people with hearing impairments, it is essential to promote access to sound. This means ensuring they have their hearing aids or bone-conduction hearing aids (BAHA) on and functioning correctly. Regular checks should be carried out to confirm that these devices are working properly.

Some children may also use additional assistive technology, such as radio aids or loop systems, which connect directly to their hearing aids. These advanced systems can link to various devices, including laptops, allowing sound to be transmitted directly into their hearing aids.

In a classroom environment, radio aids are particularly useful as they help reduce background noise. The teacher or main speaker wears a microphone, which transmits their voice directly to the child's hearing aid. This is highly beneficial in noisy classrooms, where background sounds can make it difficult for the child to hear.

When considering the best classroom setup, think about positioning – placing the child in an optimal location where they can hear clearly and avoiding areas with excessive noise, such as near fans or open windows.

Sign Language and Communication Support

The level of support needed will depend on the severity of the hearing impairment. Some children respond well to British Sign Language (BSL), which is widely used by those who are deaf. Other communication methods include Makaton and Signalong, both of which use signs alongside spoken language to support understanding.

Resources

- Hearing Aids & Cochlear Implants – Ensure they are working properly and used consistently.
- Radio Aids & Soundfield Systems – Help amplify the teacher's voice and reduce background noise in classrooms.
- Loop Systems – Assist pupils in accessing sound directly into their hearing aids.
- Speech Banana Audiogram – Helps educators understand which sounds a pupil may struggle to hear.

- British Sign Language (BSL), Makaton & Signalong – Support communication through sign language.
- Captioned Videos & Speech-to-Text Software – Provides written support for spoken content.

Support Strategies

- Use Visual Cues & Gestures – Reinforce verbal communication with pictures, written words or signs.
- Face the Pupil When Speaking – Helps with lip-reading and understanding facial expressions.
- Reduce Background Noise – Avoid placing pupils near noisy areas like fans, corridors or open windows.
- Provide Pre-Lesson Notes – Allows the pupil to follow along more easily in class.
- Check Understanding Regularly – Encourage the pupil to repeat or summarise instructions.

Visual Impairment (VI)

For children and young people with vision impairments, it is vital that the school environment is adapted to support their independence. This includes:

- Conducting a habilitation audit of classrooms and school spaces.
- Enhancing visibility by adding yellow tape on steps and installing railings to prevent falls.
- Covering potential trip hazards to create a safer environment.
- Tactile Learning and Braille
- Children with vision impairments rely heavily on tactile learning. They often explore their environment using their sense of touch, mapping out spaces by physically feeling their surroundings. They may also engage with tactile objects to aid their understanding.

For children learning Braille, it is important to introduce it early, as it is a complex skill that takes time to develop. Braille requires extensive exploration and practice to master.

Understanding a child's specific diagnosis is crucial in tailoring support. Conditions such as strabismus, astigmatism and cerebral visual impairment (CVI) all affect vision differently. A specialist teacher should conduct a functional vision assessment and provide strategies based on the child's unique needs. For instance, if a child has a limited visual field, materials may need to be presented on a specific side to optimise their vision.

Ensuring Access to Learning

Children with vision impairments need appropriate adaptations to access their learning effectively. This might include:

- Enlarging text or providing digital copies.
- Allowing them to sit closer to the screen.

- Using assistive technology, such as screen magnifiers or text-to-speech software.
- Providing one-to-one support to read materials aloud if necessary.
- For mobility, a child with a vision impairment may use a cane or other mobility aid to navigate their environment safely.

Resources

- Large Print, High-Contrast Text & Braille Materials – Ensure reading materials are accessible.
- Screen Readers & Magnification Software – Convert text into speech or enlarge text.
- Haptic Feedback & Tactile Graphics – Allow pupils to feel diagrams, maps or images.
- CCTV Magnifiers & Video Magnification Devices – Help pupils access written information.
- Mobility Aids (White Canes, Electronic Travel Aids, Guide Dogs) – Support safe movement.
- Braille Notetakers & Embossers – Enable writing and reading in Braille.

Support Strategies

- Provide a Structured Classroom Layout – Keep furniture in consistent locations to aid navigation.
- Use Verbal Descriptions – Describe what is being written or shown on the board.
- Ensure Good Lighting & Minimise Glare – Adjust lighting to reduce eye strain.
- Offer Hands-On Learning – Allow pupils to explore real objects for a better understanding.
- Teach Orientation & Mobility Skills – Support independence in moving around the school environment.

Curriculum Framework for Children and Young People with Vision Impairment (CFVI) https://www.rnib.org.uk/professionals/health-social-care-education-professionals/education-professionals/cfvi/

Multi-Sensory Impairment (MSI)

Pupils with MSI should have access to a specialist teacher, Qualified Teacher of Multi-Sensory Impairment (QTMSI) and staff should follow their expert advice. A curriculum for multi-sensory-impaired children was published by Sense in 2009: https://www.sense.org.uk/information-and-advice/for-professionals/resources-for-education-and-early-years-professionals/msi-curriculum/

A child or young person with multi-sensory impairment (MSI) has both hearing and vision impairments, making communication and access to learning even more complex. The level of impairment in each sense will vary – for example, a child may have a profound hearing loss but only a mild vision impairment. Children with hearing impairments often rely on vision, and children with vision impairments rely on touch while those with MSI require alternative methods of understanding the world around them.

To Support a Pupil with MSI

- Trained interveners should assist in their communication. https://www.seashelltrust.org.uk/deafblind-awareness-week-blog-3-the-role-of-the-intervenor/
- Multi-sensory teaching approaches should be used, incorporating touch, sound and movement.
- Real-life objects should be introduced to reinforce understanding. For example, if teaching about grass, allow the child to physically feel and smell real grass to build recognition.

The Importance of Hands-on Learning

For children with multi-sensory impairments (MSI), hands-on learning is essential. The hand-under-hand approach allows them to explore objects and movements while maintaining control. Instead of someone guiding their hands directly, the child's hands rest on top of the adult's, enabling them to observe and feel actions at their own pace. This method promotes trust, independence and confidence in learning.

By incorporating the hand-under-hand approach and other multi-sensory strategies, we can create meaningful learning experiences for children with MSI, helping them better understand and interact with the world around them.

Resources

- Hand-Under-Hand Technique – Supports exploration while allowing autonomy (Sense Hand-Under-Hand Guide).
- Tactile Sign Language & Object Symbols – Supports communication using touch-based methods.
- Multi-Sensory Learning Tools (Sensory Stories, Real Objects, Textured Materials) – Helps reinforce concepts.
- Specialist Assistive Technology (Braille Displays, Vibrating Alert Devices, Audio Descriptions) – Enhances access to information.
- Personalised Learning Spaces (Little Rooms, Sensory Environments) – Provide controlled spaces for exploration.

Support Strategies

- Use a Multi-Sensory Approach – Incorporate touch, sound, movement and scent to reinforce learning.
- Create Predictable Routines – Establish consistency to build confidence in navigating daily tasks.
- Ensure a Safe & Accessible Environment – Remove obstacles, use tactile markers and provide handrails.

- Work with a Qualified Habilitation Specialist – Develop personalised mobility and independence training.
- Encourage Interaction with Peers – Promote social inclusion through structured activities.

Habilitation Support for Children and Young People with Sensory Impairment

Habilitation support is specialised training that helps children and young people with vision, hearing or multi-sensory impairments develop essential mobility, orientation and independent living skills. Unlike rehabilitation (which focuses on regaining lost skills), habilitation is about learning new skills from an early age to help them navigate and interact with the world confidently.

Key Areas of Habilitation Support

- Teaching children how to safely move around their environment, whether at home, in school or in the community.
- Learning how to use mobility aids such as white canes, guide dogs or electronic navigation devices.
- Developing spatial awareness and learning routes to key locations (e.g., classrooms, playgrounds or public transport).
- Learning daily tasks such as dressing, cooking or organising personal belongings to promote independence.
- Teaching personal safety skills, such as navigating streets, crossing roads and using public transport.

Environmental Adaptations

- Conduct a habilitation audit of school and home environments to make spaces safer and more accessible.
- Implementing visual or tactile markers (e.g., yellow tape on steps, textured flooring, or handrails) to help children with vision impairments move around independently.
- Reducing environmental barriers for those with hearing impairments, such as minimising background noise in classrooms.

Use of Assistive Technology

- Train children to use screen readers, magnifiers, Braille displays or hearing loop systems.
- Ensuring they have access to technology that enhances learning, such as digital notetakers or speech-to-text software.

Social and Emotional Development

- Supporting children in developing confidence in new environments and social settings.
- Teaching self-advocacy skills so they can express their needs and access necessary support.

Who Provides Habilitation Support?

Habilitation support is typically delivered by Qualified Habilitation Specialists (QHS), who work alongside teachers, parents, therapists and other professionals. Support is tailored to the individual needs of the child and may be provided at home, in school or in the community.

Why Is Habilitation Important?

For children and young people with sensory impairments, independence and confidence are key to their development. Without appropriate habilitation support, they may struggle with everyday tasks, movement or accessing education. By providing the right training and resources, we can ensure they develop the skills they need to lead independent and fulfilling lives.

Physical Disabilities

Physical disability is outlined as 'limitation on a person's physical functioning, mobility, dexterity, or stamina that has a "substantial" and "long-term" negative effect on an individual's ability to do normal day to day activities' (Equality Act,2010). For some pupils, their physical impairment might be mild and for others it might be more profound. Pupils with physical disabilities will have diagnosed conditions, some of which include cerebral palsy, spinal bifida and neuromuscular dystrophies.

Pupils with physical disabilities should receive support from physiotherapists and occupational therapists. They should have an individual physiotherapy plan, which includes positional changes and necessary equipment. An exercise plan should also be created, which can be incorporated into the school timetable. Occupational therapists will assist with the use of equipment, such as slings and hoists, as well as support daily living skills (e.g. adaptive cutlery).

Positional movements are essential for wheelchair-bound pupils as they play a critical role in promoting comfort, function and health. These movements help to maintain posture, prevent secondary health issues and enhance engagement in learning activities. Here is a detailed look at why positional movements are so important for pupils who use wheelchairs:

1. Preventing Physical Complications

    - Pressure Sores
      Prolonged sitting in a wheelchair without proper positional changes can cause pressure sores (also known as bedsores). These occur when sustained pressure on

certain areas of the body cuts off blood flow, damaging the skin and underlying tissues.

Regular position changes (e.g. shifting weight from side to side, tilting the pelvis, or reclining) help distribute pressure evenly across different parts of the body, reducing the risk of pressure sores.

- Postural Support and Alignment

    Consistent postural adjustments are necessary to help maintain proper body alignment and avoid musculoskeletal problems, such as scoliosis, spinal deformities or contractures (permanent muscle tightness).

    Correct positioning can help pupils avoid pain and discomfort caused by poor posture and allow them to use their muscles more effectively for mobility and function.

2. Enhancing Comfort and Function
    - Relieving Muscle Stiffness

        Being in a static position for extended periods can lead to muscle stiffness, especially in the lower limbs, hip flexors or back.

        Regularly shifting positions and performing range-of-motion exercises (e.g. stretching, rotation) helps to keep the muscles loose and flexible, improving overall comfort and mobility.

    - Increased Independence

        For some pupils, being able to self-adjust their position (e.g. tilting their chair or shifting weight) can increase independence and self-reliance.

        Techniques such as tilt-in-space, recline and elevate leg rests on wheelchairs help pupils find a comfortable position without relying on assistance from others.

3. Promoting Learning Engagement
    - Optimal Viewing and Participation

        Proper positioning ensures pupils can easily view teaching materials, such as the whiteboard, digital displays or their own work.

        Correct posture and positioning in the wheelchair help prevent visual strain, and maximise comfort when focusing on academic tasks, enabling pupils to stay engaged for longer periods.

    - Improved Upper Body Function

        Postural support allows for better head control and upper limb function, facilitating activities such as writing, using assistive technology and engaging in physical activities.

        A well-positioned pupil is more likely to interact confidently with their environment and participate in classroom activities.

4. Supporting Well-Being and Emotional Health
    - Dignity and Social Interaction

        Maintaining a comfortable and upright position allows pupils to interact face-to-face with their peers and teachers, promoting self-esteem and social inclusion.

        It helps avoid feelings of isolation that can occur if a pupil is physically slumped or misaligned, which may make socialisation or group work more difficult.

- Autonomy in Movement
   Empowering pupils to adjust their own position or use adaptive seating features increases their sense of control over their environment, leading to improved emotional well-being. It allows them to participate in school activities with a greater sense of agency.
5. Practical Positional Techniques and Tools
   - Tilt-in-Space Wheelchairs: These allow the pupil to adjust the angle of the seat, which helps shift weight, promote comfort and prevent pressure ulcers.
   - Reclining Backrests: Helps relieve pressure and provide a change in posture.
   - Adjustable Leg Rests: Elevating legs can reduce pressure on the lower body and help with blood circulation.
   - Cushions and Pressure Relief Pads: These are designed to relieve pressure and support proper posture in a seated position.
   - Wheelchair Lap Trays: Help the pupil engage in activities like writing, drawing or using a tablet while also offering a stable surface for fine motor tasks.

For pupils with physical disabilities, it is crucial to incorporate positional changes into their daily routines and timetables. Identifying the most effective position to support engagement is key. Additionally, investing in adaptive equipment, such as easy hold grip devices (sold on Amazon), can significantly enhance the pupils' access and participation.

Physical Difficulties

> *Points of Reflection: How is support provided for those pupils that struggle with fine and gross motor skills?*

The Fizzy, Clever Hands and Write from the Start programmes are UK-based motor skills development interventions designed to support children with fine and gross motor difficulties. These programmes are widely used in schools and therapy settings to enhance physical development, coordination and handwriting skills.

Fizzy Programme (Gross Motor Skills)

A graded exercise programme designed by physiotherapists and occupational therapists, which targets balance, core strength, coordination and motor planning. This programme can be beneficial for pupils with dyspraxia (DCD), hypermobility or low muscle tone. More information can be found: https://www.nhsggc.org.uk/kids/healthcare-professionals/paediatric-occupational-therapy/fizzy-programme/

Clever Hands Programme (Fine Motor Skills)

This programme focuses on hand strength, dexterity and finger control. It can help children struggling with pencil grip, scissor skills and buttoning clothes. Clever Hands includes activities such as finger strengthening exercises, threading and pegboard tasks.

Write from the Start Programme (Handwriting Development)

A structured approach to developing pre-writing skills. This programme uses pattern drawing, hand-eye coordination activities and pencil control exercises. Suitable for children struggling with letter formation and fluent writing. More information can be found online at thedyslexiashop.co.uk

Strategies for Teaching and Learning

Supporting Gross Motor Skills	Fizzy Programme
Core Stability Exercises	Activities like sit-ups, wall push-ups and gym ball balancing.
Coordination Games	Throwing and catching, obstacle courses and skipping.
Balance Challenges	Walking on a balance beam, standing on one leg and hopping games.
Postural Support	Providing wobble cushions or supportive seating in class.
Supporting Fine Motor Skills	Clever Hands Programme
Hand Strengthening	Playdough squeezing, stress balls and theraputty exercises.
Finger Dexterity Activities	Tweezers and pegboards, threading beads and fastening buttons.
Grip and Control	Using chunky pencils, pencil grips and weighted utensils for better control.
Handwriting Support	Focus on pre-writing patterns, letter tracing and controlled colouring.
Supporting Handwriting	Write from the Start Programme
Pre-Writing Patterns	Encourage big arm movements using whiteboards or sand trays.
Letter Formation Practice	Use of sky-writing, tracing and sensory writing techniques.
Pencil Control	Practise drawing spirals, zigzags and shapes before moving on to letters.
Seating and Posture	Ensure correct desk height, foot support and pencil grip techniques.

Sensory Processing Difficulties and Physical Disabilities

It is important to consider the accessibility needs of pupils with sensory and physical disabilities. This includes making reasonable adjustments, such as altering the font size or ensuring the classroom is wheelchair accessible. Additionally, we must teach these pupils how to effectively access their learning.

Supporting pupils with physical disabilities or difficulties in teaching and learning requires a combination of adaptive strategies, assistive technologies and an inclusive environment. When considering physical difficulties, it is essential to differentiate between gross motor (large movements, e.g. walking, sitting upright) and fine motor (small precise movements, e.g. writing, using cutlery) challenges.

Key Teaching and Learning Strategies:

1. Classroom Adaptations
   - Ensure accessible seating arrangements to accommodate wheelchairs and mobility aids.
   - Provide adjustable furniture (e.g. height-adjustable desks, supportive seating) to improve posture and comfort.
   - Use non-slip mats, ramps and handrails for pupils with gross motor difficulties.
2. Supporting Fine Motor Difficulties
   - Provide larger or adaptive writing tools (e.g. chunky pencils, pencil grips, sloped writing boards).
   - Use alternative methods for recording work (e.g. voice-to-text software, typing instead of handwriting).
   - Encourage the use of Velcro fastenings for clothing and modified cutlery to support independence.
3. Supporting Gross Motor Difficulties
   - Allow extra time for movement around the classroom or school.
   - Use physical therapy exercises or activities like yoga and stretching to develop core strength and coordination.
   - Incorporate movement breaks into the school day to prevent fatigue and discomfort.
4. Assistive Technology and Alternative Learning Methods
   - Use speech-to-text software for pupils who struggle with writing.
   - Provide ergonomic keyboards, adaptive mice or touchscreen devices for accessibility.
   - Implement switch-operated devices for pupils with significant motor impairments.
5. Multi-Sensory Learning Approaches
   - Use practical, hands-on activities rather than written work alone.
   - Offer verbal, visual and auditory learning materials to cater to different needs.
   - Allow recorded responses or alternative ways to demonstrate learning (e.g. oral presentations, drawing diagrams).
6. Physical Education (PE) Adaptations
   - Modify PE activities to ensure inclusion (e.g. seated exercises, adapted equipment).
   - Encourage participation in wheelchair sports or inclusive team games.
   - Provide one-on-one support or peer buddies for physical activities.
7. Social and Emotional Support
   - Foster a culture of inclusion where all pupils feel valued and respected.
   - Offer peer support systems to promote teamwork and social interaction.
   - Educate classmates on disability awareness to create a supportive environment.

Following, are programmes that are available for those pupils with physical disabilities and difficulties. More information can be accessed via their websites.

Motor Activity Training Programme (MATP)

The MATP aims to help individuals develop both gross motor skills (such as running, jumping and walking) and fine motor skills (such as gripping, writing and other hand-eye coordination tasks).

Activities are specifically designed to help individuals with physical disabilities build strength, flexibility, balance and coordination. By improving fundamental motor skills, the MATP programme helps pupils who may have limited mobility or coordination to participate in more learning and physical activities. The programme focuses on inclusive sports and activities that enable participants to compete, interact and engage with others in a positive environment, regardless of their abilities.

It is particularly aimed at people with intellectual disabilities, offering opportunities to engage in competitive and non-competitive events.

MOVE Programme (Movement Opportunities Via Education)

The MOVE Programme is a goal-oriented, activity-based approach that helps children and young people with physical disabilities develop their mobility, independence and physical function. It is designed for those with severe physical difficulties, including children who use wheelchairs or have limited voluntary movement.

Sherborne Developmental Movement (SDM) Programme

The Sherborne Developmental Movement Programme is based on the work of Veronica Sherborne and is designed to help children and young people develop body awareness, movement control and social interaction. It is particularly beneficial for pupils with physical disabilities, motor difficulties or those who need support with gross and fine motor skills.

Pupils engage in movements that strengthen core muscles, improving their seated posture and ability to participate in classroom activities. This is especially helpful for children who use wheelchairs or have weak muscle tone.

Exercises help children understand their position in space, making movement in wheelchairs, walkers or standing frames more intuitive. Teachers can incorporate Sherborne exercises into classroom activities to support engagement, such as movement breaks, interactive learning and sensory activities. More information can be found at: https://www.sherbornemovementuk.org/

Eye Gaze Technology

Objective: Eye gaze technology allows users to control a computer, tablet, communication device or environmental control system using only their eye movements. This is particularly beneficial for pupils with severe motor disabilities who may find it difficult to use traditional input methods like a keyboard, mouse or touch screen.

Example Devices:

- Tobii Dynavox: A well-known eye gaze communication device that allows users to speak and interact with computers or tablets simply by looking at specific areas of the screen.
- Eye-tracking Software: Such as GazePoint or Windows Eye Control, which tracks the movement of the eyes and converts that into action on a screen (like moving a cursor or typing).

Application in Learning:

- Written Expression: Eye gaze technology can help pupils with fine motor challenges participate in writing tasks. By selecting letters or words on a screen, pupils can compose text, answer questions or engage in other academic tasks without needing to physically write.
- Interactive Lessons: Eye gaze enables interaction with multimedia educational content (videos, games, simulations), making it easier for pupils to engage with learning materials.
- Communication Support: For pupils with limited verbal communication, eye gaze systems can allow them to express thoughts, make choices and participate in discussions using visual symbols or text-to-speech features.

More information can be found at: https://www.inclusive.com/uk/hardware/eye-gaze-technology.html

Chapter Summary

The key takeaway from this chapter are the resources that are listed that you can implement if you are teaching pupils that have visual, hearing or multi-sensory impairments and/or physical difficulties and/or disabilities. To end the chapter is a list of equipment and where they can be found online to further support pupils.

Further Reading

- Resonance boards: https://www.sense.org.uk/activities/resonance-boards/
- Sensory vibrations: https://hirstwood.com/sensory-vibrations/
- Soundbeam: https://www.soundbeam.co.uk/
- Little room: https://activelearningspace.org/equipment/things-you-can-buy/little-room/
- Activity frames: https://livingmadeeasy.org.uk/product/wheelchair-activity-arch
- Sensory aprons: https://www.pathstoliteracy.org/make-your-own-tactile-vest/
- Body signs: https://www.ssc.education.ed.ac.uk/canaanbarrie/ and https://www.tasselstraining.com/
- Living paintings: https://livingpaintings.org/
- Clear vision: https://clearvisionproject.org/
- A network for those supporting learners with a physical disability: https://pdnet.org.uk/
- Rebound therapy: https://www.reboundtherapy.org/
- Hydrotherapy: https://www.physio.co.uk/treatments/hydrotherapy/
- Messy Play Texture Hierarchy & Food Play Texture Hierarchy – Steve Rose (2007)

Part IV
Social, Emotional and Mental Health (SEMH)

Preface

This topic can be a very sensitive area, which requires a lot of balancing in terms of incorporating views and effective strategies for mild, moderate and complex needs. Therefore, this section of the book will focus on different types of support and strategies that can be used in moments or in daily curriculums. Definitions have been incorporated to ensure clarity on mental health and SEMH in education. Most importantly, again I want to highlight that the following are ideas and theories that are for you to take and think about, research further and make them work for you and the young people that you work with.

The definition of Social, Emotional and Mental Health that I have adopted comes from The BOXALL Profile definition of SEMH in education as follows:

> 'SEMH stands for Social, Emotional, and Mental Health. In the context of education, it refers to the range of difficulties and challenges some children and young people may experience in managing their emotions, behaviour, and mental wellbeing. These challenges can manifest in various ways, such as emotional outbursts, difficulty in forming positive relationships, low self-esteem, anxiety, depression, and other behavioural issues' (Nurtureuk, 2025).

Before entering into the chapters, it is important that you read through the following key components. These key components were put together with Jade Collinge Long who has worked with pupils who have mild, moderate and complex mental health. Through her years of experience and research she has shared what she believes are fundamental aspects to successfully working with pupils who can struggle with their mental health. They are for you to think about and reflect upon when you are working with pupils who have difficulties and challenges in managing their social, emotional and mental health. These components include: the environment, relationships, connection, what is the pupil 'telling' you, trust and hope.

Key Components to Supporting Pupils' Social, Emotional and Mental Health

As an adult, supporting pupils with their social, emotional and mental health means to always . . .

Remain curious about all aspects of the young person. Be curious about their lived experiences, their narrative and the impact that these have had on the young person. Be curious and be interested in them. What does this mean: to be interested in them? It is to show an interest in them. Pupils will respond and make connections when they feel that we are genuinely interested in who they are, their interests and ambitions and relating this to their curriculum and to discussions that you have with the pupil. To be curious: this goes beyond seeing their behaviour as only communication. What is that pupil telling us, sharing with us, the story they are telling us? What makes them, them?

Adopt the idea of holistic curiosity. What life experiences have they had? What are their personal strengths and fears and how does this shape their interactions with the world? What do they need to first feel safe and then valued? We need to seek to fully understand the child before we seek support to heal (especially in cases of trauma). Although we may have seen their behaviours and profile many times before, *their* story is unique and it is our job to help guide them to understand and make sense of their own strengths, emotions and behaviours. Using the lens of nurture, a child's challenges are often unmet needs. Remaining curious helps us to think wider about the pupil and can play a key role in building connections, trust and hope.

This is the 'guiding thread' for SEMH. This is something that takes time, which is built through consistency, reliability, trust and respect. You have to factor in transference and counter transference and to remove all ego in your relationship (both the child's and our own). Encourage and influence relational dynamics. Being emotionally available is being there unconditionally, showing unconditional positive regard – accepting and valuing the child without judgement, regardless of their behaviours and past experiences. School or a class within the school should be a safe base, security and safety to take risks, explore emotions and develop their emotional literacy.

It is also important to remember that different adults will build relationships with different pupils. We (colleagues and I) have not been able to build a connection with every single young person that we have worked with. Do not take it personally. What is most important is ensuring that young person does find that connection and builds that trust relationship, it doesn't matter if that is with you or not.

Care goes beyond the words but has to be embedded in your interactions and actions. Pupils with SEMH difficulties often think that no one cares about them; they may test your ability to show them that you care, therefore you have to be willing to show this care at the most challenging times, For example when you are tested and boundaries are pushed. Pupils may continuously try to push you away as they think you are going to give up and leave anyway, so they will push you away to validate this and get it over with, proving a self-belief or to establish a feeling of safety. Will the adults around them remain consistent and safe? Care is about validating their emotions, not just managing and supporting behaviour. By being in control of the chaos, they cannot be hurt and can establish their own sense of safety.

Pupils with SEMH challenges will often find trust difficult due to lived trauma, adverse childhood experiences or their own mental health challenges. As a trusted adult, you need to be emotionally available, knowing the pupils and treating each pupil as an individual, remembering each pupil is on an individual journey.

Trust can be built between people, but also trust can be built in a whole environment. For example, trust that Mrs Grimsby is my person, I will go to her when I am anxious and she will support me in managing that.

Trust in the environment that if I communicate in some way that I am anxious, someone in my environment (school) will be able to support me in managing that.

Remember each pupil will likely be living in a world of 'what ifs', a hypervigilance where nothing feels safe. When pupils do not feel safe, they try to claw it back in some way. When we acknowledge their 'what ifs', we help them move from survival mode to a place of security.

Hope is one of the most important qualities you can have when supporting a pupil with SEMH, sharing the hope that they can build a pathway of resilience, that however they are feeling now, this can have a positive future. Sharing the success and building on the strengths. Hope – the knowledge that tomorrow is a new day (reinforcing this whenever challenges occur) and that you are on their journey with them.

Hope is not just about words but showing a child that things can improve – modelling to them daily, through consistent relationships and meaningful support that they are capable, valued and worthy of a positive future. Supporting SEMH is about building a foundation of security, care connection and possibility.

All of these components interlink and work with each other to build that enabling safe environment. Building an environment where the pupil feels safe and welcomed so they can take a break from other stresses and focus on learning and the possibility of a positive future.

> *Points of Reflection: Last but not least, I want to leave you with what a parent shared with me as an analogy that they always keep in the back of their mind: The Bottle of Pop (also known as the Fizzy Bottle Effect). Think of everyone having a bottle of pop and when something causes a 'stress' the bottle is shaken (how hard depends on how big the stress is). Sometimes there's space in between stresses and there is time for the bottle to settle and sometimes there isn't. The more the stress, the more the bottle is shaken until it explodes. For some pupils, that bottle doesn't get time to settle; instead it remains ready to explode.*

12 Research into Mental Health Strategies for Non-Speaking Autistic Pupils

Chapter Introduction

I conducted a study titled *Mental Health Strategies for Non-Speaking Autistic Pupils* first as a pilot and then on a larger scale. The study critiqued current approaches for non-speaking autistic pupils and further aims to identify new effective strategies to manage anxiety for this group of individuals. This chapter will include that study to give you further insight into others' views, adopted theories and approaches. This particular study is also incorporated to equip you with more tools to implement into educational plans.

> *Points of Reflection: Although the study focussed on non-speaking pupils, some of the theories and ideas relate to all pupils, especially in moments of upset when it is hard for the pupil to find language to explain what is going on. Think about this as you read through the study and where else these strategies could be appliable and effective.*

Aims of the Study

The research question was simply: 'What (preventative) approaches and strategies effectively support non-speaking autistic learners with their mental health needs?' Among educators, it was felt that they are not equipped to support pupils with their mental health needs especially non-speaking autistic learners; and that behaviour specialist are at their full capacity, making their services challenging to access. This is a particular group of young people, which may have been a reason why research highlighted that it is an underdeveloped area.

Therefore, the aims of the research were to identify effective preventative approaches and interventions for mild to complex cases that could be accessible to educators to implement into settings to support pupils that fall into this group.

Definition of Mental Health

The government adopted the World Health Organization (WHO) definition for mental health as 'a state of wellbeing in which the individual realises his or her abilities, can cope with the normal stresses of life, work productively and fruitfully, and is able to make a contribution to his or her community' (World Health Organization, 2022; Public Health England, 2022). This is the definition of mental health that was adopted for this particular study and used to inform and clarify mental health needs.

In relation to this definition, it seems as though those young people identified in this group may struggle due to their difficulties, which can impact on their state of well-being, this is before adding any 'normal stresses of life'. It is very difficult to be in a state of well-being when accessing daily life is a struggle on its own. According to the National Autistic Society (2021) difficulties in social situations and sensory environments can increase stress and anxiety for autistic people. A survey found that 59 per cent of autistic people said anxiety had a high impact on their ability to get on with typical daily life (National Autistic Society, 2021). Therefore, if stress and anxiety are caused by situations normal to others, it is difficult to maintain a state of wellbeing to then be able to cope with any other additional stresses deemed to be 'normal stresses of life'. As a result, the mental health needs of this group are not typical. In relation to this research, you would need to first investigate what are the mental health needs of this group then what approaches and strategies meet these needs; having a direct impact on alleviating stress and anxiety.

MacDonald and O'Hara's (1998), *Ten Elements of Mental Health*, include promoting factors such as: self-esteem, social participation and managing your own feelings. In a study conducted by Tarver et al. (2021), parents said that they avoid situations that trigger anxiety including social participation. Even though they try to find a balance between avoidance and exposure, avoidance can seem like a more attractive approach if there is nothing else on offer. The finding shows that social participation can present as a significant barrier for those individuals in this group. If avoidance to social situations is more attractive, this may mean that families are not accessing the community. Therefore, this highlights the need for approaches and support to be identified and offered, so the outcome results in families being able to socially participate and access the community to promote mental health and meet mental health needs, according to MacDonald and O'Hara. These approaches will need to provide support to autistic non-speaking individuals in managing their feelings, especially anxieties while in social situations.

Critical Analysis of Common Therapeutic Approaches

What approaches are there for autistic non-speaking individuals to support their mental health needs? When this search is put into Google, the results that come up are typically around 'how to adapt mental health talking therapies for autistic adults and children'. Most of the approaches are based upon talking. For example, asking questions, allowing processing time for their answers and talking through self-awareness of feelings and emotions. It does not appear to include support for non-speaking pupils, although there are recommendations to use visuals to support with communication difficulties and anxiety management, for example photographs; however, the therapies, even with adaptations, still all involve talking and verbal responses.

Cognitive-Behavioural Therapy (CBT)

CBT is the most researched therapy for anxiety disorders in individuals with autistic learners (Nimmo-Smith et al., 2020). Several studies (Wood et al., 2009; Ekman and Hiltunen, 2015) aimed at measuring the effects of modified CBT highlighted the need for modifying such therapies. These modifications were based around the addition of visualised language throughout the sessions (Ekman and Hiltunen, 2015). Another study enhanced the CBT manual to address social skills, adaptive skills deficits, circumscribed interests and stereotypies, poor attention and motivation, common comorbidities in autistic learners (e.g., disruptive behaviour disorders), and school-based problems (Wood et al., 2009). Making modifications to further support individuals, the more individuals that can access it the better. It did leave one group out as none of the studies addressed communication barriers. According to Koegel et al. (2019), there are no current routinely recommended interventions for nonverbal or minimally verbal autistic children. Here is an opportunity to advocate for a greater understanding of communication differences.

Behaviour Analysis Tools

Antecedent, Behaviour and Consequence charts as well as behaviour recording and tracking sheets and other behaviour analysis tools can provide data which can highlight themes. These themes help to examine when the behaviour is more likely to occur, with whom and in what setting, providing information about the possible purpose of the behaviour. A lot of behaviour management resources weave these into their training and programmes.

Analysis of Effective Approaches

The following diagram represents how strategies interlink between managing emotional distress in the moment and how these can also be effective as regular tools. It also highlights the role that communication tools can play.

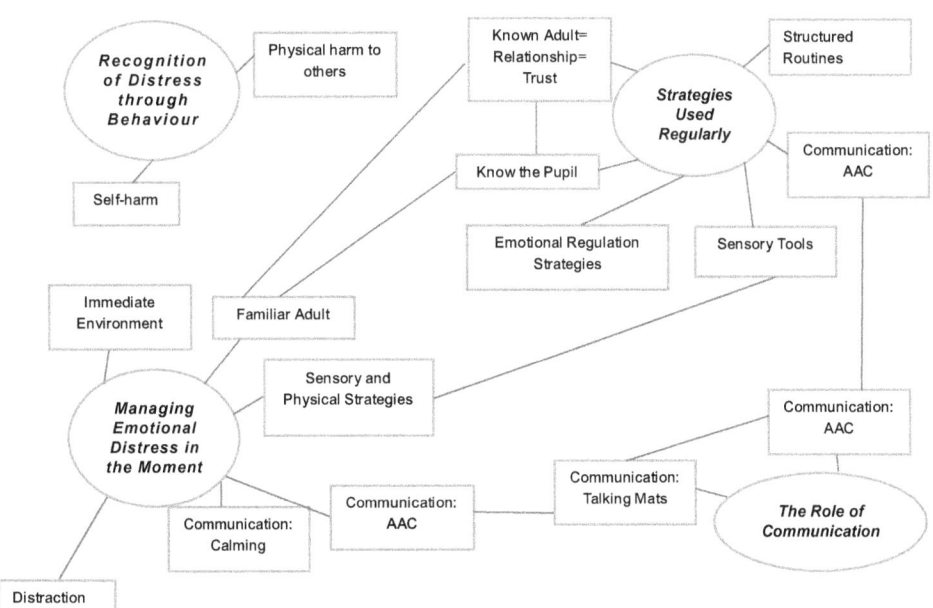

Theory: Need + Acknowledgement and Environment = Trust = Managing Anxiety

This is based on a pupil having a need and seeking it to be met. If the environment meets that need (including if the particular need cannot be met then it may be met in another way or redirected) then it builds trust that the need will be met in some way somehow. This manages the anxiety. Therefore, becoming a learned pattern making the environment safe and predictable.

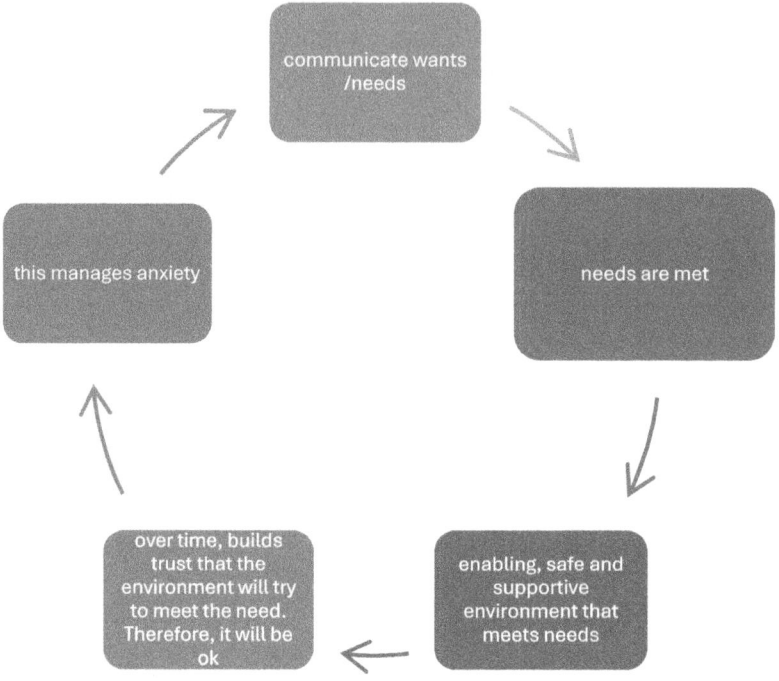

However, the crucial role that we play as educators is in creating the environment. Need/Want + acknowledgement and environment = trust = manages anxiety

Communication:
Providing for those pupils that are non-speaking/limited language/lack of emotional language so they can communicate their want/need.

Behaviour regulation:
In the moment and daily curriculum. To provide times to regulate and manage sensory and/or anxiety related needs.

Provision:
Accessible to promote self-esteem, progress, independence and build confidence.

Step 1: The child develops a need or want. They will communicate this in some way. This is where we first play a role. We provide, in the immediate environment, ways for that pupil to communicate that need or want, however this may look. That communication is a key part in managing anxiety. If they have clear communication routes then this manages the build-up of anxiety and frustration. (Remember that symbol cards etc. will be built up over time as you learn and navigate your way through the pupil's needs and wants.)

Step 2: Next is acknowledging and meeting the pupil's need or want in some way. This builds that trust in the environment that the pupil has a voice, is heard and that their need or want will be met and/or managed in some way. Pupils get the feedback that they want (feeling good inside), therefore they will repeat the behaviour to get the need (and the feeling) met, chasing that feeling good inside.

Step3: Overtime, the pupil builds trust in the environment including the people in it. They learn that if the need cannot be met, that it is still ok and trust something will be met in some way. This manages the anxiety.

> ### Case Study: Year 2 Pupil Who Attended a Complex Special Needs School from Year 2–Year 11.
>
> This case study has been shared by a parent, which is an example of this theory and their journey as a family.
>
> Our child was diagnosed at the one-year point in their life. Unfortunately, I was working away for six months so my wife started the process of engaging with Portage by herself. She talks about how the Portage support worker started introducing symbols using quartered Jaffa cakes being exchanged with our child for the symbol. My wife had no faith at this point that it would ever work, as it understandably seemed such a huge challenge.
>
> When I returned to the UK we fully engaged with visuals around the house. We had visuals on the fridge and slowly our child began to understand that if they gave us a picture, we would make sure that the food/activity was there for them. They began to trust us that if they requested something we would ensure they had it. Even if it meant a trip to the shops! Other examples of visuals being used, are when they scroll through our photos on the iPad to find a place or item, sometimes zooming in on a photograph to specific sweets within a photograph!
>
> When this trust was made between them and us (and school) then the challenging behaviours appeared to lower. They do still get upset, but it seems to be when we have misunderstood a situation or if they are feeling unwell.
>
> This following example highlights the impact this approach has had on our child's mental health and anxiety.
>
> Usually, the car is parked close to the house and our child either gets in the back behind me or lately, since they are getting older, they wait patiently by the front gate and I pull the car out making space for them to get in the front passenger seat.
>
> On this occasion, the roof of our house was getting replaced, and we had scaffolding around the house, so we could not park in the usual place. Instead, I parked on the main road which is very busy, facing the way which meant that they were getting in the safer side of the vehicle. To enable a smooth transition into the new procedure we used visuals of where the car was moved to and discussed how dangerous the road was. They trusted us that they would be safe and that they would still get in the car but would have to follow the rules. In previous years, this change

would have caused heightened anxiety and possibly harming themselves or others. Instead, when they walked out of the house and the car was not where it usually was, they looked at me, I responded by reminding them that it was ok and that the car had been moved and that we were still going to school as normal. We have that trust built already, therefore they trusted me, followed me, got to the car and then their routine ran as normal. Their anxiety was managed through trust in me (the environment) that the need of following routine and going to school would still be met even though things didn't start as normal.

Case Study: Year 11 Pupil Attending Alternative Provision.

This case study also highlights the cycle of behaviour where a pupil develops a need and how that need is met. Therefore, every time that need arises, they seek out how it was previously met, creating a learned behaviour.

The first incident happened when the pupil left the class due to an issue with another pupil. They got into a disagreement, which led to swearing and shouting at each other. The pupil got up and left later saying that they felt angry, upset and embarrassed. They wanted to punch the other person. The pupil made their way to the Head Teacher's office. The Head Teacher spoke to the pupil and was able to de-escalate the situation, taking control of the situation, restoring order and safety.

Now, whenever there is an issue for that particular pupil, they go only to the Head Teacher, who has a chat with them and then they go back to class. This is now a learned behaviour because that pupil has learned that:

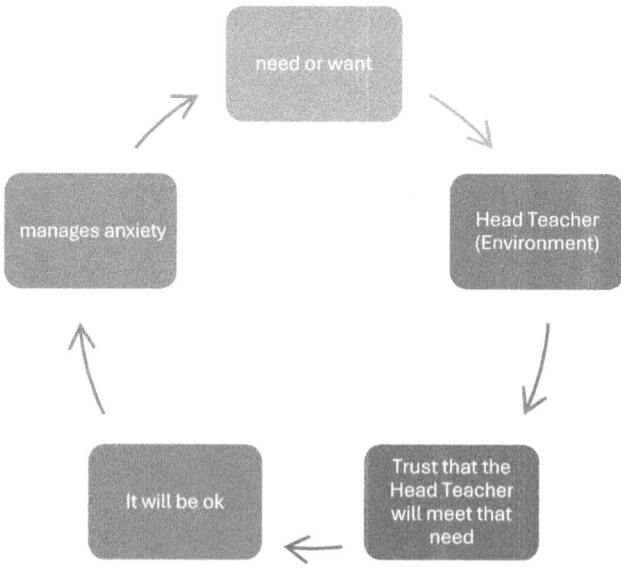

> When the pupil has a need/want then the environment, that is, the Head Teacher will meet that need. The pupil trusts that it will be ok, which manages the anxiety through the day and anytime there is an issue. The pupil doesn't escalate, they ask to take a break and go and seek out the Head Teacher.

Neuroception and Attunement

Neuroception refers to the subconscious process by which individuals assess the safety of their environment, while attunement refers to how well adult responses align with the emotional state of the student. Both neuroception and attunement are key components of creating a responsive and emotionally safe learning environment for students.

This is particularly significant because it touches on the unseen processes that influence students' behaviour and emotional states. Neuroception helps explain why students may react to their environment in ways that are not immediately understandable. For example, students may feel discomfort or stress due to environmental cues that they subconsciously register – like smells, lighting, or noise – even though they may not be able to articulate the cause of their distress. Attunement, in turn, is the adult's ability to read these cues and respond with appropriate strategies to ensure that the pupil feels safe and understood. Both concepts are crucial for creating a safe, emotionally responsive environment where students can feel secure enough to learn and engage.

Talking Mats

According to Tarver et al. (2021) communication resources such as Talking Mats, are an effective way to allow individuals with intellectual disabilities, or those who speak few or no words, to express their views. Therefore, these may be an effective addition to supporting this group of pupils in meeting their mental health needs and any communication barriers in accessing talking-based therapies. Brief information can be found in Chapter 2 or visit Talking Mats at: https://www.talkingmats.com/

According to a study by Murphy and Cameron (2008) on the effectiveness of Talking Mats used by people with intellectual disability, this resource helped them to understand and to say what they feel about their lives. The study concluded that Talking Mats increases the number of people with intellectual disability who can meaningfully be involved in decision making and provides a structure for carers and staff to interview, discuss and ascertain opinions (Murphy and Cameron, 2008). The National Autistic Society (2021) conducted a survey incorporating the views of over 1,500 autistic people: 80 per cent of the participants ranked 'How to communicate how I was feeling' as the highest priority. Almost eight in ten would have liked to have been able to communicate how they felt when they were younger. Therefore, in relation to this research, this approach may be effective in breaking down communication barriers and used to support communicating anxieties and emotional distress; most importantly giving individuals a voice, enabling them to communicate how they are feeling from a young age.

Sensory-related Strategies

Most parents discussed the importance of understanding sensory needs and sensory strategies when managing anxiety (Tarver et al, 2021). Anxieties heightened if their children were not given enough opportunities to express and release. Examples such as deep pressure, massage and ear defenders were given by parents (Tarver et al., 2021). These are examples of sensory approaches, which according to Moore (2016) are used in mental health treatments for adults and adolescents. Sensory diets were first created by occupational therapist Wilbarger (1991). According to Bennie (2021), the main goal of a sensory diet is to prevent sensory and emotional overload by meeting the nervous system's sensory needs; however, it can also be used as a recovery technique. Sensory diets include proprioceptive, vestibular, tactile, auditory, visual, smell and taste input (Bennie, 2021). Parents said that by using these strategies, that autistic individuals requested or sought out, help to regulate their child, thereby reducing anxiety (Tarver et al., 2021).

Distraction

The strategy most discussed to manage anxiety in the short-term was distraction (Tarver et al., 2021). Hackney Learning Trust (2017) published a positive handling document incorporating Team Teach de-escalation training and strategies stating that distraction and diversion are extremely useful. This helps when students are aggressive and are responding with their own fight-or-flight instincts and not thinking about their actions, distraction engages their thinking brain (Hackney Learning Trust, 2017). Therefore, this highlights what parents had said, that this strategy would be typically used to manage anxiety more in the moment.

Accessing the Community

Many parents in the interview discussed exposure and avoidance. Parents shared that to reduce anxiety, they would not expose their child to anxiety-provoking situations and avoid situations that may be a trigger. Tarver et al. (2021) argue that while a likely effective short-term strategy, avoidance may not be the most optimal strategy for long-term anxiety management. They believe that avoidance can work to inadvertently maintain the anxiety cycle, by removing opportunities for the individual to obtain mastery experience in overcoming anxiety. Instead, the study shares that the approach that needs to be invested in or changed is societal changes such as expanding the availability of autism-friendly events. This may help parents and autistic individuals feel more able to engage in community and recreational activities (Tarver et al., 2021). In relation to this research, if the community is more user friendly, then it may give parents what they need to be confident and comfortable in accessing it with the individual, alleviating stress for both. This is something research could explore further: how activities can be accessed by schools and families. The possibility of professionals or families approaching venues and supporting them in putting these types of events in place.

Visual Aids

According to the National Autistic Society (2024), visuals are a communication tool commonly used with autistic people in most situations. They are used in most educational settings as a tool to support communication for pupils with educational needs.

Structured Routines

This was a common answer among all participants. The consensus was that structured routines can take away uncertainty which alleviates anxieties. Timetables can include what, where and who. Parents shared that they have built a routine and that they do struggle to 'spring' things on their young person; however, they have learned how to build things into their routine. A participant said that they use a surprise visual and add that to daily timetables to prepare pupils for change. There was a debate around sudden changes to staffing and how this can cause anxiety. The parent shared that their young person has trust in the building, therefore he trusts all the adults in the setting, no matter who they are.

Decoding the Environment

This was brought up in the focus group by a parent and then supported by all the other attendees, who were professionals and parents. The parent described their young person as being successful in managing their anxieties most of the time. Something that the parent feels largely contributed to was what they labelled as 'direct input' which I call 'decoding their environment', similar to what pupils do. When the young person was distressed in the moment, parents would unpick their immediate environment, thinking about: Has there been a change in routines? Time of the day? Has something stopped working? For example, was it that specific cakes and sandwiches were not available at a cafe? Or a toy had stopped working? After unpicking the environment and finding out what was the cause parents were then able to unpick what the need was and then try to meet it in some way. In relation to the cake and sandwich example, it was to explain they needed to go to another cafe to get the food. The discussion around the idea of unpicking the environment evolved into unpicking and reflection and/or anticipate and plan (adaptive approaches to teaching). The parent said that in the reflection stage, they had added several different cafe options to the young person's device.

A key phrase that stuck with me throughout the study came from a parent who said, 'We are guiding and supporting him through those times of distress and anxiety rather than commanding and demanding'.

Chapter Summary

In conclusion to the study and to the chapter, this particular study highlighted that this area is very much underdeveloped. Most common therapies are talking based which require the participant to be verbal. Therefore, if this group of individuals are unable to access those common therapies, then we need to think about what can be accessed and how. It may seem as though this study has highlighted the obvious, it has, but it has also identified approaches and theories that we can apply and move forward with. Therefore, key takeaways from this study and this chapter are:

- Key components that adults working with and supporting pupils with their social, emotional and mental health should consider.
- Using the theory: need/want+ acknowledgement and environment= trust= managing anxiety. This implies a holistic approach and those approaches together build trust, which essentially altogether manages the anxiety.
- The crucial role that the environment plays in building trust and managing anxiety.
- Anticipate and plan using knowledge of the pupil to guide and support pupils through their journey.
- The role of neuroception and attunement as effective strategies.
- Strategies that professionals and parents deemed effective include those that can be used both in the moment and those that can be incorporated into daily activities.

Further Reading

- Sites to support with managing anxiety:

http://www.calmerclassrooms.co.uk/
http://www.elsa-support.co.uk/the-huge-bag-of-worries/
http://www.ferryhalim.com/orisinal/g3/spider.htm
https://www.gozen.com/50-calm-down-ideas-to-try-with-kids-of-all-ages/
www.innovadesigngroup.co.uk/news/how-can-design-help-minimise-student-stress-in-the-classroom/
https://www.moodcafe.co.uk/media/19579/cyp_parents_1_2_web.pdf
https://www.nhs.uk/conditions/stress-anxiety-depression/anxiety-in-children/
https://www.pshe-association.org.uk/curriculum-and-resources/resources/guidance-preparing-teach-about-mental-health-and
http://parentingchaos.com/anxiety-apps-kids/

13 Mental Health Support

Chapter Introduction

This chapter is largely focussed on sharing specific resources available online or in books that are aimed at managing anxiety, trauma, promoting resilience and positive mental health. These resources include those that are well-known as well as introduces some of those not so well-known resources. Before the chapter begins, following are points for you to reflect upon specifically relating to pupils' struggles, managing anxiety and our role.

> *Points of Reflection:*
> - *BBC Children in Need: The Heaviest Backpack. Watch this clip and think about the following: The Heaviest Backpack + rigour + expectations. For some, this is their life: difficult homelife in the morning and evening and school life throughout the day, repeat, repeat, repeat. If this is their world, are there things that we can do so accessing their world is a little easier?*
> - *If the child has already had fights, disagreements and difficulties at school, then they will be on high alert before entering. They will be coming in heightened and nervous. Without safety and security children cannot settle to learn and explore. Therefore, think about creating safety right from entering. Does an adult stand at the gate greeting all of the pupils as they come in? Do we create that safe feeling for the pupil who is coming in ready to fight or is scared, so they can in themselves feel like they have a chance to access their learning?*
> - *Risk factors for SEMH can include but are not limited to Childhood ACEs, for example domestic violence, poor mental health within the family (including poor perinatal mental health in the mother), childhood poverty and physical disabilities.*
> - *Protective factors can include positive, secure attachments, nurture including consistent, safe environments, being taught emotional literacy, building resilience, healthy lifestyles including diet and exercise, hobbies and interests to build self-esteem and confidence and a positive educational experience. Do we incorporate risk factors and promote protective factors?*

DOI: 10.4324/9781003596820-21

- *Social Attunement.* The previous chapter highlighted the crucial role this plays in ensuring that the pupil feels safe and understood. For those pupils with trauma, no matter what you do, you will at some point trigger that child, even if you are their safe adult; therefore, everyone around that pupil will need to be attuned to that child in that moment. We can look at this in two ways:

  1. If you are not having a good day and your cup is near full then you may not be the best person to go as they may say or do something that fills up your cup. Then your reaction (which is natural by the way) will re-escalate the situation.

  2. Become attuned to that pupil in the moment and pull strategies out of your teacher toolbox that you think are the best ones for that pupil in that situation. For example, 'I can see you're not happy, I'm just going to wait here out of the way'. Rather than, 'You shouldn't be here, hurry up and get back to class'. The adult that uses one strategy for every situation is probably not the most effective in those moments.

If you are a safe adult for that young person then they will respond to you; however, if you are not, but are the only adult in that moment that is available, then you need to make sure that you are as attuned to the situation as much as you can be. This is where having a behaviour support plan that everyone is aware of, or having a bunch of strategies that you can pull from helps.

The best piece of advice I was given was from a Head Teacher of a high school who said to me that sometimes the best approach is to just listen to the pupil. That is sometimes all they want, for someone to listen to them. They just want an adult to listen and in that moment that they offload, you take it from their shoulders. Sometimes that is all they need, every now and again. If you don't think that you are a great listener, here is a good place to start: https://www.youngminds.org.uk/professional/resources/how-to-be-a-good-listener/

If you google mental health and well-being for children and young people, you will get an extensive list of websites and agencies that are available to you. The following are different types of resources that have been used and proved to be effective; there are also resources that may not be as well-known as the ones that pop up first on our Google search (do we really go any further than the first page of a Google search?). Remember that this is a very limited list and one of the best ways of knowing what works, why and how is through sharing and discussing effective tools between each other.

Teaching Emotions

Using different approaches and research, I have put together a Teaching Emotions Progression. The progression starts with the basics and then moves through to Zones of Regulation. It is so that any pupil can access the teaching of emotions, no matter what their level of understanding is or what their abilities are (similar to that of the Reading Framework): Emotions for All. It also includes the links between emotions and the senses, which was covered previously.

[Emotion Recognition] [Interocpetive Curriculum (Kelly Mahler)] [Zones of Regulation]

Emotion Recognition

Some of the pupils that myself and Charlotte Housden have worked with have not responded to a lot of the existing approaches as they never stepped back enough. Due to the complex nature of the setting we worked in, we decided to make a step-style recognition programme to start off teaching emotions and linking them to sensations, like a stepping stone to other programmes. Emotion Recognition focusses on the first four emotions with the addition of 'ok', the identification of these and then matching the emotion with the sensation.

1. Use the first five emotions to model the correct use of naming and labelling a feeling. These emotions include happy, sad, ok, cross (angry) and excited.
2. Teaching Emotions: In the moment

Teach these in the moment that the pupil is feeling/showing this emotion. When the pupil is showing that they are happy, sad, excited or angry we can use the correct vocabulary to show them the 'name' of how they are feeling. Matching the name of the feeling to the sensations of the feeling. For example, when the pupil is obviously happy, we can show the symbol card for happy. Depending on the level of the pupil, we can also label the sensations associated with the emotion. Happy is laughing and smiling. Embed this throughout the day. This makes up a pupil's 'provision' thus making their curriculum relevant and purposeful to the pupil.

3. Teaching Emotions: Naming emotions in the moment

In the moment when the pupil is clearly showing one of the emotions, give the pupil a communication sheet or symbols cards showing the four different emotions. Ask the pupil '(name) is feeling . . .' and the pupil will then respond by pointing to the emotion.

4. Regulation strategy

This can be used as a restorative approach after a crisis and a form of regulation around many emotions. Sometimes it can be used as an 'in the moment' regulation strategy to re-engage the thinking brain and re-engage interaction (you need to know the pupil).

Again, this was designed to support pupils who need that first step to identify emotions as a label to sensations that they are feeling. Then support the pupil in meeting any need that comes from those sensations.

Practical Strategies

Clear and Communicated Expectations

> *Points of Reflection:* Often, we will ask pupils if they are calm; however, do they know what we expect to see when we say they need to be calm? This is the same with 'ready'. Do pupils know what 'ready' looks like? Have we communicated what we will see when they are 'ready'?

First of all, we need to ensure that the pupil understands the expectations we are communicating to them, otherwise we are setting the pupil up to fail before we even begin. If the pupil understands these expectations, then we need to ensure that we are communicating to the pupil clearly what we expect and/or want to see. Highlight what it looks like and feels like so it is very clear to the pupil. For example, 'Ready looks like . . . sat on chair, hands on table and looking at the board, like this (adult to model).' You have communicated to the pupil what 'ready' looks like to you, so they clearly know what is expected.

Pupil Voice

There are several ways to capture pupil voice.

- An effective way of capturing pupil voice is through scaling questions. These can be accessed on the internet. There are several types that are split into categories, for example home, school. They are a great way to highlight explicitly what the pupil is feeling and where and when.
- For non-speaking pupils this could be through Talking Mats or just using pen, paper or a whiteboard and writing out two options for them to choose from.

When a Pupil Is Not Yet Ready to Talk Using Words

This is especially effective if a pupil does not want to talk but you can see that they want to 'get it out'. As a starting point or an 'in', simply write and draw on a piece of paper 'I feel' and draw happy, sad, angry and ok faces. Then leave the pen for when they are ready and often they will just mark the responding face. I follow it up with 'who' or 'where' may have upset the pupil, for example 'home' or 'school'. Then 'adult' or 'child'. Continue on writing options to unpick what may have upset the pupil.

The Incredible 5-Point Scale

This helps identify and regulate emotions. If you search for this or the 5-Point Scale you will see a variety of templates that you can tailor to the pupil and their interests. These scales can also be a good way of teaching emotions and regulation strategies but also highlight appropriate responses.

Mental Health Support

Breathing Techniques

When we are upset or in moments of crisis, one of the only things that we can control is our breathing. Therefore, we can support pupils to breathe using lazy 8 maps and/or breathing templates that come in all different shapes. Another quick tool is to use our hands: breathing in as you trace up the outside of your finger and out when you trace down the inside of your finger.

Grounding Techniques

These techniques I used specifically when pupils have had panic attacks or have high levels of anxiety to re-engage the thinking brain and come back into the now. These can be found on the internet. I use simple scripts of 'Tell me five things that you can see'. 'What did you eat for breakfast?'

Team Talks

> *Points of Reflection: Do any of your staff sometimes feel isolated, struggling to move past balancing complex behaviours? Are they experiencing the feeling that they have hit a wall that they cannot get around? The following is a case study about a setting that incorporated team talks once every half term focussing on pupils' behaviours that were a priority for the setting.*

Dip Dive: Pupil Focus Group Meetings.

At a setting where there were a high percentage of pupils with SEMH needs, we set up an hour meeting where staff working with those pupils met together. The aim of the meeting was to identify functions of behaviour, highlight barriers to strategies and how to overcome the ones we could and get around the ones we couldn't. The Head Teacher chaired the meeting and a specialist from within the trust joined the meeting to offer support and strategies where needed. The meeting was clearly outlined as a focus group and working party. The specialist was involved as part of the discussion but not as a lead as they didn't know the pupil, so a lot of it would come from the group.

Three pupils were identified and discussed. One person who knew the pupil would share an overview, strategies would be discussed and barriers would be shared. Through the discussion we were able to dissect and analyse. The barriers began to slowly lessen. Adults shared interests of that pupil, which started a discussion around bringing outsiders in to do workshops, outside agency support and CPD sessions. Staff started to think about how and what we were talking about could be transferred to other pupils and across the whole school. The adults started to mind shift and think about their actions as well as actions as a team, creating consistency.

Approaches

> *Points of Reflection: When looking into different resources, think about the pupil and scale their need - mild, moderate and/or complex - as this will play a part in deciding the most appropriate type of support. Often general services and resources will be aimed at mild to moderate and specialist services at moderate to complex.*

Boingboing

Focussed on **resilience**, Boingboing has a large number of resources aimed at young people and their resilience.

PACE Model

This is used to support those who have experienced **trauma** and, as a result, do not respond the same way their peers would. In the following site: https://www.oxfordshire.gov.uk/sites/default/files/file/children-and-families/PACEforteachers.pdf you will find a leaflet and what is especially useful is the section providing practical examples with language pupils may use and responses that adults may use. This makes it a useful tool to help build those connections and de-escalate situations more quickly, increasing that important trust between you and the pupil.

Neurosequential Model of Therapeutics (Perry's Core Principals)

Dr Bruce Perry states that 'Heading straight to the reasoning part of the brain cannot work if the brain is dysregulated and disconnected from others'. For example, when you have felt frustrated or upset, has someone ever told you to 'calm down'? What effect did it have? More than likely, you felt even more irritated.

That is because the person was trying to *reason* with you before you were *regulated and ready to listen*. And that is never going to work, because it pays no attention to the structure and organisation of the brain (Pace, 2025).

This model is an approach that integrates core principals of neurodevelopment and traumatology. The model's roots are in support for children who have experienced trauma; however, some believe its core principals are relevant to all children.

Emotional Literacy Support Assistant (ELSA) Intervention

Delivered typically by Teaching Assistants or other specialist school roles who have been through ELSA training. Once trained, following are areas that an ELSA can help with:

- Loss and bereavement
- Emotional literacy
- Self-esteem
- Social skills

- Friendship issues
- Relationships
- Managing strong feelings
- Anxiety and worries
- Bullying
- Conflict
- Emotional regulation
- Growth mindset
- Social and therapeutic stories
- Problem solving

Thrive

Thrive is another organisation that provides a huge range of support for pupils' well-being. It has been successfully implemented in several primary schools that I have worked in. More information can be found at: https://www.thriveapproach.com/

Talkabout Book Series

These are a series of books by Alex Kelly and Brian Sains. There are books aimed at developing self-esteem, social and friendship skills. There are books aimed at children and at teenagers. These books have been really effective in supporting those educators when they have had a cohort of pupils where the dynamics have been tricky to balance.

Nurture International

Nurture International, an independent company founded by two former teachers and advisers from the authorities in the North West of England. Their commitment to fostering an inclusive, developmentally led, trauma-sensitive nurture approach to education sets them apart, creating environments where all learners can thrive.

The founders, with their extensive experience and passion for education, envisioned a system where inclusivity is not just an ideal but a reality. While keeping the fidelity of Nurture, their training is based on up-to-date neuroscience with a digital developmental portrait, quick and easy, effective tool that can show the developmental needs of all learners, along with developmental strategies that can be employed in the classroom.

Trauma on the body: we believe that schools really need to focus on sensory as the external senses send signals to the brain that will be interpreted and the physical response will follow, according to past experiences. Schools need to offer as many positive experiences as possible in order to change neural pathways for the better. Nurture International's Nurture Approach offers training and support in these areas as an Inclusive, Developmentally Led, Trauma-Sensitive Nurture Approach for Learning. Implementing this approach is definitely not a quick fix, as when stressed, the brain prefers to respond in the way it is used to rather than what others may perceive as the 'right way', so needs to be implemented correctly.

If teachers and educators really want to support learners to heal from trauma and become valued citizens, then they need to know themselves too and what can trigger them. Working through and embedding the six nurture principles for learning fully throughout their setting supports them and builds a framework for all they do.

Nurture international work globally, supporting as many schools as possible to encourage all learners to be able to achieve their potential.

Assessment Tools

BOXALL Profile Online

The BOXALL Profile Online is a measurement tool used in schools to identify children and young people's particular mental health needs. I have used this a lot as it helps to identify targets and specific resources to support pupils' mental health needs, giving them the support so they can engage in their everyday curriculum.

Jade Collinge Long who has worked in mental health and complex needs for over 20 years created this 'Path of Support' document for families, staff and pupils.

General mental health	**Young Minds** is a UK charity focussed on supporting the mental health and well-being of children and young people: https://www.youngminds.org.uk
	Mentally Healthy Schools is an initiative providing free mental health resources, information, and training for school staff: https://www.mentallyhealthyschools.org.uk
	Childline provides free, confidential support for children and young people, offering advice and counselling on various issues, including mental health: https://www.childline.org.uk
	NSPCC offers support for children and young people, especially those who have experienced abuse or are struggling with emotional and mental health issues: https://www.nspcc.org.uk
SEMH	Methods to support children and young people with social, emotional and mental health needs: www.semh.co.uk
	SEMH Tools for School: https://www.educationsupport.org.uk
	Department for Education offers guidance and resources for supporting pupils with Special Educational Needs and Disabilities (SEND): https://www.gov.uk/government/organisations/department-for-education
	ELSA provides schools with training for staff to help them support children with emotional difficulties, including those with SEMH: https://www.elsa-support.co.uk/
Mental health and emotional support	**Anna Freud Centre**: Specialises in children's mental health and emotional well-being: https://www.annafreud.org/
	Talk 2 Nish: Provides mental health support for secondary school students: https://www.talk2nish.com/
	Calm Harm: An app offering tasks to help manage the urge to self-harm: https://calmharm.stem4.org.uk
	Clear Fear: An app to help manage anxiety in young people: https://www.clearfear.co.uk
	Beat Eating Disorders: Provides support for individuals affected by eating disorders: https://www.beateatingdisorders.org.uk
	Hub of Hope: A platform to find local mental health support services: https://hubofhope.co.uk

	Winston's Wish: For child and adult bereavement: https://www.winstonswish.org
SEND	Place2Be offers mental health support in schools, providing counselling and therapeutic services for children with SEND, including those experiencing emotional and behavioural difficulties: https://www.place2be.org.uk/
	The ADHD Foundation provides resources and support for children with ADHD, a common SEND, offering mental health support, educational tools, and training for parents and educators: https://www.adhdfoundation.org.uk
	National Association for Special Educational Needs (NASEN)
	NASEN provides advice, guidance, and resources for educators working with children with SEND, including those requiring mental health support. They offer training and resources for managing SEND and mental health issues in the classroom. Website: https://www.nasen.org.uk
Sites that provide resources, training and support for pupils/parents/carers and staff.	Barnardos: Barnardo's Education Community Platform (BEC) that have a range of resources, training
	NSPCC
	YoungMinds
	BBC Children In Need: https://www.bbcchildreninneed.co.uk/changing-lives/mental-health/mental-heath-wellbeing-resource-hub/
	NHS: Every Mind Matters
	Gov.Uk; Promoting and supporting mental health and well-being in schools and colleges
	UNICEF Mental health and well-being
	Dr Pooky Knightsmith
	Pathway 2 Success: Social, Emotional Learning and Executive Functioning
	What survival looks like in school: a resource for understanding children with trauma and/or sensory processing difficulties.
Sites that provide resources and service packages.	Anna Freud Early Support Services
	Trauma Informed Schools UK
	Nurture International
	Nurture UK

Chapter Summary

There are a lot of resources online that you will have access to. If you are finding it difficult to sift through then you can use some of the previously mentioned tools, that is, the Evidence Based Practice Unit (EBPU) model to help find the most effective intervention or ask yourself those key questions. Where you can, ask for free trials. A lot of resources will do this or ask to meet with the service you are looking into so you can gather more information if you need to. Ensure you know who the proposed audience is and that intervention matches to the cohort that you have in mind. What are you exactly getting for your money? Take the time to ask yourself and your team those questions to ensure it is the best-fit intervention. Remember, if down the line it is not effective, do not just let it tick over in the background. If it is not being utilised then stop it and use that knowledge to refine, reflect and look for something else that is a better fit.

Further Reading

- The A-Z of Trauma Informed Teaching - Sarah Naish et al (2023)
- Michelle Garcier Winner books:
  Social Thinking and Me (two book bundle, 2016)
  Social Thinking Worksheets for Tweens and Teens Learning to Read in Between the Social Lines (2009)
  Think Social! A Social Thinking Curriculum for School-Age Students (2005)

14 TOOLBOX: Practical Regulation and De-escalation Strategies for Both Speaking and Non-Speaking Pupils

Chapter Introduction

This chapter is written in collaboration with Sophie Finney who has worked with learners who have complex special needs and challenging behaviour. She has shared her research and experience with me, with the intent of giving you strategies to create a teacher toolbox and a pupil toolbox to support regulation and de-escalation. The toolboxes can be used in two ways:

- implemented daily/routinely to regulate the pupil, which are used as preventative approaches,
- in the moment strategies for when you need effective strategies to de-escalate the situation and co-regulate or prompt self-regulation.

The idea is that you have an invisible 'toolbox' that you carry around with you (I call it tricks in my sleeve that I pull out until one works) that you can 'open up' when you need to and use. This chapter contains the tools to put into that toolbox. These 'tools' are both evidence-based and from experienced colleagues who have worked with mild, moderate and complex behaviours. The chapter begins with some discussion on implementing strategies and barriers that can occur, followed by listing strategies that can make up a 'toolbox' and which have been grouped according to their theme.

Implementing Strategies

Part III of the book highlighted the idea that pupils develop a need or a want. Here, I view it in the same way. When a pupil's behaviour changes and begins to escalate, think: **What is the need/want that the young person is trying to meet?** What are they trying to tell me? What can I do right now to somehow meet that (or distract) and is there anything I need to do daily or in the short term? Think about: do I need to stop the behaviour and redirect or am I going to substitute it?

In the Moment of Distress

When a pupil is distressed, sometimes it is because they have not had that predicted desired response and are communicating this through some form of distressed behaviour. In that moment think about: What is the need/want? Can I meet it? If not, what am I going to do instead (behaviour strategy: toolbox)? Then think about how you will communicate this to the pupil. Having this formula can be effective when supporting pupils that are distressed in the moment.

Acknowledge behaviour (is it appropriate or not?), attach to a feeling – meet the need (use a strategy: toolbox).

For the following script example, the strategy that you would put in place would depend on the pupil. If you did not know the pupil, then you would use your toolbox dependent on your environment such as offering generic things that typically work and/or using what you have to offer, for example outside or time and space.

'Hitting has finished. It is not safe. You look angry. Walk outside with me'

OR

'Hitting has finished. You look angry (I think you look angry). Sit down, hand massage'

Then when the pupil is engaged, take the time to think about what is next and what strategy do I need to put in place to get them there. As a reflective follow-up at the end of the day, take the time to think about if there is anything that you could add into the day to support the pupil or was this just a moment? If so, what could be put in place? Specific strategies are listed further below.

Being Attuned to the Pupil and the Situation

> *Points of Reflection: Social attunement when implementing strategies: if the adult is not attuned to the child and the situation then you may not get the desired impact. An obvious example would be having a busy, heightened staff member lead a calming yoga session or an annoyed adult supporting a child in crisis.'*

Sometimes, the most effective way forward is for someone to observe the child over a short period of time to identify triggers that lead to dysregulation and aggressive behaviour. This could be done through a simple Antecedent, Behaviour and Consequence (ABC) chart. Common triggers can be sensory overload or underload (hypersensitive and hyposensitive), transitions, changes in routine, not having a predicted and desired response or difficulties with communication.

Finally, when implementing these strategies, monitoring is key to ensure that toolboxes are in place and if not, why not? What barriers do we need to overcome? It is important to monitor their impact and amend as you go along through behaviour and educational support plan meetings.

We Have Tried That

'What do I do when this happens? They don't listen when we try that. When we do that, they just escalate more. We have tried that . . .'

TOOLBOX: Practical Regulation and De-escalation Strategies 221

This is often what we are confronted with when sharing strategies. Sometimes, it becomes a discussion in which we end up Scenario Matching. One person says one thing, it is matched with a strategy, then another behaviour matched with another strategy and so on. Sometimes this does work, but other times when you are going around in circles or in a continuous back and forth, it is more effective to give a 'tool box' approach of ideas. This way you are building up a variety of strategies for someone to pull from. What this chapter is about is building a 'tool box' so when one does not work you have more to choose from. You know the child, therefore, you have tools to choose from.

The Pupil Does It for You, But They Don't Do It for Me . . .

This can be because the adult that it works for is anticipating, planning and dynamic risk assessing in the moment. That may sound a lot but basically by anticipating, they are a step ahead of the pupil, making them more prepared, whereas the other adult is a step behind the pupil playing catchup. It comes back to anticipating behaviours and putting strategies in place, rather than being reactive.

Following are strategies to support regulation and de-escalation. These are in no particular order, but grouped according to their theme.

Regulation

Co-regulation Techniques

Co-regulation is an approach that involves the adult working together with the pupil to regulate their behaviour and emotions. Co-regulation techniques, such as providing physical support, using nonverbal cues and modelling positive behaviour, can help the pupil regulate their emotions and behaviour.

Gestural Prompt

The best line I heard regarding using this strategy was, 'You can't argue with a gestural prompt!' Instead of saying anything, using a gestural prompt shows the pupil what you would like them to do without adding in a verbal cue that can add in an extra factor and heighten the situation.

Instead of Using 'No'

Some pupils can become heightened and distressed when they do not get a predicted response and are met with the word 'no'. A substitute for this word can be 'wait and see' or 'maybe later'. Sometimes if you are unable to give a predicted response then saying nothing can be effective, then redirecting with a gestural prompt. Overall, co-regulation is about working together with the pupil to support their regulation and behaviour. Here are some examples of how adults can support pupils with co-regulation.

222 *Developing Educational Plans for Learners with SEND*

Establish a consistent routine and environment:
Pupils with complex needs often benefit from a structured and predictable routine. Establishing a consistent routine and environment can help the pupil feel safe and secure, which in turn can support with co-regulation.

Use calming activities:
Calming activities, such as deep breathing, sensory activities or mindfulness exercises, can help the pupil regulate their emotions and behaviour.

Provide physical support:
Physical support can be a powerful tool for co-regulation. For example, teachers can provide a calming touch or a hug to help the pupil feel safe and secure.

Use nonverbal cues:
Teachers can use nonverbal cues, such as facial expressions, tone of voice and body language, to signal to the pupil that they are there to support them. This can be particularly helpful for pupils who have difficulty with verbal communication.

Use visual aids:
Visual aids, such as picture schedules, emotion charts or visual cues, can help the pupil understand what is expected of them and how to regulate their behaviour.

Use social stories:
Social stories are a helpful tool for pupils with complex needs to understand social situations and appropriate behaviour. Teachers can create social stories to help pupils understand how to regulate their emotions and behaviour in specific situations.

Model positive behaviour:
Teachers can model positive behaviour and emotion regulation to help the pupil learn how to regulate their own emotions and behaviour.

Collaborate with parents and caregivers:
Collaborating with parents and caregivers can be an effective way to support co-regulation. Teachers can work with parents and caregivers to establish consistent routines and strategies for supporting the pupil's regulation.

Create a calming space:
Creating a calming space in the classroom can be helpful for pupils who need a break from the classroom environment to regulate their emotions and behaviour. The calming space can include sensory tools, such as weighted blankets or fidget toys, and calming activities, such as breathing exercises or mindfulness activities.

Use positive reinforcement:
Positive reinforcement can be a powerful tool for supporting co-regulation. Teachers can provide positive feedback for positive behaviour and emotion regulation.

Self-regulation Skills

Self-regulation is an essential skill for pupils to develop as it helps them manage their emotions and behaviours effectively. Self-regulation skills can be taught through activities such as deep breathing, counting or using a self-talk script. For example, a pupil can be taught to take five deep breaths when feeling overwhelmed or to count to ten before responding to a trigger. Social stories or visual aids can be used to support this process. Resources that may help include visual breathing charts, counting games and social stories.

Here are some detailed examples of how teachers can support pupils with self-regulation:

Sensory breaks: Fidget toys, or a calming sensory space.	**Visual supports:** Schedules, checklists, taskboards, social stories.	**Physical activitiy:** Dancing, jumping, running, P.E. circuit, sensory circuit or walking.	**Mindfullness activity:** Deep breathing, meditation, colouring or yoga.
Pre-teaching: Prepare pupils for challenging situations by pre-teaching skills such as calming techniques or problem-solving strategies.	**Modeling:** Model self-regulation skills such as taking deep breaths, identifying emotions or using positive self-talk.	**Choice-making:** Provide pupils with choices such as choosing between two activities, or choosing how to complete a task.	**Task modifications:** Modify tasks to meet the needs of the pupil. Break tasks into smaller, manageable steps or simplify instructions.
Social skills training: Teach pupils social skills such as turn-taking, sharing, and problem-solving to help them interact positively with their peers.	**Time and Space:** Provide pupils with a safe space to take a break when they feel overwhelmed or need to regulate their emotions.	**Sensory integration therapy:** Provide pupils with sensory integration therapy to help them regulate their sensory processing.	**Co-regulation:** Encourage pupils to seek support from teachers or peers to co-regulate when they are struggling to self-regulate.
	Goal-setting: Help pupils set realistic goals for themselves to improve their self-regulation skills.	**Relaxation techniques:** Teach pupils relaxation techniques such as guided imagery, progressive muscle relaxation, or listening to calming music.	

Create a Calm-Down Space

Creating a calm-down space can be an effective strategy to support pupils with regulating their behaviour. Create a calm-down space: a designated space in the classroom or school where the pupil can go to calm down can be created. This space should be quiet and comfortable, with dim lighting and calming music or sounds. For example, a sensory tent can be set up in a quiet corner of the room. This helps to support the child in the classroom, rather than leave the classroom and require additional staff. The pupil can be encouraged to use this space when feeling overwhelmed or dysregulated. Resources that may help include sensory tents, calming music and mood lighting. Here are some examples of how a teacher can create a calm-down space.

Choose a quiet and calming location	The space should be away from the classroom noise and activity. It should also be a place where the pupil feels safe and comfortable.
Use calming colours	Colours such as blue, green or purple, which are known to have a calming effect on the mind.
Provide comfortable seating.	Soft cushions or bean bags can be a great option to provide comfortable seating.

Copyright material from Darleen Matoe Grimsby (2026), *Developing Educational Plans for Learners with SEND*, Routledge

Use calming lighting	Use low lighting or natural lighting if possible, to create a calming atmosphere.
Provide sensory items	Provide sensory items such as stress balls, fidget toys or weighted blankets, which can help pupils to regulate their emotions and behaviour.
Use calming scents	Use essential oils or a calming scent diffuser to create a soothing atmosphere.
Display calming images	Display calming images such as nature scenes or animals.
Provide noise-cancelling headphones	Noise-cancelling headphones can help pupils to block out noise and create a calming environment.
Use a visual timetable	A visual timetable can help pupils to know what they can expect next, which can help to reduce anxiety and prevent challenging behaviour.
Use a feelings chart	A feelings chart can help pupils to identify and communicate their emotions which can support with regulation.
Provide a timer	A timer can be used to help pupils manage their time in the calm-down space and give them a sense of control.
Have a box of distractions	Provide a box of distractions such as puzzles, colouring books or storybooks, which can provide a distraction and help pupils to regulate their emotions.
Use a soft toy or comfort item	A soft toy or comfort item can provide comfort and reassurance to pupils.
Encourage deep breathing	Teach pupils to use deep breathing exercises to calm themselves down.
Allow pupils to personalise the space	Allowing pupils to add their own personal touches such as pictures or posters can help them to feel more comfortable and relaxed in the space.

Copyright material from Darleen Matoe Grimsby (2026),
Developing Educational Plans for Learners with SEND, Routledge

Resources that can be used to support pupils in a calm-down space include sensory items such as stress balls, fidget toys or weighted blankets. Essential oils or a calming scent diffuser can also be used. Soft cushions or bean bags can provide comfortable seating. Noise-cancelling headphones can help pupils to block out noise and create a calming environment. Additionally, calming images such as nature scenes or animals can be displayed, along with a visual timetable and a feelings chart.

Use Calming Tools

Use calming strategies: Calming strategies such as mindfulness, meditation or yoga can be used to help the pupil regulate their emotions and behaviour. For example, a pupil may benefit from a guided meditation video or a mindfulness app. A yoga mat can be used for yoga exercises. Social stories or visual aids can be used to support this process.

Deep breathing exercises	Teach the pupil to take deep breaths, counting to five while inhaling and exhaling slowly. This can help regulate their breathing and reduce anxiety.
Sensory breaks	Allow the pupil to take a sensory break when they become overwhelmed, providing sensory toys or other calming resources.
Progressive muscle relaxation	Teach the pupil to tense and then release each muscle group, starting with their toes and working their way up to their head.
Visualisations	Encourage the pupil to imagine a calming scene, such as a peaceful beach or a forest, and guide them through a relaxation exercise using the visualisation.
Yoga poses	Incorporate simple yoga poses, such as child's pose or downward dog, to help the pupil release tension and calm their mind.
Guided imagery	Use a guided imagery script to guide the pupil through a calming and relaxing experience.
Mindfulness exercises	Teach the pupil to focus on the present moment and their surroundings, using techniques such as body scans or mindful breathing.
Listening to music	Provide the pupil with calming music to listen to, or encourage them to create their own playlist of calming songs.

Copyright material from Darleen Matoe Grimsby (2026),
Developing Educational Plans for Learners with SEND, Routledge

Aromatherapy	Use essential oils or other calming scents to help the pupil relax and reduce anxiety.
Progressive counting	Encourage the pupil to count slowly from one to ten, or count backwards from ten to one, to help them focus and calm down.
Positive self-talk	Encourage the pupil to use positive self-talk, such as 'I can handle this' or 'I am calm and in control'.
Hugging or cuddling a stuffed animal	Provide the pupil with a stuffed animal or blanket to hug or cuddle for comfort and security.
Exercise or movement breaks	Allow the pupil to take a movement break, such as stretching or walking, to release energy and reduce stress.
Creating a calm-down box	Provide the pupil with a box of calming resources, such as stress balls, fidget toys or calming colouring books.
Relaxation apps	Use relaxation apps or guided meditation apps to guide the pupil through relaxation exercises and calm their mind.

It is important to note that different calming strategies may work better for different pupils. Find what works best for each individual. Additionally, it is important to teach and practice these strategies with pupils **when they are not in a state of crisis**, so that they can more easily access them when needed.

Communication

Provide Visual Supports

Visual supports can be a powerful tool for supporting pupils with regulating themselves and de-escalating challenging behaviours. Visual supports such as a visual timetable, schedule or a choice board can be used to help the pupil understand their day and anticipate changes in routine. For example, a pupil may benefit from a visual schedule that shows the sequence of activities throughout the day. Visual supports can be customised to suit the pupil's needs and preferences. Resources that may help include: communication boards, objects of reference, visual schedule, Augmentative and Alternative Communicayion (AAC) devices and choice boards, which have all been covered in Part 1: Communication and Interaction.

It is important to note that when using visual supports, it is essential to consistently provide the visuals and not take them away. This can help to build the pupil's sense of predictability, structure and control, which can ultimately lead to improved self-regulation and decreased challenging behaviours. Professionals can also work with the pupil's team, including parents and therapists, to develop visuals that are tailored to the pupil's specific needs and preferences

Communicate with the Pupil

Communication with the pupil should be calm and non-judgemental. Teachers can encourage the pupil to express their needs and feelings using their preferred mode of communication. It is important for relationships to be developed to build a mutual trust. Listen and honour, where safe, what the pupil is saying. For example, a pupil who uses symbols can be encouraged to use these to express their wants and needs. Visual prompts can be used to support this process. Resources that may help include social stories, communication boards and visual prompts. Intensive interaction, Zones of Regulation and creating a safe environment will help.

Collaborating with other professionals such as Speech and Language Therapists and Occupational Therapists can help identify specific communication and sensory needs and provide appropriate interventions.

Quick Tip: When asking someone to put something down, instead of asking for it in your hand, find a neutral place.

Routines

Provide a Consistent Routine

(When there is a change in the timetable, add in a ? symbol.)

Consistency and predictability are essential for pupils as it can help to reduce anxiety and increase their feelings of safety and security. Consistent routines provide structure and familiarity, which is important for many pupils with complex needs who may struggle with change and uncertainty. By having a consistent routine, pupils can better anticipate and prepare for what is going to happen next, leading to increased feelings of control and independence. It can also help them to develop their self-regulation skills and reduce challenging behaviours.

Here are some examples of strategies that could be used to support a consistent routine.

Create a visual timetable	Use visual aids such as pictures or symbols to represent the different activities and events of the day. This can help pupils to understand what is going to happen next and give them a sense of structure and routine. Use a marker like a peg to show where you are up to in the timetable or take the symbol off and put it into a finished container.
Use objects of reference	Objects of reference can be used to represent different activities or parts of the day, such as a toy car for playtime or a book for storytime. This can help pupils to understand and anticipate what is coming next.

Copyright material from Darleen Matoe Grimsby (2026),
Developing Educational Plans for Learners with SEND, Routledge

Establish consistent routines for specific activities	For example, establish a consistent routine for snack time or a consistent routine for transitioning between activities. This can help to create a sense of predictability and security.
Use visual cues to signal transitions	Use a visual cue such as a picture or a timer to signal transitions between activities. This can help pupils to prepare for the change and reduce anxiety.
Use social stories	Social stories can be used to explain social situations and routines to pupils with complex needs. They can help to provide a consistent framework for understanding and anticipating social situations.
Create a sensory calming area	Create a designated area that pupils can go to when they need to regulate themselves. This can help pupils to feel safe and secure and provides a consistent coping mechanism for stress and anxiety.
Establish consistent expectations and consequences	Be consistent in your expectations and consequences for behaviour. This can help to create a sense of structure and accountability for pupils.
Provide warning before changes to the routine	Give pupils plenty of warning before any changes to the routine are made. This can help them to prepare for the change and reduce anxiety.
Use a visual schedule to break down larger tasks	Use a visual schedule to break down larger tasks into smaller, more manageable steps. This can help pupils to understand what is expected of them and reduce feelings of overwhelm.
Use a consistent communication method	Whether it is through the use of AAC devices, sign language or simple words and phrases, ensure that there is a consistent method of communication between the pupil and the teacher. This can help to build trust and understanding between the two parties.

Music

Playing calming music can be an effective way to support regulation and de-escalate challenging behaviours. For example, if a pupil is feeling agitated, playing soft music or white noise can help them to relax.

Calming music	Slow, soft and calming music can help to reduce anxiety, stress and other challenging behaviours in pupils. Teachers can play this music during transitions, independent work time or quiet time.
Upbeat music	Energetic and upbeat music can be used to help pupils with low energy levels, fatigue or depression. Teachers can use this music during exercise or movement breaks.
Familiar songs	Familiar songs and music can provide a sense of comfort and security for pupils with autism and complex needs. Teachers can incorporate these songs into daily routines, such as during circle time or transitions.
Sensory music	Music with a variety of sensory experiences, such as vibration or different textures, can be beneficial for pupils with sensory processing difficulties. Teachers can provide instruments and sensory materials for pupils to explore and engage with during music time.
Music therapy	Teachers can work with a music therapist to provide individual or group sessions for pupils with complex needs. Music therapy can help to improve communication, social skills and emotional regulation.
Music as a reward	Teachers can use music as a reward for positive behaviour or completion of tasks. This can be motivating for pupils and encourage them to engage in positive behaviours.
Music as a cue	Teachers can use music as a cue to signal transitions or changes in activities. This can help pupils with autism and complex needs to understand what is happening next and reduce anxiety.
Personalised playlists	Teachers can work with pupils to create personalised playlists of their favourite music. This can help to increase motivation, engagement and overall well-being.
Music and movement	Teachers can incorporate music into movement activities, such as dance or yoga. This can help to improve gross motor skills, coordination and sensory regulation.
Music as a communication tool	Teachers can use music to support communication for pupils with complex needs who may have difficulty with traditional forms of communication. For example, using music to teach vocabulary or to support nonverbal communication.

Copyright material from Darleen Matoe Grimsby (2026),
Developing Educational Plans for Learners with SEND, Routledge

Movement Breaks

Providing movement breaks throughout the day can help pupils regulate their emotions. For example, taking a walk outside or participating in a structured movement activity can help pupils release energy and reduce stress.

Here are some examples of how movement breaks can be implemented:

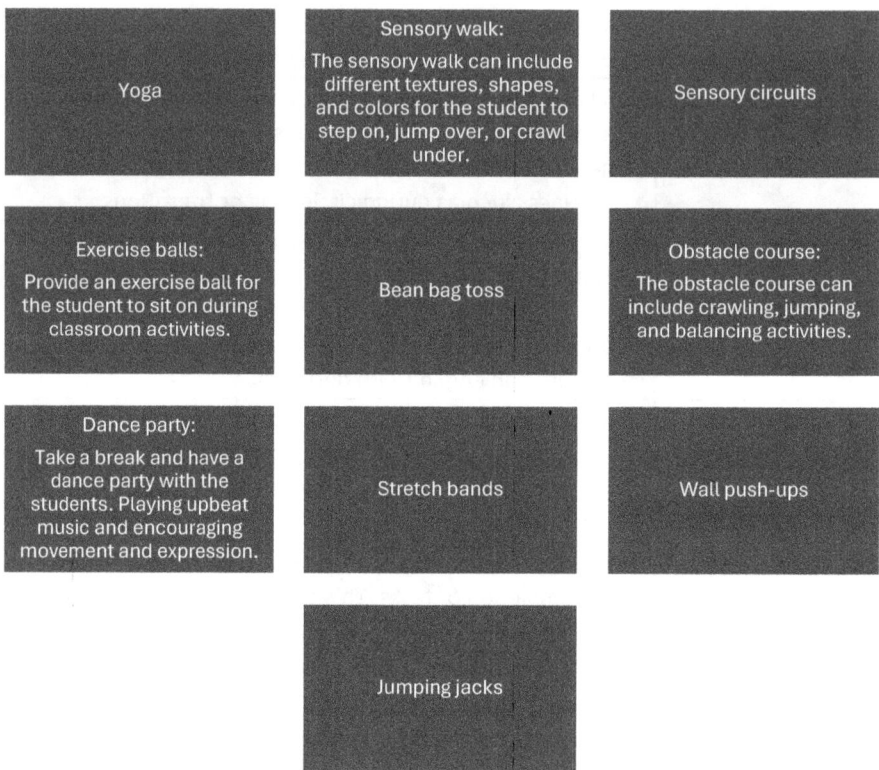

It is important to note that movement breaks should be incorporated into the student's daily routine and individualised to meet their specific needs.

In the Moment

When a pupil is in some form of distress/upset, there may not always be an obvious trigger; it could be a memory that has come to mind and if the pupil cannot share that then it is not obvious to us. You will know the pupil best so you will build your toolbox for that knowledge. Following are strategies that are additional ideas to help build up your 'toolbox'.

Distraction

Providing a preferred activity or object can be a great way to distract a pupil from a challenging situation. For example, if a pupil is feeling upset, providing them with a fidget toy or a favourite book can help them regulate their emotions.

Here are some other additional examples of distractions that can be used to help regulate and reduce challenging behaviours for pupils.

- Sensory activities – sensory activities such as playing with sand, water or other tactile materials can help pupils feel calmer and reduce challenging behaviours.
- Special jobs – give pupils jobs that can make them feel valued such as taking an important note to the office.
- Puzzles and games – puzzles and games can help distract pupils and reduce challenging behaviours.
- Drawing or colouring – providing pupils with paper and colouring materials can help them calm down and express their emotions in a nonverbal way.
- Role play – role-playing situations that trigger challenging behaviours can help pupils learn how to respond in a more appropriate way.
- Snacks – providing pupils with a small snack can help regulate blood sugar levels and reduce challenging behaviours.
- Pets – bringing in a therapy dog or other animal can help pupils feel calmer and reduce challenging behaviours.
- Rhythm in your voice – this can calm and distract pupils.
- Massage – some pupils when upset will respond to a foot or hand massage.

It is important to note that not all distractions work for every pupil, and it is important to assess the needs and preferences of each individual pupil to determine which distractions will be most effective. Some pupils will use physical communication to tell you that they just want everyone to go away. Be aware of this and update plans accordingly, so others know which techniques are effective.

Humour

Sometimes, using humour can help to defuse a tense situation. For example, if a pupil is feeling frustrated, making a silly joke or using a funny voice can help to lighten the mood and reduce tension.

Here are some examples of how humour can be used to support regulation:

Use silly voices and facial expressions to make a task more engaging.	Playful activities	Use funny stories or jokes to help ease anxiety and tension.
Use humour to diffuse a tense situation. For example, if two pupils are arguing, use humour to make them both laugh and deescalate the situation.	Create silly or exaggerated gestures.	Use humorous videos or memes to introduce a lesson or concept.
Use silly costumes or props to make a task more enjoyable. For example, if the class is doing a science experiment, wear a lab coat and safety goggles to make it more fun and engaging.	Use humour to redirect negative behaviors. For example, if a pupil is upset, use a silly voice to say something like, 'Oh no, I think you've turned into a grumpy monster!'	Use puppets or stuffed animals to engage pupils in imaginative play.

It is important to note that the use of humour should be appropriate and respectful of individual pupils' needs and sensitivities. Additionally, it should not be used to undermine the seriousness of challenging behaviours or situations.

Redirecting Attention

Sometimes, redirecting a pupil's attention to a different activity can help to de-escalate a situation. For example, if a pupil is feeling anxious or upset, suggesting they take a walk around the classroom or look out the window can help them calm down.

Offer a preferred activity	If a pupil is engaging in a challenging behaviour, redirect their attention to a preferred activity. For example, if a pupil is becoming frustrated during a math lesson, the teacher can redirect their attention to a sensory bin or a fidget toy. This can also open an opportunity for dialogue to gather the pupil's voice as to why they were frustrated. You could then make reasonable adjustments, e.g. adding in concrete materials to re visit the task.
Change the environment	Sometimes, changing the environment can help redirect a pupil's attention. For example, if a pupil is becoming overwhelmed during a crowded assembly, the teacher can redirect their attention to a quieter area.

Copyright material from Darleen Matoe Grimsby (2026),
Developing Educational Plans for Learners with SEND, Routledge

Provide a task	Give the pupil a specific task to complete to redirect their attention. For example, if a pupil is becoming agitated during a group activity, the teacher can redirect their attention to an individual task such as colouring or sorting objects.
Use humour	Using humour can help redirect a pupil's attention and diffuse a challenging situation. For example, if a pupil is becoming upset during a transition, the teacher can use humour to redirect their attention and make the transition more enjoyable.
Offer a sensory break	Providing a sensory break can help redirect a pupil's attention and regulate their emotions. For example, if a pupil is becoming agitated, the teacher can redirect their attention to a sensory area or provide a sensory activity.
Use positive redirection	Redirect the pupil's attention by offering positive reinforcement for appropriate behaviour. For example, if a pupil is engaging in a challenging behaviour, the teacher can redirect their attention to a positive behaviour and praise the pupil for their efforts.
Change the topic	If a pupil is becoming upset or agitated during a conversation or activity, the teacher can redirect their attention to a different topic that the pupil is interested in.
Use visual supports	Visual supports can help redirect a pupil's attention and provide structure to their day. For example, if a pupil is becoming upset during a transition, the teacher can use a visual schedule to redirect their attention and provide a clear understanding of what is coming next.
Offer choices	Providing choices can help redirect a pupil's attention and give them a sense of control. For example, if a pupil is becoming upset during a task, the teacher can offer a choice of which activity to complete next.
Use music	Music can help redirect a pupil's attention and regulate their emotions. For example, if a pupil is becoming agitated, the teacher can redirect their attention to calming music or a preferred song.

Copyright material from Darleen Matoe Grimsby (2026),
Developing Educational Plans for Learners with SEND, Routledge

Offering Choices

When students are presented with choices, they feel a sense of control over their environment, which can help to decrease anxiety, frustration and other challenging behaviours. Sometimes when the pupil seems overwhelmed, offering a choice takes that away, still allowing that sense of control; it also takes away any uncertainty that could be causing anxiety. For example, offering a choice between two activities or two types of sensory input can help pupils feel more comfortable and engaged.

Here are some ways offering choices can be used:

- Presenting choices in daily routines: offering choices in daily routines can be a useful way to reduce challenging behaviours. For example, a student may be given the choice to use the bathroom before or after snack time. This empowers the student to make a decision that affects their life and may help to prevent meltdowns or frustration.
- Providing choices during academic tasks: choices can be given during academic tasks, such as choosing which subject to work on first or which book to read. This can help the student feel more invested in the learning process and reduce the likelihood of challenging behaviours.
- Giving choices for break time activities: students may be offered a choice of activities they can engage in during break time. This can help reduce anxiety or frustration as it provides the student with control over their free time. For example, they may choose to play a board game, draw or go for a walk.
- Providing choices for sensory input: some students with complex needs may require a certain amount of sensory input. Providing choices of sensory input can help reduce challenging behaviours. For example, they may be offered a choice of different fidget toys or weighted blankets.

Examples of what these choices could be:

- During a math lesson, a student may be given the choice of which problems to work on first.
- During a break time, a student may be given the choice to play on the swings or climb on the jungle gym.
- A student who needs sensory input may be given the choice of using a fidget spinner or squeezing a stress ball.
- When transitioning between activities, a student may be given the choice to walk to the next activity or skip.

Change of Face

Remember, do not take this personally! If someone else comes along and the pupil goes with them it is just a strategy that has worked in that moment. 'A change of face' is a strategy that involves introducing a new staff member to work with a pupil who is exhibiting challenging behaviours. The new staff member or volunteer can provide a fresh perspective and approach to working with the pupil, which may help to reduce or regulate the challenging behaviour. This can be an exit for the pupil as the 'new' person has not been involved already so it can feel as though they have come to take the pupil away and out of the situation. This can double up as a form of distraction or an exit out of the cycle. This can also reduce dependence on one staff member as some pupils may become dependent on a particular staff member. This dependence can lead to challenging behaviours when the staff member is not available. Introducing a new staff member or volunteer can help to reduce this dependence and provide the pupil with alternative sources of support.

Case Study: Year 4 Pupil Attending a Mainstream School.

A female Year 4 pupil who had been through a traumatic experience did not like leaving her favourite grandparent at the school gate to enter school and do work. From the transition, she would show behaviours that challenge to communicate she didn't want to be at school but she wanted to go home. The aim was to build an environment that enabled the pupil:

- to feel safe
- regulate through strategies so the adult could switch out
- communicate

  Over a period of time:
  - a timetable was introduced with her day, home was featured at the end so she knew she was always going home
  - 'now' and 'next' to show her that first was phonics and then her choice
  - the adult remained calm and patient throughout the timetable, using distraction techniques when they needed to
  - 3, 2, 1, finished during transition times, so she knew that at 'finished', they would move on to what was next
  - sensory circuits twice throughout the day
  - 'when' and 'then' script

When	Then
Screaming Shouting Finished	Calm: Walking next to me chatting go inside

- Script: 'I think you are upset because you are (biting your hand). (I want to help you, what do you need?')
  Show visual: with choices, for example hug, massage, sensory room.

- Transition from Nana to teaching assistant: Big hug. I will countdown from 3 to finished. Nan leaves at finished. TA while walking into school, 'Let's get into the warm'. Distraction chat.

- Use of small sensory room to regulate:
- Movement breaks (sensory circuit, trampette etc.)
- Time and space
- Zones of regulation used to communicate emotions in the moment, for example you are laughing, you look happy, you move to happy. You look angry, let's move you to angry and see what you need when you are angry.

Once these were in place, the pupil was able to regulate through the day. They are now accessing a timetable with subject-specific learning and has made 1.5 years progress in reading age. The pupil has remained focussed following her daily timetable.

This highlighted success in identifying the right provision and putting it in place over time.

Chapter Summary

If pupils want to meet a need, they will continue to escalate until some need is met. A lot of the time it is through co-regulation, which does need adult intervention while teaching them techniques they can access to regulate on their own. A huge barrier is staffing but if the pupil needs an adult, they will escalate anyway until that adult comes.

The key takeaway from this chapter is to build a 'toolbox' of strategies that you can use to de-escalate behaviours and support regulation both in the moment and by implementing them into the pupil's daily curriculum and routines.

Conclusion
Putting It into Practice

First of all, I would like to thank you for taking the time to go on this journey with me in the hope to effectively support those learners with SEND. Although it may seem that we are at the end of the book, it is not my intention for it to be finished here. The intention is for the book to be used as a 'toolbox' for you to refer to, consult and discuss. Use it during 'focus groups' and 'discussions' to initiate thinking and bounce ideas around. It does not have the only answer, it is a starting point for you to create from. Refer to it when you are writing Education, Health and Care Plans. When you are writing Behaviour Support Plans, implement into the plan strategies from the 'toolbox' section and amend as you review plans. Remember the chain from the introduction section of the book: keep the chain going so that the approaches reach the pupil in the chair.

The key takeaway is that our role is to provide an environment in which a pupil can be open to learning. An environment that enables the Four Areas of Development to work together, so that the pupil can feel, process, regulate, communicate and they can learn.

Finally, I would like to thank Routledge Education for giving me this opportunity to share my passion for supporting learners with special educational needs.

Darleen Matoe Grimsby

References

Aubin, G. (2024). What Is Adaptive Teaching? [online]. Available at: EEF https://educationendowment foundation.org.uk/news/eef-blog-five-a-day-for-pupils-with-send-a-cluster-of-adaptive-approaches.

AutismSpectrum Australia (2024). Aspect Positive Behaviour Support. [online]. Available at: https://www.autismspectrum.org.au/uploads/documents/Aspect%20Practice/PBS/Aspect-Practicet-BB-Positive-Behaviour-Suppor-Early-Years.pdf.

Beck, C. (2024). Heavy Work Activities. [online]. Available at: https://www.theottoolbox.com/heavy-work-activities/.

Bennie, M. (2021). What Is a Sensory Diet? [online]. Available at: https://autismawarenesscentre.com/what-is-a-sensory-diet/.

CambridgeshireCommunity Services NHS Trust (2025). Just One Norfolk NHS. [online]. Available at: https://www.justonenorfolk.nhs.uk/.

Connect, Humber Teaching NHS Foundation Trust (2024). What Is Sensory Processing? [online]. Available at: https://connect.humber.nhs.uk/service/humber-sensory-processing-hub/what-is-sensory-processing/.

Department for Education (2015). Special Educational Needs and Disability Code of Practice: 0 to 25 Years. [pdf]. Available at: https://www.gov.uk/government/publications/send-code-of-practice-0-to-25.

Ekman, E. and Hiltunen, A. (2015). Modified CBT using visualization for Autism Spectrum Disorder (ASD), Anxiety and Avoidance Behavior – A Quasi-experimental Open Pilot Study. *Scandinavian Journal of Psychology*. [online]. 56(6): 641–648. Available at: https://www.ncbi.nlm.nih.gov/pmc/articles/PMC4670704/.

Essex Partnership University NHS Foundation Trust (2025). Children and Young People Experiencing Sensory Processing Needs. [online]. Available at: https://eput.nhs.uk/patient-carer-and-visitor/children-and-young-people-experiencing-sensory-processing-needs/.

Farrell, P., Dyson, A., Polat, F., Hutcheson, G. and Gallannaugh, F. (2007). SEN Inclusion and Pupil Achievement in English Schools. *Journal of Research in Special Educational Needs*, [e-journal] 7(3): 172–178. Available through EBSCO Host Library website.

Hackney Learning Trust (2017). Positive Handling: Guidance for Schools and Settings. [online]. Available at: https://www.hackneyservicesforschools.co.uk/system/files?file=extranet/HLT%20Positive%20Handling%20Guidance.pdf.

Hodkinson, A. (2012). Illusionary Inclusion: What Went Wrong with New Labour's Landmark Educational Policy? *British Journal of Special Education*, [e-journal] 39(1): 4–11. Available through EBSCO Host Library website.

Jones, A.P., (1995). IMPACT – IMPlementing Augmentative Communication Training Nottingham: Talksense Publications. Available from Liberator Ltd- Swinstead.

Koegel, L. K., Bryan, K. M., Su, P. L., Vaidya, M. and Camarata, S. (2019). Intervention for Non-verbal and Minimally-verbal Individuals with Autism: A Systematic Review. *International Journal of Pediatric Research*. [online]. 5(56). Available at: doi.org/10.23937/2469-5769/1510056.

MacDonald, G. and O'Hara, K. (1998). Ten Elements of Mental Health, its Promotion and Demotion: Implications for Practice. Glasgow: Society of Health Education and Health Promotion Specialists.

McLachlan, H. and Elks, L. (2017). *Communication Builders for Complex Needs. Advice and Activities to Support Pupils with Severe or Profound Complex Needs*. Cornwall: Elklan.

Maher, A. and Macbeth, J. (2014). European Physical Education Review [e-journal] 20(1): 90–103. Available through EBSCO Host Library website.

Mahler, K. (2020). What is Emotional Intelligence and How Does Interoception Come into Play? [online]. Available at: https://www.kelly-mahler.com/resources/blog/what-is-emotional-intelligence-and-how-does-interoception-come-into-play/.

Maths No Problem (2025). [online]. Available at: https://mathsnoproblem.com/en/approach/concrete-pictorial-abstract.

Marnell, L. (2023). Non-Speaking versus Non-Verbal: What Is the Difference in Autism? [online]. Available at: https://www.kidsmasterskills.com/post/non-speaking-versus-non-verbal-what-is-the-difference-in-autism.

Money, D., and Thurman, S. (1994). The Means, Reasons and Opportunities Model of Communication [online]. Available at: https://library.sheffieldchildrens.nhs.uk/the-means-reasons-and-opportunities-model-of-communication/.

Moore, K. (2016). Following the Evidence: Sensory Approaches in Mental Health. [online]. Available at: http://www.sensoryconnectionprogram.com/pdf/follow_the_evidence.pdf.

Murphy, J. and Cameron, L. (2008). The Effectiveness of Talking Mats with People with Intellectual Disabilities. *British Journal of Learning Disabilities*. [online]. Available at: https://web.p.ebscohost.com/ehost/pdfviewer/pdfviewer?vid=1&sid=1fb69f4d-df1a-4635-ac4a-8857a07e1c21%40redis.

National Association for Special Educational Needs (NASEN) (2015). The SEND Code of Practice: 0 to 25 years. A Quick Guide to the SEND Code of Practice: 0 to 25 years (2014) and its Implications for Schools and Settings [pdf]. Available at: https://www.yorksj.ac.uk/media/content-assets/schools/education/initial-teacher-education/NASEN-mini-guide-to-2014-CoP.pdf.

National Autistic Society (2021). Good Practice Guide for Professionals Delivering Talking Therapies for Autistic Adults and Children. [online]. Available at: https://s2.chorus-mk.thirdlight.com/file/24/asDKIN9as.klK7easFDsalAzTC/NAS-Good-Practice-Guide-A4.pdf.

National Autistic Society (2024). Visual Supports. [online]. Available at: https://www.autism.org.uk/advice-and-guidance/topics/communication/communication-tools/visual-supports.

Nimmo-Smith, V., Heuvelman, H., Dalman, C., Lundberg, M., Idring, S., Carpenter, P., Magnusson, C and Rai, D. (2020). Anxiety Disorders in Adults with Autism Spectrum Disorder: A Population-Based Study. *Journal of Autism Development Disorders*. [online]. 50(1): 308–318. Available at: https://www.ncbi.nlm.nih.gov/pmc/articles/PMC6946757/.

Nurtureuk (2025) Supporting You to Meet Your Pupils' SEMH Needs. [online] Available at: https://www.nurtureuk.org/supporting-you/

Oxford Health NHS Foundation Trust (2014). Sensory Processing. [online]. Available at: https://www.oxfordhealth.nhs.uk/wp-content/uploads/2014/05/Sensory-Processing-presentation-February-2014.pdf.

Pace (2025). Neurosequential Learning. [online]. Available at: https://thepacecentre.org/advice-items/neurosequential-learning/.

Porges, S. W. (2004) Neuroception: A Subconscious System for Detecting Threats and Safety. *Zero to Three*, 24(5): 19-24.

Positive Behavioural Support Coalition UK (2015). Positive Behavioural Support. A Competence Framework. [online]. Available at: http://pbsacademy.org.uk/wp-content/uploads/2016/11/Positive-Behavioural-Support-Competence-Framework-May-2015.pdf.

Public Health England (2022). Wellbeing and Mental Health: Applying All Our Health. [online]. Available at: https://www.gov.uk/government/publications/wellbeing-in-mental-health-applying-all-our-health/wellbeing-in-mental-health-applying-all-our-health#fn:4.

Smartbox (2025). [online]. Available at: https://thinksmartbox.com/.

Smith, M. and Broomhead, K. E. (2019). Time, Expertise and Status: Barriers Faced by Mainstream Primary School SENCos in the Pursuit of Providing Effective Provision for Children with SEND. *Support for Learning*, [e-journal]34(1): 54-70. Available through EBSCO Host Library website.

Speech and Language UK (2025). [online]. Available at: https://speechandlanguage.org.uk/educators-and-professionals/resource-library-for-educators/creating-a-communication-supportive-environment-early-years/.

TACPAC (2025). [online]. Available at: https://tacpac.co.uk/.

Tarver, J., Pearson E., Edwards G., Shirazi A., Potter L., Malhi, P. and Waite J. (2021). Anxiety in Autistic Individuals Who Speak Few or No Words: A Qualitative Study of Parental Experience and Anxiety

Management. *Autism*. [online]. 25(2): 429–439. Available at: https://journals.sagepub.com/doi/10.1177/1362361320962366.

United Nations Educational, Scientific and Cultural Organisation (UNESCO) (1994). The Salamanca Statement and Framework for Action on Special Needs Education. [online]. Available at: https://unesdoc.unesco.org/ark:/48223/pf0000098427.

Wilbarger, P. and Wilbarger, J. (1991). *Sensory Defensiveness in Children Ages 1–12: An Intervention Guide for Parents and Other Caretakers*. Santa Barbara, CA: Avanti Educational Programs.

Wood, J., Drahota, A., Sze, K., Har, K., Chiu, A. and Langer, A. (2009). Cognitive Behavioral Therapy for Anxiety in children with Autism Spectrum Disorders: A Randomized, Controlled Trial. *Journal of Child Psychology and Psychiatry*. [online]. 50(3): 224–234. Available at: https://doi.org/10.1111/j.1469-7610.2008.01948.x.

World Health Organization (2022). Mental Health. [online]. Available at: https://www.who.int/news-room/fact-sheets/detail/mental-health-strengthening-our-response.

Index

Entries in **bold** refer to tables; entries in *italics* refer to figures.

AAC (Augmentative and Alternative Communication) 28-9, 67, 226, 228; Android apps for 54; *see also* visuals
ABC (Antecedent, Behaviour and Consequence) 165, 201, 220
abstract concepts 42, 142
Abstract Language Comprehension 47
accreditation, acquiring 23
achievement orientation 23
adaptations 86, 140
Adcock, Emma 83
addition, column 142-3
ADHD 92, 217
adult support 43
alphabetic stage, in Reading For All framework 116-22
Android devices 54
Anna Freud Centre 216-17
anticipate and plan approach 144
anticipation 59, 69, 75; in Engagement Model 151
anticipatory skills 37
anxiety management 57, 140, 157, 209; for autistic people 200; and communication tools 47, 70; and countdowns 44, 64; for non-speaking pupils 199, 202, 204-8; and sensory processing 159, 174; and visuals 33, 42, 57, 65; and waiting 66
App Wheels 54
arm movements 188
aromatherapy 226
Assessing Reading 144
assessment 80, 152; of blank levels 28; of interventions 146; for maths 145-6; for reading 144; in Reading Intervention Framework 97; of SEND 6-7; of writing 145
assistive technology: ensuring access to 180; and habilitation support 184; and physical disability 186, 189; and vision impairments 182; and working memory 93
attention: control over 92; redirecting 151, 232-3
Attention Autism 25, 65; and Curiosity Programme 99; and Engagement Model 151
attunement xii, 205, 208; social 210, 220
audiogram 179-80
auditory memory 33
Augmentative and Alternative Communication *see* AAC
autism-friendly events 206
autistic learners: and music 229; and sensory interventions 174, 176; and writing interventions 139-40
autistic non-speaking individuals 199-208
automaticity 95, 122
autonomy, and physical disability 183, 187
avoidance: of sensations 157, 161-2, 164; of social interaction 200, 206

backrests 187
backward chaining 23
ball games 169
bandwagon approach xiii, 18
barriers, anticipating 6
BBC Children In Need 209, 217
bean bags 169, 223, 225

Index

Beat Eating Disorders: 216
behaviour analysis tools 201
behaviour regulation 79, 87, 157, 202
behaviour support plans 176, 210, 237
bespoke curriculum 7, 18
Birkinshaw, Sam 10
blank levels 47, 122, 133
blankets, weighted 45, 174, 224-5, 234
Bob Books 117
body language 28, 55
body signals 166
Boingboing 214
Boo game 151
bottle of pop 198
BOXALL Profile Online 195, 216
Braille 181-4
brain space 93
branch maps 24, 80, 149
breathing techniques 93, 101, 171, 213, 222, 224-5
bridging programme 129
bubble wrap 169, 172

Call Scotland 54, 124
Calm Harm 216
calm-down boxes 226
calm-down space 174, 223-5, 228
calming down, and transitions 64
calming strategies 12, 225-6
care, in SEMH 196-7
carousel teaching 116, 119-22
carrots, frozen 71, 178
CBT (Cognitive-Behavioural Therapy) 200-1
cerebral palsy 6, 185
challenging behaviours 28
change of face 234-5
checklists 24, 45, 172; and independence 33; in writing programme 134-5, 140
Childline 216
choices, providing 233-4
Choose/Request board 44, 60-1
chunking 88, 92
Clear Fear 216
Clever Hands Programme 187
CLT (Cognitive Load Theory) 87
clutter, reducing 91, 93, 174
Coe, Rob 86
cognitive load 86-91, 93-4

cognitive systems 83-4
colouring: for brain break 173; for distraction 224, 226, 231; in grab bags 120; for motor skills 188; using task board 58
communication, and visuals 31
communication boards 47, 64, 226-7
communication books 24, 47, 49-53, 50, 52-3, 60-2; opportunities to use 70-1, 73
communication devices 47, 68
communication difficulties 19, 21, 200, 220
communication preferences 56, 73
communication skills, opportunities to practise xi, 27, 69, 71
communication strategies: demonstrating 72; for regulation and de-escalation 226-7
communication support 180, 191
communication tools 54; access to 73; music as 229; opportunities to use 69-70, 72-3, 75
communication tracker **146-8**, 152
communication-supportive environments xi, 27, 55-6, 69
compensatory strategies 85
Complex Special Needs Schools xii, 25, 71, 116-17, 138, 163, 176, 203-4
confidence-building: and communication skills 73; and impairments 183, 185; and mental health 209; and writing interventions 80, 135, 138, 140, 145
confusion 33, 42, 88, 161
connection, in SEMH 196
consent, and tactile touch 175, 177
consistency 40, 64
coordination 161, 187, 189-90, 229
core boards 29, 46
core strength 187, 189-90
core words 73-4, *74*, 115
co-regulation 219, 221, 236
countdowns 42, 44, 63-4, 235
counting, progressive 226
CPA (Concrete, Pictorial and Abstract) 142-3
critical thinking 141
cue cards 93
cultural differences 177
cumulative knowledge-building 91
Curiosity Programme 99
curriculum: alternative 80, **81**; inclusion through 6; well-sequenced 89, 91-2; *see also* National Curriculum

cushions 169, 173, 187, 223, 225
cutlery 185, 189
CVI (cerebral visual impairment) 181

daily tasks 183-4
days of the week, learning 99-104, **100-1**, *100, 102-4, 107*
decoding the environment 109, 207
de-escalation xiii, 204; distraction and 206; like and don't like boards 46; practical strategies for 219-36; sensory diet and 170
DfES (Department for Education and Skills) 6
dietary requirements 100
discomfort 161
distraction: and anxiety management 206; box of 224; like and don't like boards 65; reducing 91; strategies for 231
distress: articulating cause of 205; in the moment of 219-20, 230
distress management 57, 67-8, 72, 201
distressed behaviour 219
Dolch sight word lists 114
Down syndrome children 114, 118
drawing out 46
Dual Cascade Model 95
dual-coding principles 89-90
dyslexia 8, 124
dysregulation 20, 175, 220

EBPU (Evidence Based Practice Unit) logic model 146, 217
Education Endowment Fund 9
educational psychologists 10
EHCPs (Education, Health and Care Plans) xi, 25, 152, 237; and SEND Support Plans 10
ELSA (Emotional Literacy Support Assistant) 214, 216
emotion cards 72
emotion recognition 211
emotional distress 68, 178, 201, 205
emotional granularity 28
emotional health *see* SEMH
emotional literacy 196, 209, 214
emotional regulation 93, 157, 201, 215; and interoception 165-7
emotional safety 93-4
emotional support 189, 216

emotions, teaching xii, 210-12
enabling environments xi, 27, 56, 72, 79
Engagement Model 24, 79, 144, 149-52
environmental design 91
equal value *see* time and value
equipment, labelling 33
escalation, preventing 57
essential oils 100, 172, 224-6
Evan-Moor Daily Reading Comprehension 120
expectations: clear and communicated 212; consistency of 40, 45, 228; rigour and 26
explicit teaching strategies 88
extraneous load 87
eye contact 56, 113
eye gaze technology 190-1

facial expressions 28, 151, 181
fear of failure 93, 138
feelings chart 224-5
fidget toys 57; in calm-down space 224-6; choice of 234; as distraction 231; and sensory regulation 162, 168, 171-2, 174
fine motor activities 132, 169, 187-91
Finney, Sophie 219
First and Then Boards 39, 40-1, *41*, 62-3
Fizzy Hands 120, 130
Fizzy Programme 187-8
flashcards 31, 112, 119
flight mode 164-5, 169
focus groups 207, 213, 237
food sensitivity 161-2, 175
foundational knowledge 86, 89, 91
Frith, Uta 95
frustration: and communication tools 72-3, 202; and hyper-sensitivity 161; talking out 65; and visuals 33, 42, 44
fun activities 71, 120-1
functionality 18

games: in communication 60; as distraction 231; and eye gaze 191; and learning 72
gaps, identifying 116, 141, 143-4
gardening 169
germane load 87
gestural prompt 221
gestures 28, 65, 89-90, 181
grab bag activities 65, 73, 119-21, 157

gradual release model 91
grey areas 33, 42, 59
gross motor activities 22, 157, 169, 187-90, 229
grounding techniques 213
group activities: and communication practice 72; and countdowns 64
guided imagery 225
guided reading 116, 119-22, 124

habilitation audit 181, 184
habilitation support 179, 184-5
handrails 183-4, 189
hands-on learning 183
headphones, noise-cancelling 171-2, 174, 224-5
hearing aids 180
hearing impairments (HI) 8, 179-82, 184
hearing loop systems 184
heavy touch 161
heavy work 163, 169, 174-5
Hertfordshire Reading Age Test 144
high frequency words 117-18
high-tech AAC 28-9
hitting 166, 176, 220
holistic approach 81, 208
holistic curiosity 196
hope, in SEMH 197-8
Housedon, Charlotte 66, 211
Hub of Hope 216
hugs: giving 163; in regulation and de-escalation 235; safe and appropriate 176-7; seeking 161
humour, as distraction 231-3
hyperactivity 100, 162-3
hyperlexia 122
hypersensitivity 161-2, 220; sensory integration for 169-70
hyposensitivity 161-2, 220; sensory integration for 169

ice 45, 166, 172, 178
images, calming 224-5
inclusion 26; achievement through planning 7-9; building in 73; culture of 189; in mainstream schools 6, 23-5; origins of 7; use of term 5
inclusion support documents 8
inclusive practice 5, 7, 25
inclusive schools 7, 23

independence xi; building 75; and visuals 31, 33, 42; working towards 23
independent writing tasks 91, 140, 145
individualised support 6-7, 9
initial observation, in Engagement Model 150
instructions, multi-step 84, 86
intellectual disabilities 190, 205
intensive interaction 13, 227
interleaved practice 91
interoception 101, 124, 157, 165-6

Kelly, Alex 215

language development 28
language experience books 115-16, 136
lanyards 29, 47
lavender 172
layouts, well-organised 91
learned behaviours 75, 204-5
learning goals, personalised **19-22**, *23*
learning spaces, personalised 183
less preferred activities 40
letter formation 131, 145, 188
light touch 29, 161, 176
lighting, controlling 174
Like and Don't Like boards 45-6, 51, 64-5
limited language xi, xiii, 33, 56; learning goals for 19
literacy, curriculum offer for 24
logographical stage, in Reading For All framework 109-16
Long, Jade Collinge 195, 216
long-term memory 84-5, 90

mainstream schools 6-7, 235
Makaton 113, 180-1
management, task 92
massage 163, 175-6; and anxiety management 206; in regulation and de-escalation 231, 235
maths assessment 145-6
maths interventions 141-3
maths skills, early 141-2, 146, 153
MATP (Motor Activity Training Programme) 190
Means, Reasons and Opportunities model *4*
meditation 225
Meeting Record 16, 18

memory-friendly teaching practices 88-91
mental health: definition 199; see also SEMH
mental health support 209-17; approaches 214-16; assessment tools 216-17; practical strategies 212-14; teaching emotions 210-12
metacognitive abilities 88
mindfulness 93, 225
mind-maps 88
mistakes, normalising 94
mobility aids 182, 184, 189
motor skills development 187-8
mouthing 162-3
MOVE Programme 190
movement breaks 157, 169, 189-90, 226, 229-30, 236
multiple choice 120
multi-sensory approaches 124, 183
multi-sensory impairment (MSI) 179, 182-4
multi-step problems 83-4, 86, 93
muscle stiffness 186
muscle tone 187, 190
music 90, 107, 169; in regulation and de-escalation 223, 225, 228-9, 233

name writing 130, 145
NASEN (National Association for Special Educational Needs) 217
National Curriculum 5-6; access to 7, 9, 79, 118; stepping stones to 80
need, profile of 8
neuroception xii, 205, 208
neurodevelopmental conditions 92
neurosequential model of therapeutics 214
neutral space 63
new learning, connecting to existing learning 88-9
noise levels 33, 174, 180-1, 184
non-speaking pupils xi-xiii, 27, 56, 71; and communication opportunities 70; learning goals for 19; mental health strategies for 199-208; and Talking Mats 46
non-verbal pupils xi, xiii
Norfolk County Council's Provision 8
note-taking 85, 88
Now and Next boards 24-5, 48, 49, 57-8, 58, 62-3, 151

NSPCC 216-17
Numicon Breaking Barriers 81, 141-3
Nurture International 215-17

Objects of Reference (OoR) 29, 33-4, *34-7*, 38, 61-2; decoding 109; in regulation and de-escalation 226-7; stages of development for **62**
observation sheets 151-2
obstacle courses 169
occupational therapists 10, 170-1, 173, 185, 187, 227
open-ended questions 73
opportunities to communicate 70-5
oral processing 171, 177-8
orthographic stage, in Reading For All framework 122
outdoor area, access to 169
overwriting 19, 129, 131, 139

PACE Model 214
pain threshold 161-2
pairing 44, 56, 60-1
pattern recognition 141
PEaSS (Provision Expected at SEN Support) 8
peer support systems 189
pencil grips 130, 157, 187-9
pencils, chunky 188-9
pen-ended question 73
Perry, Bruce 214
personal boundaries 176
personal safety skills 184
phonics xii, 41; and whole-word approach 114, 118-20; and working memory 85; and writing assessment 145; see also PPSEN
Phonics for Pupils with Special Educational Needs see PPSEN
phonics test 144
physical activities, and countdowns 64
physical difficulties 187-91
physical disability (PD) 179, 185-7, 190-1; and sensory processing disabilities 188-9
physical education 92, 189
physical environment xi, 6, 27
physiotherapy 185, 187
Pictophonics 124

PKSS (Pre Key Stage Standards) 24, 79–80, 136–7, 140, 145
play-based learning 72
playdough 124, 172, 188
PMLD (Profound and Multiple Learning Disability) 95, 142
POLE (person, object, location, event) 37–8, 61
positional changes 185–7
postural adjustments 186, 188
posture 161, 185–90
PPSEN (Phonics for Pupils with Special Educational Needs) 97, 116–19, 152
practice times 72
Pre Key Stage Standard *see* PKSS
precision teaching 114, 118
predictability 41–2, 63–4, 226–8
pre-formal learners 65
pre-learning skills 19; tracking **146–8**, 152
pre-National Curriculum 7, 18
pre-programme stage 24, 79, 95, 116; and maths 143; in Reading For All framework *98–109*
pressure sores 185–7
prior knowledge 83, 86, 88
problem dumping 6
problem solving 141, 215
processing time 59, 66–7, 72, 200
progressive muscle relaxation 171, 177, 225
proprioception 101, 123, 173–4
pupil focus group meetings 213–14
pupil voice 212
puzzles 120, 173, 224, 231

QHS (Qualified Habilitation Specialists) 185
quality first teaching 7–9, 157
queuing an emotion 165
Quigley, Alex 86

radio aids 180
reading acquisition, three-stage model 95
reading age 144
Reading Comprehension Sheets 120
reading difficulties, addressing *127*
Reading For All framework 95–8, **96**, 122–7, **125–6**, 210; alphabetic stage in 116–22; logographical stage in 109–16; pre-programme stage in *98–109*
reasonable adjustments 5, 7, 9, 144, 188, 232

reasons to communicate 70–3
recalling 27–8, 129
regulation, zones of 101, 210, 227, 236
regulation enablers 57
regulation strategies 211–12, 221–6; implementing 219–21
rehearsal aloud 93
relaxation apps 226
repetition 67, 72, 88, 90; in Engagement Model 151
request boards 45, *50*, 60–1, 72–3
resilience 197, 209, 214
resonance boards 109
resource cupboards 73
response to communication 75
restorative tools 65
retelling 27–8, 116, 122
retention 89, 92
retrieval, spaced 91–2
retrieval practice 88, 90–1
rhymes/songs 72, 97–8, 108, 125, 170
role-playing 72, 231
routines: changes in 207, 220, 226; consistent 33, 183, 227–8; offering choices in 234; structured 201, 207; visual 42

safe adults 210
safety: and anxiety management 204–5; creating 209; fleeing without regard to 164; personal skills 184; and SEMH 196–7; and touch 175; and working memory 93
Sains, Brian 215
Salamanca Statement 7
Salford Sentence Reading Test 144
Sandwell Numeracy Test 145–6
scaffolding 7, 18, 86, 91, 144
scaling questions 212
Scenario Matching 221
scents, calming 224–6
scripting 59
SDM (Sherborne Developmental Movement) 190
seating: comfortable 171, 174, 223, 225; supportive 188–9
seating arrangements 33, 189
See and Learn Programme 114–15
selective mutes xi, xiii, 65–6
self-advocacy 185

self-assessments 46
self-awareness 200
self-esteem: for autistic non-speaking individuals 202; and mental health 200, 209, 214-15; and physical disability 186; in writing and maths interventions 135, 138, 140
self-monitoring 85
self-regulation 20, 93, 219, 222, 226-7
self-scaffolding framework 86
self-talk, positive 226
SEMH (Social, Emotional and Mental Health) xii-xiii; alternative provisions 28; key components in support 195-8; and physical disability 186; risk factors for 209; and sensory information 167
semi-formal curriculum 19
SEN (special educational needs): in inclusive schools 6; Referral Form 8
SENCO (special educational needs and disability coordinator) 7, 9
SEND Code of Practice 7
SEND support plans 10-16, **11-15**, 18, 152
sensology 65, 99, 163
sensory activities 168, 171, 190, 231, 233
sensory boxes 175
sensory breaks 171, 225, 233
sensory circuits 43, 152, 163, 170, 235-6
sensory craving 163-4
sensory diet 168, 170-1, 206
sensory drama games 65, 96, 124
sensory environments 183, 200
sensory input 99, 170-1, 234
sensory integration 168-9, 171
sensory processing: activities 169-70; difficulties 160-5, 168, 188-9, 217, 229; use of term 159-60
sensory regulation xii, 157, 163, 229
sensory rooms 38, 111, 171, 235-6
sensory stories 109, 113, 122-3, 171-2, 183
sensory strategies 206
sensory support xii
sensory toolkit 171-3
sensory tools 109, 168, 171, 174, 201
sensory toys 174, 225
sensory-friendly environment 171, 173-4
sentence starters 133, 138
sentences, short and clear 72
sight word teaching 114

sign language 28, 180-1, 228
Signalong 180-1
Simple View of Reading 95
skills progression 114-15, 136, 140-1
small group work 138, 169
SMIF (Suffolk Mainstream Inclusion Framework) 8
snack time 37, 60, 71, 114; routine for 228
snacks: as distraction 231; sensory 171-2
Social, Emotional and Mental Health *see* SEMH
social interactions 6; emotion cards in 72; and physical disability 186; and sensory processing 160
social participation 200
social skills 201, 214, 229
social stories 46, 54, 215, 222, 227-8
spaced retrieval 91-2
spatial awareness 184
special schools 19, 71, 80, 118; inclusion in 25
specialist provisions 23, 173
specialist support xi, 73, 179
specific learning difficulties 8, 120
Speech and Language: screeners 27-8; specialists in 9-10
Speech and Language Therapists (SaLT) xii, 37, 46, 227
speech development, and hearing impairment 179-80
speech-to-text software 181, 184, 189
story massage 108
storytelling 108, 124
storytime skills sessions 122
strengths-based approaches 92
stress 198; and autistic people 200; and sensory processing 161, 171, 175
stress balls 172, 188, 224-6, 234
stretch bands 173, 230
structured choices 71
Suffolk County Council 8
switch access 54
symbol cards 44; going outside 169; like and don't like 65; opportunities to use 70-1, 73; requesting food 166; tactile touch 176; teaching to use 60-1
symbol charts 73

tablets 29, 47, 54, 187, 190-1
TACPAC 107, 163

tactile learning 181
tactile markers 183-4
tactile touch 175-7
Talk 2 Nish 216
Talk 4 Writing 129, 140
Talkabout Book Series 215
Talking Mats 46, 111, 205, 212
target setting meetings 23
targeted provision 23
targets, personalised 10, 19, 73
task analysis 23, 140
task boards *43*, 58-9, 120-1, 140
task initiation 86, 93
teacher toolbox 210, 219
Teachers Handbook: SEND Embedding Inclusive Practice 9
teaching assistants 18, 26, 214, 235
team talks 213
temperatures 161, 174-5
textures 123, 178, 229; avoidance of 161; exploring different 165, 172, 175
thinking time 93
3, 2, 1, Finished 44, *51*, 63-4, 71, 151
Thrive 215
tilt-in-space wheelchairs 186-7
time and value 5-7, 25
time to communicate 74-5
timers *42*, 63; in calm-down space 224; in Engagement Model 151; to signal transitions 228; and waiting 66-7
timetable strips, personalised *49*
timetables: and anxiety management 207; bespoke 24; personalised 33; positional changes in 187; visual 33, 41-2, 63, 93, 224-7
trampoline 169-70
transference 196
transitions 38; being upset by 162, 220; and checklists 45; and countdowns 42, 44, 63-4; key indicators 109; signalling 228-9; and task boards 58
trauma 27, 196-7, 209-10, 214-17
Trim Trails circuits 163
trip hazards, potential 181
trust: and anxiety management 201-4; building 33, 60, 73, 208, 227-8; in SEMH 196-7
tunnels 169, 173
turn-taking 72

understanding, supporting 40, 42, 121, 180
universal provision 23
unpicking behaviours 79, 157, 167
unpreferred tasks 64
upper body function 186

Velcro fastenings 189
verbal cues 151, 221
verbal information 89-90
vestibular activities 101, 123, 206
vests, weighted 171, 173
vision impairment (VI) 8, 61, 179-82
visual cues 33, 64, 228; and hearing impairments 180-1
visual schedule 72, 172, 226, 228, 233
visualisation techniques 85
visualisations 225
visualised language 201
visuals 23-4, *30-1*, *31-3*; for autistic non-speaking pupils 207; communication through 74; in maths 143; pairing language with 89; questions around implementing 56-9; in regulation and de-escalation 226, 233; in sensory-friendly environment 174; for specific people 46; and working memory 86-7; in Writing Progression Programme 135
vocabulary, pre-teaching 89
vocabulary mats 120, 122
volume, regulating 64

waiting, support for 66-7
wall push-ups 188, 230
wheelchairs 185, 187-90
Where's Wally 117, 121
White Rose Maths 6, 81, 141, 143
whiteboard: and pupil voice 212; schedule on 121; in sensory toolkit 173; viewing from wheelchair 186; visuals on 40, 58-9; in writing progression 133, 137
WHO (World Health Organization) 199
whole-word approach 114, 118-20
Widgit software 31
Winston's Wish 217
wobble cushions 173, 188
Word Aware 124
word banks, personalised 111-13
word sets xii, 109-10

working memory xii, 83–4, 94; and curriculum design 91–2; importance in learning 85–6; managing 88; misconceptions about 84–5; profiles in SEND 92–3; reducing load on 33, 87–90; spotting challenges to 86–7
Write from the Start Programme 188
Writing on a Page 129–31, **130–2**
Writing Progression programme 133–41; assessment cycle 140; skills progression 136–40, *139*; teaching progression 133–6, *134–5*
writing rope 129

yellow tape 181, 184
yoga 157, 169, 173, 189, 225, 229
Young Minds 216

Zones of Regulation 101, 210, 227, 236

For Product Safety Concerns and Information please contact our EU representative GPSR@taylorandfrancis.com
Taylor & Francis Verlag GmbH, Kaufingerstraße 24, 80331 München, Germany

www.ingramcontent.com/pod-product-compliance
Lightning Source LLC
Chambersburg PA
CBHW080802300426
44114CB00020B/2801